Abolition and Plantation Management in Jamaica, 1807–1838

Abolition and Plantation Management in Jamaica 1807–1838

Dave St Aubyn Gosse

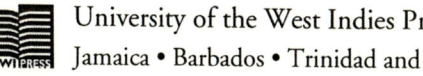
University of the West Indies Press
Jamaica • Barbados • Trinidad and Tobago

University of the West Indies Press
7A Gibraltar Hall Road, Mona
Kingston 7, Jamaica

www.uwipress.com

© 2012 by Dave St Aubyn Gosse

All rights reserved. Published 2012

A catalogue record of this book is available
from the National Library of Jamaica.

ISBN: 978-976-640-269-3

Cover illustration: Hopeton D. Bartley, *Antiquity*.

Cover and book design by Robert Harris.

Set in Adobe Garamond 11/14.5 x 27

Printed in the United States of America.

TO THE LATE

IVY BUCHANAN MAUD WILLIAMS

Contents

List of Illustrations / *viii*

Acknowledgements / *xi*

Introduction / *1*

1   The Impact of the 1807 Abolition Act / *11*

2   Ambiguous Management / *32*

3   Worthy Park: Example of Management for Survival / *63*

4   The Impact of Abolition on Labour Procurement / *92*

5   Health and Reproduction / *120*

6   Management Initiatives / *153*

Epilogue / *178*

Appendix 1: Injustices in the Jamaican Legal System, 1817–1822 / *189*

Appendix 2: Injustices in the Jamaican Legal System, 1826–1832 / *190*

Appendix 3: Company for Importing Chinese Workers in Jamaica in 1808 / *191*

Notes / *193*

Selected Bibliography / *219*

Index / *229*

Illustrations

Figures

2.1 Sugar production in Jamaica, 1800–1838 / *35*
2.2 Crop accounts on Hermitage estate, 1801–1809 and 1817–1828 / *41*
2.3 Yearly hogsheads of sugar produced at Golden Grove, 1802–1836 / *46*
2.4 Amity Hall yearly production of sugar, 1802–1838 / *52*
2.5 Production figures for Tharp's eight plantations, 1805–1837 / *59*
3.1 Worthy Park sugar production, 1800–1838 / *66*
3.2 Individual jobbing contracts at Worthy Park, 1793–1795 / *72*
3.3 Mortality by age group at Worthy Park, 1813–1834 / *76*
3.4 Inventory of food items at Worthy Park, 1813 / *84*
3.5 Inventory of food items at Worthy Park, 1815 / *84*
3.6 Food items received from Spring Gardens Pen, 1792 / *85*
4.1 Summary of ages of Africans at Hermitage estate in 1824 / *109*
5.1 Sugar production at Mesopotamia plantation, 1799–1835 / *138*
5.2 Sugar production at Island estate, 1799–1835 / *139*
6.1 Sugar production at Denbigh, 1806–1837 / *158*
7.1 Net profits at Goulburn's Amity Hall plantation, 1805–1825 / *184*
7.2 Net profits at Tudway's Jamaican plantations, 1800–1834 / *186*

Tables

1.1 Account of Trade Between Jamaica and the United States for the Year 1804 / *15*
1.2 Licensed Imports and Exports of Africans, 1808–1822 / *22*
1.3 Early Nineteenth-Century Rebellions in Jamaica / *29*

2.1 Slave Productivity on Hermitage Estate, 1817–1828 / *42*
2.2 Slave Productivity at Amity Hall, Selected Years 1803–1836 / *53*
2.3 Slave Productivity at Tharp's Sugar Plantations, 1805–1837 / *60*
3.1 Rate of Productivity at Worthy Park, 1812–1837 / *67*
3.2 Jobbing Charges in Jamaica, 1793–1799 / *71*
3.3 Mortality and Fertility Rates of Africans at Worthy Park, 1792–1834 / *73*
3.4 Health Indicators of Worthy Park's Enslaved Africans, 1813–1836 / *74*
3.5 Analysis of Mortality Rates at Worthy Park, 1813–1834 / *75*
3.6 Average Volume of Sugar at Worthy Park, 1800–1838 / *77*
3.7 Cost of Maintaining Africans Annually / *78*
3.8 Additional Food Items Given to Africans at Worthy Park, 1795 / *86*
3.9 Land Utilization on Rose Price's Plantations, 1813 / *88*
4.1 Division of Africans at King's Valley Estate, 1 February 1808 / *96*
4.2 Division of Africans at Amity Hall, 1 January 1825 / *99*
4.3 Division of Africans at Radnor Plantation, 1825 / *100*
4.4 Apprentices at Pepper and Bona Vista Pens in 1838 / *101*
4.5 Enslaved Africans at Pepper and Bona Vista Pens in 1826 / *102*
4.6 African Women under Forty Years at Amity Hall: Number of Children, 1827 / *106*
4.7 African Women under Forty Years at Amity Hall without Children in 1827 / *107*
4.8 Average Prices of Captive Africans, 1793–1799 / *110*
5.1 Sickness and Mortality on Mesopotamia and Island Plantations, 1801–1826 / *128*
5.2 Morbidity on Other Jamaican Estates, 1802–1812 / *130*
5.3 Analysis of Morbidity Listed in Tables 5.1 and 5.2, 1801–1826 / *131*
5.4 Africans Condemned in the Vice-Admiralty Court up to 31 August 1816 / *135*
5.5 Enslaved Population of Mesopotamia and Island, 1799–1831 / *137*
5.6 Increases and Decreases of Enslaved Africans in Five Parishes, 1817–1829 / *143*

5.7 Increases and Decreases of Enslaved Africans at Bog Estate, Vere, 1803–1817 / *146*

5.8 Increases and Decreases of Enslaved Africans at Three Estates in Vere, 1825–1831 / *146*

6.1 Levels of Productivity at Denbigh, 1808–1828 / *158*

6.2 Amity Hall Production Figures, 1802–1837 / *161*

6.3 Logwood Production on Penrhyn and Barham's Plantations, 1803–1835 / *166*

6.4 Pepper and Bona Vista Crop Accounts, 1826–1838 / *173*

6.5 Value of Sales at Pepper and Bona Vista, 1826–1835 / *174*

7.1 Merchants' Accounts on Tharp's Plantations, 1815–1833 / *182*

Acknowledgements

MY RESEARCH WAS CONDUCTED PRIMARILY in the United Kingdom and in Jamaica. I wish to specially thank the staff at the Jamaican Archives: Sophia, Lloyd and Marsha, for their willingness to go beyond the call of duty in finding the necessary materials. I also wish to thank the staff at the Elsa Goveia Library at the University of the West Indies, in particular Joan Vaciana and Frances Salmon. The staff at the Island Record Office and the National Library of Jamaica was also most helpful. In the United Kingdom, I wish to thank the staff at the Surrey Historical Society, especially Mary Macky. At the University of North Wales, Bangor, Ann Lennegan went beyond the call of service to aid my research. I also wish to thank the staff at the Bodleian Library at Oxford University; the staff at the manuscript reading room at the University Library of Cambridge; the staff at the Cambridge County Office; the staff at the Institute of Commonwealth Library; and the staff at the British Library and the Public Record Office.

For my sojourn in London on two separate occasions, my profound gratitude to Sean, Zara, Sadie, Pastors Handy and Harvey, Monique, Phillip, Rhona, Andre, Enid and her family, and Brothers Steele and Campbell and all the other members of the Church of God in Tottenham and Thornton Heath. Their generous hospitality towards my material comforts while conducting research in London was exemplary.

I am also indebted to Professor S.H.H. Carrington, my academic advisor at Howard University, for his excellent advice and critical support from the inception of this study to its completion. I wish to also thank all of the other faculty members of my doctoral committee for offering invaluable support and critique while this book was at the dissertation stage: Drs Tolbert, Medford, Peloso, Knight and Palmer. The Department of History and its chairman, Dr Tolbert, were also most helpful in offering financial aid in travelling to London. The Graduate School's Sasakawa fellowship in 2002–3 was also useful in my last year of research and writing the dissertation. I also have to thank my fellow graduate students in the Department of History, Howard University, who aided in the process of research and writing, particularly Gordon Gill, who has always been most helpful in photocopying materials and in providing stimulating discussion relevant to the topic

I also express my profound thanks to Professor Patrick Bryan of the Department of History and Archaeology, University of the West Indies, Mona, who provided valuable critique.

Most important is my wife, Deirdre English Gosse, whose constant encouragement and support were vital and whose sacrifice helped in completing the final edition of the manuscript. Last, to McKayla Gosse, my daughter, whose presence inspired me to complete the project. Hopefully, she will become cognizant of her history and her roots.

Introduction

THE 1807 BRITISH ABOLITION ACT to end the slave trade continues to be a controversial topic of debate among historians. Was its goal economic, humanitarian or a combination of both? In 1806, in events leading to the implementation of the Abolition Act, management reforms within the British West Indies were at the centre of discussions between the Jamaican assembly and the British Colonial Office. The Jamaican planters cautioned the British authorities not to surrender to the humanitarians and pass the dreaded abolition bill, because it would drastically reduce their levels of production and productivity. Their plantations were already in financial distress and the levels of economic protection they enjoyed had to remain.[1]

The Colonial Office, in response, stressed the economic necessity of passing the abolition bill, which was aimed at encouraging the planters to implement drastic managerial reforms. These reforms were necessary in the area of health care, especially among enslaved children.[2] The Jamaican planters were told that the abolition bill was an imperative since it would force planters in the older sugar colonies, like Jamaica, to restructure their operations and become as economically competitive as the newer sugar colonies.[3]

For the Colonial Office to have introduced management reforms in the discussion on abolition first suggests that the 1807 Abolition Act had an economic motive. Second, it seems to validate the argument of some historians who argue for early decline within the British West Indies.[4] It is the intention of this study, then, to investigate how the lack of new enslaved labourers after the 1807 Abolition Act affected the Jamaican plantation economy. This study will also investigate the relationship between plantation management and productivity in a time of enormous labour transition. I will argue that plantation management, especially human resources management after 1807, was poor. The planters wasted time fighting political battles with the metropolitan authorities rather than concentrating on the economic implications resulting from the abolition of the slave trade. Instead of restructuring their plantations to face the new economic order that was being forced on them, the Jamaican planters engaged in political propaganda with respect to slavery. In the end, they hastened their own demise. The Jamaican planters, those residing both in Great Britain as absentee owners and in Jamaica as steward managers, failed to make drastic managerial changes regarding labour reforms, as was stressed by the metropolitan office in London.[5] They didn't heed the new ameliorative direction of their government, failing to institute the radical changes that were necessary in a competitive world market. Instead, they resisted bitterly, creating a culture of paranoia. This further escalated their desire to control and tighten their grip on the enslaved population rather than becoming more sensitive to their needs.

This study of early nineteenth-century plantation management in Jamaica is centred on the larger context of amelioration. This was one of the most important socio-political reform initiatives promulgated by Great Britain, geared particularly towards its older sugar colonies and beginning in the late eighteenth century.[6] Entering the early nineteenth century, ameliorative reforms made it necessary for these older sugar colonies, including Jamaica, to resolve the pressing question of slavery, which had run its course and was no longer cost-effective. Metropolitan initiatives such as slave registration, from its beginning in 1812 to its final adoption in 1819; Parliament's 1823 adoption of amelioration; the abolition of slavery in 1833; the apprenticeship period that followed; and the eventual emancipation of slaves in 1838, were all reforms on the same continuum. They were aimed at implementing social, economic and political changes in the British West Indian colonies. The Jamaican planters' vigorous resistance to amelioration coupled with the colony's increasing slave rebellions, which culminated in the Sam Sharpe Rebellion of 1831, contributed significantly to the "early" termination of slavery in 1833. Most officers of the Crown seem to have preferred a more gradual approach, until the institution of slavery withered away.[7]

In measuring the planters' levels of success, this study will use the concepts of both "crude production" and "productivity". Historians have used the latter term to describe the overall efficiency of the enslaved Africans and, by extension, the plantations. However, calculating productivity is problematic in and of itself, and even more so when evaluating the contribution of plantation managers in this regard. There are too many incalculable variables that have a significant bearing upon production;[8] for example, a plantation's geographical location. This was influenced by the weather, which in turn had an enormous effect on the health of the plantation's enslaved Africans and its eventual production figures. Other factors included the quality of the soil and the levels of erosion taking place; the kinds of cane planted and their eventual effect on the soil; the plantation's method of planting; the availability of stock to manure the soil of new cane fields; and the state of the plantation's infrastructure and technology. Most important was the proper treatment of enslaved Africans and stewardship of their health. After 1807, the number of those reported as unhealthy on plantation lists continued to rise even as new enslaved Africans became harder to obtain.

There are many incalculable factors that econometrics cannot accurately evaluate in examining productivity. Despite this difficulty, however, productivity levels will still be considered, as they provide an idea of the efficiency of a plantation. When levels of productivity are combined with the crude production figures for the plantation's staples, a picture emerges of the economic health of a plantation. When both concepts are studied together, the relationship between plantation management and production can be better understood. Although most of the plantations that I examined do show evidence of decline in the early nineteenth century, the primary aim of this study is not to discuss the decline thesis; rather, it is to investigate the factors behind such decline and the extent to which the planters' management affected production.

Chapter 1 of this study will outline the economic, political and social contexts of the late eighteenth and early nineteenth centuries. Chapter 2 will examine the plantation management structure as practised in Jamaica. Chapter 3 will take a closer look at Worthy Park, one of the more productive plantations in Jamaica, to determine the extent to which its management practices affected production. Chapters 4 and 5 will show how the lack of good leadership made it difficult for the planters to procure and maintain enslaved labour. Chapter 6 will examine management initiatives and the production of other commodities, to determine how those planters faced with declining profits from sugar diversified their operations and the effect this had on their overall production.

This study theoretically builds on the work of historians who have highlighted the role of economics in the understanding of both the 1807 abolition of the slave trade and the eventual abolition of slavery. Such scholars include Eric Williams, who argues in *Capitalism and Slavery* that the economic motive was the principal concern of both abolition and emancipation. Williams's work represents the first significant challenge to historians of slavery who were more sympathetic to the humanitarian cause.[9] Other supporters of Williams's thesis include Barbara Solow. Solow argues that the abolition of the slave trade in 1807 came at a time when the trade would no longer have a negative impact on the British economy. She indicates that if abolition had taken place half a century earlier, it would have devastated the British economy.[10] William Darity Jr agrees, arguing that not only was the plantation system no longer valuable in furthering the interests of British industrial capitalism, but there was a fundamental transition in the thinking of Britain's governing elite, who were moving away from the principles of mercantilism towards the laissez-faire principles of Adam Smith. As an example, he cites the sugar manufacturers in Great Britain who joined in support of the abolitionist movement out of the desire to protect an important element of the British economy.[11] There are, however, very strong critics of the Williams thesis, chief among them being Seymour Drescher. In *Econocide: British Slavery in the Era of Abolition*, Drescher argues that Britain was altruistic in abolishing the trade at the precise time the country stood to gain significant profits from it.[12]

The debate surrounding the economic decline of the planter class in the British West Indies is much wider, however, than that of the Williams school versus that of Drescher. There are other significant social and political realities that contributed to this decline. One such factor, which has been understated by Caribbean historians, is that of poor plantation management in an era that called for bold, creative leadership. Most planters could not transcend their racist and sexist stereotyping of Africans, which compromised their management. As a result, they refused to treat the enslaved Africans as a highly intelligent workforce that could be motivated to work without the whip. This prevented them from adopting critical management reforms. The low fertility rate among enslaved women is a case in point. Most planters never saw this as a management failure. Instead, they chastised the enslaved women in their correspondence as barbaric, crude and uncivilized. In their view, the enslaved women could not do any better since it was in their nature. Such an ideology inhibited plantation growth.

Eugene Genovese said it best when he stated, in *The Political Economy of Slavery*, "[The] debate over a seemingly economic question cannot be understood unless studied in its political context, the main feature of which was the intention of the rural slaveholders to maintain their hegemony at all costs."[13] This can be clearly seen in the Jamaican scenario. The majority of Jamaican planters, despite the withering of the economic protection that they badly needed and the decreasing sugar prices in London in the early 1800s, nevertheless refused to adhere to ameliorative reforms. As a result, they resisted important and necessary discussions centred on labour reform and property rights, much to their detriment. This was because slavery was more than an economic institution; it was also a social and political reality that was deeply embedded in the very fabric of colonial life. In refuting the argument that Cuban planters had little emotional attachment to slavery in the 1870s and thus pushed for abolition, Rebecca Scott argues that while this might have been true for a few planters, the majority maintained a high degree of control over their workforce and inhibited rather than facilitated emancipation.[14] This was true in Jamaica as well.

To understand fully the need for this important study of plantation management and its relationship to production, the following historiography has to be examined. The literature on plantation management falls into three categories. First, there are older works, which more or less approach the aspect of management in the manner of a manual or textbook and describe the ideals of management. *The Jamaica Planter's Guide* by T. Roughley is an example of this type of book. Roughley gives advice on the care and handling of enslaved Africans, the planting of provision grounds, the season to plant and the kinds of items to be planted.[15] A similar work is Dr Collins's *Practical Rules for the Management and Medical Treatment of Negro Slaves in the Sugar Colonies*. Collins describes himself as a professional planter and divides his work into two parts. Part one gives practical advice on the "seasoning" of enslaved Africans, and on their diet, clothing, labour and discipline. Part two gives medical advice on the care and handling of the sick, including establishing hospitals and treating individual cases of fever and other illnesses.[16] The works of well-known planters such as Edward Long and Bryan Edwards are also most instructive. In the first volume of *The History of Jamaica*, Long offers twelve points for the management of estates and laments the lack of available manuals to encompass what experience taught older Jamaican planters. He saw sugar planting in Jamaica as extremely difficult in comparison to many of the other sugar islands because of the constant changes in climate, soil and conditions.[17] Edwards, on the other hand, in the second volume of *The History, Civil and Commercial, of the British Colonies in the West Indies*, makes three recommendations to Jamaican planters which could strengthen amelioration and lead to increased production. First, he advocates the abandonment of gang work in favour of task work, which meant paying the enslaved Africans cash for extra plantation work. Second, he recommends the institution of "slave courts" adjudicated by enslaved Africans to cultivate distributive justice. Third, he insists that the Sabbath day of rest for the enslaved Africans be rigidly enforced.[18]

In the second category of management literature, we find several publications aimed primarily at examining the larger issue of plantation production. The work of Lowell J. Ragatz is one such example. Ragatz is extremely critical in refuting the traditional humanitarian argument and implicitly establishing an economic paradigm. In *The Old Plantation System in the British West Indies*, he argues that Caribbean plantations were designed to produce artificial wealth and thus could not resist serious economic competition and drastic changes in world market prices.[19] In *The Fall of the Planter Class in the British Caribbean*, Ragatz refutes the claims that abolition and emancipation destroyed the British West Indian planter class. He argues instead that its decline began with the Seven Years' War (1756–63) and was accelerated because of improper management, as the planters' eighteenth-century wealth was mainly a result of the high price of sugar in the international market.[20] In "Absentee Landlordism in the British Caribbean, 1750–1833", Ragatz's indictment of management is even more explicit, as he shows the direct link between planter absenteeism and decline. Ragatz states that because of the planters' enormous mid-eighteenth-century profits they were able to retire in luxury in England, and in doing so they left a weakened infrastructure in the existing plantation system in the British Caribbean. Added to this, the inexperience of the next generation of planters reduced their competitive edge, resulting in lost ground in the international sugar trade.[21] It was Ragatz's work that provided the ideological underpinnings for Williams's economic critique and for supporters of the decline thesis.[22]

B.W. Higman's *Slave Population and Economy in Jamaica, 1807–1834*, with its emphasis on the productivity of the Jamaican plantation, extended the debate from the role of British West Indian economies in its larger international context to an internal examination of the plantation system. Higman shows how abolition in 1807 affected the changing demography of the Jamaican slave system, which in turn impacted its overall economic performance. He argues that Jamaican economic decline was also attributed to internal factors.[23] As a result, issues relating to plantation life, such as health, fertility, nutrition, population, structural composition of the slaves, and their effect on the economy had to be examined.[24] Another critical work in this category was J.R. Ward's *British West Indian Slavery, 1750–1834*. Ward argues that by the early 1900s, the British public had come to associate economic progress with industrial development; the British West Indian planters failed to meet this expectation with their primitive agricultural methods and they could not eliminate the cruel and inhumane treatment of enslaved Africans because of slave labour.[25] On the other hand, Ward argues that absentee management in Jamaica was to be blamed for the failure of the Jamaicans to procure a natural increase in enslaved Africans, unlike the planters in Barbados. He estimates the productive capacity of enslaved Africans on Jamaican sugar estates to have risen by 35 per cent, or 0.4 per cent annually, from 1750 to 1830. Ward even indicates that Jamaica's per capita output in 1830 approached that of Great Britain around the same time and that the material conditions of the enslaved Africans improved to the point where it was comparatively better than that of manual workers in the very early stages of the industrial revolution in Great Britain.[26]

As a result of the important studies in this second category, further studies related to plantation slavery and management arose. Among such works in this third category, centred on management, is Heather Cateau's dissertation, "Management and the Sugar Industry in the British West Indies, 1750–1810". Her work could be considered one of the first major studies to investigate the role of plantation management in the British West Indies. She argues that from 1750 to 1810, planters throughout the British West Indies rapidly adopted necessary innovations for the survival of their industry.[27] Selwyn H.H. Carrington has also examined some aspects of management and production in a chapter entitled "New Management Techniques: Adjusting to Decline" in his recent publication, *The Sugar Industry and the Abolition of the Slave Trade, 1775–1810*. Carrington concludes that by the end of the eighteenth century, planters in the British West Indies had to face the reality that an in-depth restructuring was needed. Most estates then adopted the "Modified System of Management", as practised in Barbados.[28] Carrington further elaborates on the nature of such management restructuring in an article in the *Journal of Caribbean History*. He shows that better-qualified managers were chosen who could exercise greater professionalism and who were paid an annual salary rather than the regular commission.[29] He also argues that the planters implemented technological changes only when the opportunity was afforded them. Changes such as the introduction of the steam engine to replace or supplement the windmill were considered. Most significant, however, was the attempt at planter amelioration, which was introduced by individual planters and dictated by several colonial assemblies. As part of this initiative, laws were passed for better government of the enslaved Africans, with the hope that their production and reproduction levels would increase.[30]

Higman, however, in a later work, *Plantation Jamaica 1750–1850: Capital and Control in a Colonial Economy*, has defined the pertinent issues surrounding plantation management. He analyses the important but overlooked role of the attorneys who managed estates chiefly for absentee proprietors. He assesses their efficiency and concludes that they are not to be blamed for the fall of the Jamaican planter class as they were highly efficient and productive. In fact, he asserts that these planters were very successful to the extent that they could be considered the precursors to modern managers.[31] Higman also charts the complex structure of managerial hierarchy and includes information about plantation life, labour, technology, trade, investment profits and the postal service.[32]

John Campbell, in his dissertation, has also written about aspects of plantation management in Jamaica. In "Managing Human Resources on a British West Indian Sugar Plantation, 1770–1834", he argues that by the late eighteenth century the demanding nature of sugar production had forced plantation managers to seek new strategies for sustaining and increasing estate production. While coercion was often used, management soon realized that voluntary compliance from the enslaved workforce provided much higher returns. Thus, management supported new policies that accommodated labour dialogue and ameliorated conditions within its managerial schemes.[33] Another dissertation, "Producing a Peculiar Commodity" by David Ryden, also examines aspects of plantation management. In his work on Jamaica, which spans the years 1750 to 1807, Ryden makes two significant contributions to understanding eighteenth-century labour practices. He indicates that the sugar planters during the pre-abolition period had little regard for the health of enslaved labourers because purchasing enslaved Africans was cheaper than rearing them. This accounts for the annual 2.5 per cent death rate over the birth rate. Planters after the 1807 Abolition Act, however, were more concerned about massive labour shortages. Thus, they implemented various strategies such as purchasing new, illegally imported enslaved Africans and removing enslaved Africans from other sectors such as coffee to augment their labour force in the sugar industry.[34] Second, Ryden argues that the size of the enslaved population on a plantation was not a guarantee of high productivity as many of the enslaved were invalids and sickly. As a result, most of the efficient estates in the mid-eighteenth century had only small populations of healthy enslaved Africans.[35] Even the size of plantation pens, Ryden indicates, had no direct bearing on productivity.[36] Ryden thus identifies the critical link between good management and increased production.

The studies of Higman, Campbell and Ryden highlight the need for a more critical and general assessment of the role of good management in increasing productivity. Although those publications concentrate on Jamaica, they are still limited. Campbell concentrates on the dynamics of management on one plantation, Golden Grove. Ryden stops his study at 1807; although he mentions some management strategies implemented after 1807, he does not detail the nuances of plantation management in the period after abolition leading up to emancipation in 1838. He also does not show how the economic changes in the world caused primarily by the implementation of a free trade philosophy in the early nineteenth century influenced Britain, and how Britain in turn sought to influence its colonies through its assigned institutions and individuals. Higman comes the nearest to defining plantation management and describing its essential features. He does not, however, test the relationship between plantation management and productivity on several plantations, over a period of years, to determine their overall efficiency. What he has done, however, is refute the argument that attorneys contracted by absentee owners were inefficient.

The story of plantation management and its impact on productivity in Jamaica after 1807 has not yet been told. This account is significant since Jamaica was the largest British West Indian sugar colony, containing nearly half of all the enslaved Africans in the British West Indies. Furthermore, some of the arguments postulated by scholars such as J.R. Ward and B.W. Higman still need further investigation. Ward states, on the one hand, that in general the planters in the British West Indies were resistant to amelioration. Yet on the other hand, he argues that amelioration helped to improve the food eaten and clothes worn by enslaved Africans. As a result the planters were correct in saying that the enslaved Africans in the British West Indies were as well fed and clothed as the poor working-class labourers in England.[37] Ward, in his attempt to give a general picture of the effect of amelioration on the entire British West Indies, does not take into account the regional differences and as such contradicts himself.[38]

Higman is convinced that the majority of attorneys of absentee owners were productive and actually saved many Jamaican plantations from falling into ruin sooner. This study will show, however, that on several of the leading plantations the attorneys were not as efficient and productive as Higman claims. They did not halt the general trend of declining crude production figures and declining productivity levels in the early nineteenth century.

Let me hasten to state that the methodology used for this study was an examination of numerous random plantations rather than a representative sample of the over seven hundred plantations in Jamaica. The major plantations were chosen based on two important factors. First and foremost was the availability of yearly crop accounts, spanning from 1800 to the 1830s. This was important in determining the yearly levels of crude production of staples and in plotting the productive capacity of the plantations. I also chose plantations that, in addition to having crop accounts, had frequent and yearly correspondence between the various managers from 1800 to the 1830s. It was necessary to read the stories behind the production figures and to determine productivity levels by comparing the slave lists to the crude production figures. As a result of these two important factors my sample was limited to a select number of plantations. It also meant that my sample was random. The primary plantations examined were Amity Hall in the parish of Vere; Island and Mesopotamia, owned by Joseph Foster Barham, in the parishes of St Elizabeth and Westmoreland; Lord Penrhyn's plantations in the parish of Clarendon; Worthy Park in St Catherine; Tharp's eight plantations in Trelawny; and Golden Grove in St Thomas in the East.

CHAPTER 1

The Impact of the 1807 Abolition Act

Economic Context

Generally, Jamaican planters of the early nineteenth century would not accept the fact that the 1807 Abolition Act had serious social, economic and political implications. They ignored the new reality that enslaved Africans would not be readily available for purchase from the slave ships and that they had to implement new management initiatives to maintain the health of their existing enslaved population.

Historians such as Lowell Ragatz, Eric Williams and Selwyn H.H. Carrington argue that the British West Indies had begun to decline economically in the last quarter of the eighteenth century.[1] It is not my intention to reiterate arguments for an early decline; nevertheless, the 1807 Abolition Act was significant to British economic policy and to the planters' economic profitability.

Adam Smith, one of the foremost eighteenth-century British economists, concluded in his seminal work, *The Wealth of Nations*, that slave labour in the British territories ought to be abolished, since it was no longer cost effective. Smith's theory regarding the high cost of maintaining slave labour towards the close of the eighteenth century seems to have been a reflection of a new economic paradigm in British economics: a shift from mercantilism to free-market capitalism, with a new concentration on the gradual withdrawal of protected colonial markets and the emergence of free or unshackled trade.[2] The Jamaican planters should have accepted the policy of free trade by the early nineteenth century, since as early as 1770, they had been petitioning unsuccessfully against the loss of economic protection.[3] Of particular impor-

11

tance was the reduction of the drawback, which were the duties on re-exported sugar. Reducing the drawback lessened their profit margins and was economically discouraging.[4]

The British West Indian planters wanted higher duties to be placed on foreign imported sugar since they were already sharing preferential duties with sugar from the recently captured "Ceded Islands" (Grenada, Tobago, Dominica and St Vincent), which had already left them economically vulnerable.[5] This "West Indian body" of planters and merchants had once been a very influential lobby group in London. However, they were now outrivalled by the British sugar refiners, who wanted cheaper sugar for the British consumers. This meant an increase in sugar consumption and extra financial revenue for the kingdom of Great Britain. In response, the Association of West India Planters and Merchants argued that if they were to lose their monopoly due to the introduction of cheaper foreign sugar, it would not only be catastrophic to the British West Indies, but it would also devastate the overall navigation and commerce of Great Britain.[6]

The West Indian body even employed a solicitor, one Mr Potts, to represent them in the House of Commons. They also encouraged each other to pressure their members of Parliament to be present at the hearings by the select committee of the House of Commons and to speak on their behalf.[7] However, in August 1783, the West Indian merchants and planters learned that their petition had failed and their exclusive monopoly was under threat.[8] To underscore the clear intention of the British government, the prime minister, William Pitt, who was also former chancellor of the exchequer, issued a most important trade policy to the West Indian planters in February 1792. In a meeting chaired by the renowned Jamaican planter Simon Taylor, Pitt acknowledged the historic reciprocal nature of trade between Great Britain and the British West Indian colonies. The West Indian planters had borne the sacrifices and had contributed immensely to the revenue of the mother country by breaking the previous monopoly enjoyed by the Portuguese. Nevertheless, that was the past. The West Indians had enjoyed not only a full monopoly but also enormous wealth. They had to accept that the context had changed. Wars were now incessant and high taxes were necessary to maintain those wars. In addition, the British public and indeed all of Europe demanded cheaper sugar.[9]

Pitt conceded that the West Indian planters were at a disadvantage due to

Great Britain's navigation laws, which benefited the mother country over the colonists. Because of these laws, the West Indians were forced to obtain expensive provisions, could not always use cheaper vessels to carry their sugar, and were most vulnerable to market prices.[10] Nevertheless, in the new era of unrestricted free trade that had emerged, Great Britain had no other choice but to restructure their operations to remain competitive in the new market environment. As a result, they were forced to reduce the West Indian planters' bounty on re-exported sugar, as well as to lower the price of sugar at home through the importation of cheap foreign sugar.[11] These innovations meant the possible loss of economic protection to the British West Indian colonies. However, it would benefit the British consumers and manufacturers and, indirectly, the British West Indian colonies.[12]

The admission of cheap East Indian sugars with duties lower than or similar to the British West Indies' was economically unfair to the British West Indies, based on their long historic principle of mutual monopoly. Nevertheless, it was the medicine the British planters needed in their bid to restructure their plantations.[13] It was also true that the East Indian producers did not spend their profits in Great Britain as the West Indian planters did. Greater reliance on the East Indies could even destroy trade with the British West Indies. Nevertheless, the East Indian trade was the source of the future, and as imperfect as their markets were, economic prudence dictated that they had to be encouraged.[14]

Despite this clear message, the Jamaican assembly, along with their colleagues in Great Britain, continued to object to the British Parliament's new economic philosophy. Other resident Jamaican planters, including Simon Taylor, launched a bitter attack on Chancellor Pitt and the other leading ministers of state for their free trade policy on the grounds that it would ruin their plantations. Taylor even lambasted the British authorities for incursion into the local affairs of the island's assembly. He labelled Pitt's economic policies as "madness" and charged that from the very moment Pitt had come into power, his plan had been to destroy the British West Indian colonies. Only an immediate change of policy could save Jamaica. Taylor strongly believed that the loss of the British West Indian colonies would be such a blow to British commerce that they could never recover.[15] Taylor now had second thoughts about returning to live in England. Instead he thought about the republic of North America.[16]

British policymakers, in their search for cheaper sugar, also explored possible plantations in Africa.[17] As early as 1791, Lord Penrhyn and other members of the Committee of West India Merchants and Planters in Great Britain objected to a proposal by the British government to establish sugar plantations in Sierra Leone. The West Indians viewed it as counterproductive to the reciprocal monopoly between Great Britain and themselves.[18] The West Indians continued to protest, but this did not halt the British officials from pursuing the initiative.[19] One would think that by then the West India Merchants and Planters would have realized that the sugar monopoly they had enjoyed for decades would be removed. The British economic policy of free trade seemed fixed and unmovable. Thus, their best alternative was to prepare their plantations for change.

The West India Merchants and Planters, however, were conservative men whose main goal was to protect the savings they had amassed from the exploitation of enslaved Africans in the British West Indies. Similar to the old Wild West movies, these men migrated to the British West Indian colonies in search of their El Dorado; instead, they found King Sugar. However, conditions were too inhospitable: a very hot tropical climate, too few white women, inadequate social life and a multitude of enslaved Africans within their midst. Very early on, they decided that their aim was to amass as much wealth as quickly as they could, since they had protected markets. Now that the world economic order had changed and they were living comfortably in Great Britain, their goal was confined predominantly to lobbying to preserve as much of their assets and way of life as possible. Going back to colonies like Jamaica, even for a short time, to re-structure their entire operations, as wisdom dictated, was no longer a viable option. They intended to remain in Great Britain and run their plantations through local attorneys.

If the lobbying by the West Indian planters in Great Britain yielded minimum success, then one is left to question the wisdom of their persistent lobbying over and against helping their managers in the colonies to accept the bitter medicine of amelioration. Ironically, while the West Indian planters in Great Britain were afraid of free trade and its implications, a number of planters and merchants in Jamaica understood the benefits of free trade. Some of these Jamaican planters and merchants traded openly and illegally with whomever they could.[20] The Jamaicans were faced with the high prices of lumber, high freight charges and insurance rates, and the reduction of the drawback.[21] Although the Jamaican planters occasionally received permission for trading with the North Americans, based on the shortage of commodities in the island, many planters wished the trading relationship with the United States were permanent. The planters viewed the revival of trade with North America as central to increasing productivity since their businesses desperately needed the cheaper American goods.[22]

The Jamaican merchants in the main towns sold their imported provisions at high prices. This occurred as British trade restrictions forced some Jamaican merchants to travel to places as far away as India to purchase commodities. The cost of travel and freight forced these merchants to retail their goods at high prices to the Jamaican planters. Taylor supported free trade, as his twenty years of experience had taught him that British territories could not continuously supply the West Indies with their much-needed provisions. Consequently, the sugar colonies desperately needed the unlimited trade with the United States, as seen in table 1.1.[23]

Economic desperation thus resulted in a thriving illegal trade in Jamaica. British navigation laws further encouraged the North Americans to supply the French markets at the expense of British colonial markets, placing enormous economic pressure on the Jamaican planters to procure large quantities of cheaper commodities for their enslaved Africans.[24]

The irony is that despite the acknowledgement by Jamaican merchants and planters that they needed further free trade options, their associates in Great Britain still relied on economic protection. This is not to suggest that the planters in Jamaica did not desire economic protection. In fact, the Jamaican planters and their colleagues in Great Britain, having been accustomed to

Table 1.1 Account of Trade between Jamaica and the United States for the Year 1804

Imports	£'000	Exports	£'000
Imports in American bottoms	£982,642	From Jamaica to United States	£538,052
Imports in British bottoms	£166,851		
Imports from British colonies	£99,572		
Total imports	£1,249,065		

Source: CO 137/115, 232.

economic preference, still wanted the best of both worlds. They needed economic protection to sell their staples and free trade to import the necessary commodities at the cheapest price. Thus, while the British policymakers were thinking globally and attempting to influence their colonies to fall in line with their economic vision, the Jamaican planters were thinking only of themselves. They did not accept the fact that the abolition of the slave trade in 1807 had profound implications for the management of their plantations.

Social Context

The abolition of the slave trade also had implications for the social context of early nineteenth-century Jamaica. The metropolitan authorities encouraged the planters to take amelioration seriously. J.R. Ward and Heather Cateau offer two contrasting yet complementary views of amelioration. Ward sees amelioration as a series of reforms initiated by the Crown, which the British West Indian planters largely resisted but which largely benefited the enslaved Africans, who were better maintained and more lightly worked in comparison to earlier standards. Ward, however, acknowledges that despite the enslaved Africans' better treatment they were still liable to arbitrary punishment and likely to be denied Christian instruction or marriage.[25] Although Ward does not offer substantial proof that in Jamaica the enslaved Africans' material conditions were better, he is nevertheless correct in demonstrating that amelioration was an attempt by the British Parliament to institute managerial changes in the British West Indies, starting in the latter part of the eighteenth century. Cateau, on the other hand, views amelioration as an initiative not just of Parliament but also of the West Indian plantation managers, many of whom could be termed "progressive planters". She illustrates that the British West Indian planters in the late eighteenth century initiated amelioration as a practical measure and as a component of their endeavours to respond to the changing economic climate. These planters demonstrated their willingness to accept amelioration by consolidating the slave laws prior to 1781 and revising them in 1787, 1788 and 1792. Cateau concludes, however, that planter amelioration had its weaknesses. Many such laws amounted to nothing more than "window dressing"; the planters used the Consolidated Slave Laws of the last decade of the eighteenth century as a pre-emptive attempt to discourage metropolitan threats of abolition.[26]

Cateau's arguments are in keeping with the Jamaican social context of the late eighteenth and early nineteenth centuries. Amelioration as practised by the Jamaican planters was, at best, minimal and was mainly an attempt to thwart British metropolitan efforts to legislate social and political reform in the colonies. One of the reasons the Jamaican planters were so much against the abolition of the slave trade in 1807 was because it was designed in part to stimulate management initiatives in the British West Indies. As a result, it would gradually change the status of the enslaved Africans to responsible free labourers. This would reduce the high levels of African mortality while restructuring the plantation economy on a more competitive basis.

Many of the proponents of abolition in Great Britain argued that abolition was necessary to force the British West Indian planters to practise better management and to achieve natural increases of their African population. As early as 1777, the Society for the Abolition of Slavery, or the African Institution, stated explicitly that the slave trade was not only immoral but was bad economic policy. The society, whose membership included such persons as William Wilberforce, observed in 1790 that the abolition of the slave trade was in the best interest of the West Indian planters because it would lead to better management of their African population, resulting in desirable natural increases. Furthermore, "[The planter's] interest must be to recruit his stock of laborers by natural increase rather than by purchase, for such as are born in the islands and bred up in the habits of labor are by the unanimous testimony of all parties of much superior value to those dragged from Africa."[27] The Society for the Abolition of Slavery believed it was important for the planters to concentrate on the managerial issues of gender and health because the failure of the planters to procure such natural increases stemmed clearly from the high levels of infant mortality. They further believed that if proper material attention – better food, less labour and less severe punishment – were not given to African mothers and their children, they would continue to have extremely high mortality from diseases.[28] The Jamaican planters, in their defence, noted that some of their own planters had already procured such natural increases and did not need the abolition of the slave trade as encouragement.[29]

The correspondence between the Colonial Office and the Jamaican authorities also underscores the point. The Second Earl of Camden, the secretary of war, notified Governor Nugent in 1804 that the abolition bill against the slave trade would very soon become law. It had already been passed by the House of Commons but subsequently dropped by the House of Lords. He stated that whenever it was passed it would not damage permanently the immediate interests of the planters in Jamaica. In fact, the prohibition against the importation of captive Africans would provide greater long-term security, in light of the recent rebellion of the enslaved Africans in Haiti. Abolition would encourage proper management of the Africans, resulting in their greater commitment to the planting class and to an increase in their numbers.[30] The Earl of Camden further assured Nugent that, from the perspective of the British government, the cost of purchasing an African adult was greater than that of rearing an African infant to manhood. Thus, the rearing of Africans was also socially and politically advantageous.[31] Governor Nugent even agreed that the Jamaican planters needed the Abolition Act to force them into proper management, since many of the smaller planters along with the owners of jobbing gangs had an inadequate number of enslaved Africans whom they overworked, thereby shortening their lifespan. This was the planters' deliberate policy to maximize profits, since the money they gained by working the Africans to death could be used to purchase fresh supplies. Nugent blamed the Jamaican managers for maintaining a culture of neglect of their enslaved Africans. However, with abolition, greater priority would have to be given to the pre-natal and post-natal care of newly born Africans by the medical staff on all plantations.[32]

After the abolition bill was passed, it was clear that the British Parliament viewed abolition as a necessary part of the bitter medicine that the British West Indian planters had to swallow. Lord Castlereagh, foreign secretary to Prime Minister Liverpool, expressed deep regret to the Jamaican assembly in the passing of the Abolition Act. Their disappointment was understandable, he wrote, but he hoped that they would see that it was in their best interest. They now had to learn to increase their enslaved Africans through good management and good morals. They also had to increase their provisions to their enslaved Africans as was practised in Tobago and St Vincent, which were models of care. Furthermore, he said, they were to concentrate on the promotion of healthy enslaved families by encouraging marriages and consequently the increase of children. Most important, they were to investigate seriously the reasons behind the prevalence of tetanus, which had killed so many enslaved children. The British government believed that its pervasiveness was due to the overworking of pregnant mothers either during their gestation period or too soon after childbirth. Hence, Lord Castlereagh suggested a special medical investigation be undertaken, sponsored by the Jamaican assembly and conducted by leading medical members of the Jamaican community, which would enable the assembly to pass adequate legislation on health. This was to be followed by adequate incentives rewarding managers who had maintained the highest increase of children being born among the enslaved for a period of around five years.[33]

These pieces of correspondence both before and after abolition highlight the fact that the abolition of the slave trade was primarily economic in focus, as it would aid the British West Indian planters in the better organization of enslaved labour. Abolition would further act as an economic incentive to the British West Indian planters in their attempt to concentrate more on the quality of production than its quantity.[34]

The relationship between the abolition of the slave trade and British economic policy becomes even more evident when one examines correspondence between members of the House of Lords. Lord Wellington, one of Great Britain's outstanding military heroes, was informed in 1814 by one of his colleagues (unnamed) that the desired economic results behind the 1807 Abolition Act had not materialized and the issue was becoming embarrassing. Despite this, however, they could still utilize the act as one of the key strategies in their diplomatic manoeuvres to end the war with France. The unnamed colleague proposed the surrender to France of the strategically located British colony of Trinidad in exchange for a decision by France to terminate their slave trade. If the French were not interested in Trinidad then they could negotiate with them a financial compensation package of two to three million pounds sterling for their decision to end their slave trade. Wellington was further warned that the correspondence was confidential and had to be kept hidden from Wilberforce and his colleagues at the African Institution. British success in convincing the French to end the slave trade, then, would restore the confidence of those who believed that humanitarianism was at the centre of the campaign to abolish the slave trade.[35] Ironically, James Stephens, one of the more prominent moral crusaders of the African Institution, heard about the private negotiations with the French and supported the idea. Stephens hoped that the British administration would be able to balance successfully moral considerations along with economic interest. If they influenced France to suppress their slave trade, it would result most importantly in British colonial produce receiving a great boost in the European markets, and the British administration would be recorded in history as the moral conscience of the world, since they would be repairing the damage done to the Africans for the horrendous slave trade.[36]

The scepticism and outright anger of many Jamaican planters in reaction to the abolition of the slave trade arose partly because they recognized this economic design and partly because of ensuing economic policies, which had lasting social and political ramifications that they found unacceptable. As a result, they used a number of methods to try to hinder metropolitan reforms. First, they resorted to political propaganda that played on fear, arguing that complete abolition would destroy the colonies by allowing the brutish Africans to rise and slaughter the white people, as was done in St Domingue. Second, as a pre-emptive attempt to thwart meaningful metropolitan reforms, the planters revised their Consolidated Slave Laws, granting, however, only minimal compromises to the enslaved Africans. Third, the planters resisted other meaningful changes, such as judicial, prison and legal reforms. As a result, amelioration had only a limited effect on the enslaved population. This is significant because some Caribbean historians claim that planter amelioration achieved a measure of success, such as better material conditions for the enslaved Africans.[37] They base their arguments primarily on the various laws passed by the Jamaican planters in the assembly. But most of these laws were limited and easily evaded by the planters; in reality, they were strategies to prevent tougher metropolitan laws.

Cateau describes the eighteenth-century Consolidated Slave Laws as acts intended to cover the following five basic requirements: increased quantity and quality of food, improved clothing and better health; reduction in the severity of punishments; improvement in the fairness of trials; the spread of religion; and the fostering of natural increase.[38] The early nineteenth-century laws should have also covered the five basic requirements, but they were never substantially addressed at that point. Even in 1831, when the British Parliament finally ratified the Consolidated Slave Laws of Jamaica, it was done with much reservation, as the five basic requirements were still not substantially met.[39]

The more Parliament pressured the Jamaican planters, the more entrenched became their record of social and human rights abuses. This was especially true of the legal profession, specifically the very magistrates who represented the British government. The Consolidated Slave Laws that the Jamaican assembly passed signalled a step forward, but the harsh actions of their members to protect the institution of slavery nullified the laws, taking them two steps backwards. The Jamaican planters' non-enforcement of these laws and the conduct of the magistrates in the execution of justice up to 1822 contributed to Parliament's decision to insist on more speedy and qualitative ameliorative reforms in the 1823 House of Commons.

The rights afforded to the enslaved population by the new reforms of 1823 were as follows: compulsory manumission, task work replacing day labour, the acquisition of property that could be legally given to their posterity, and even the right of personal banking, with which the Africans could leave their assets to whomever they wished.[40] It is clear that the British Parliament by then was preparing the enslaved Africans for wage labour. The Jamaican planters strongly disapproved. One of the manifestations of their displeasure was the unusual number of enslaved transported from the island as punishment from the slave courts. Between the years 1808 and 1822, approximately 1,779 Africans were transported from the island's seven ports, a yearly average of 127 enslaved Africans (table 1.2). If transportation only represented one form of punishment, it was symbolic of how draconian the planters' punishments were. Most of these enslaved Africans were sent to Cuba – which explains why so many returned to Jamaica – and to other places on the Spanish mainland. Others were sent to the United States, Honduras, the Bahamas and Florida.[41] If the 2,923 enslaved Africans imported in 1808 and 1809 are taken out of the total of 3,922 from table 1.2, then it shows that only 999 enslaved Africans were imported legally into the island by the Jamaican authorities from 1808 to 1822. When the 1,779 transported enslaved Africans are compared with the 999 imported, we see not only the high number transported, but also that for every enslaved African imported by the Jamaican authorities, approximately one and a half were transported as a means of punishment.

The Jamaican planters' punishment of the enslaved Africans was so severe that the Colonial Office in 1823 reprimanded the Jamaican authorities for the deportation of such a high number of Africans and demanded an immediate explanation, as it contradicted their navigation laws. The crown indicated that the high figure was discussed in the House of Commons in its meeting of 14 May 1823. The members reacted with shock.[42] The lieutenant governor, Henry Conran, could not give a direct answer, as he did not have the documents. However, he surmised that they were enslaved Africans deported as a means of punishment. To make matters worse for Lieutenant Governor Conran,

Table 1.2 Licensed Imports and Exports of Africans, 1808–1822

Year	Imports	Exports
1808	161*	375
1809	2,762*	91
1810	–	83
1811	17	41
1812	–	72
1813	–	81
1814	–	157
1815	–	175
1816	59	147
1817	138	83
1818	95	76
1819	139	91
1820	–	140
1821	48	86
1822	503	81
Total	3,922	1,779†

*Unlicensed and hence illegal imports for 1808 and 1809.
†The 1,779 are all transported enslaved Africans but in a later document, CO 137/155, the Colonial Office has a figure of 1,392. Thus, my figure of 1,779 could be disputed.
Source: CO 137/154, 58, 257–58.

Custos Vassal in the parish of Hanover had an enslaved African, Neptune, hanged based on a faulty interpretation of the ninety-sixth clause of the 1816 slave law. Conran subsequently changed the law regarding capital punishment because of its frequent abuse by the planters, who were both the jurors and magistrates in the slave courts. Under the new law, magistrates at the slave courts had to apply to him before they could administer capital punishment.[43]

In 1829, the Right Honourable George Murray, the secretary of state for the colonies, further changed the law for capital offences. He informed all his governors that in cases of capital convictions, all judges had to send to the governor's office all the relevant information relating to the case along with a transcript of the judge's notes based on the evidence of the trial. All of this had to be then submitted to Parliament. This meant that capital convictions now had to be sanctioned by Parliament before the Jamaican authorities could take action.[44] This had become necessary because of many magistrates' negligence in recording detailed notes. In one prior case, magistrates had been accused of having the court minutes written in pencil. They were later transcribed in pen and sent to the governor under oath.[45]

The Colonial Office's reprimand over the large numbers of enslaved Africans deported prior to 1822 seemed to have an impact in the ensuing years. Between the years 1821 and 1825, there were 818 Africans imported into Jamaica, mainly from Nassau and Bermuda, under consent from the Jamaican authorities; only fifteen were deported to Cuba between 1823 and 1825.[46] This was in stark contrast to the previous years, 1808 to 1822, when there were 1,779 Africans deported.

The planters' desire to maintain the institution of slavery by punishing enslaved Africans with deportation for non-capital crimes becomes very evident when the results of slave court cases are examined. In one particular court in the parish of St Dorothy in the Vale, between the years 1814 and 1818, enslaved Africans were sentenced to deportation for minor offences such as the stealing of clothes and cattle. Although most of the sentences for deportation from the same slave court in St Dorothy in the Vale consisted of runaways who had been gone for over a year, there were nevertheless a few cases in which enslaved Africans were transported for running away for a little over six months.[47] Of the eighty-nine cases brought before the magistrates, eighty-eight involved charges against the enslaved Africans and one involved a charge against a white person for flogging his slave. The white person was acquitted. Of the eighty-eight charges against the enslaved Africans, seventy-eight resulted in guilty convictions: fifty were sentenced to deportation, five to life imprisonment, and the other twenty-three were imprisoned with hard labour and sentenced to be publicly flogged.[48]

In the area of prison reform, Governor Belmore in 1831 apologized to the Colonial Office for not sending sufficient returns regarding the number of enslaved Africans in jails. He too was shocked that such a large number of enslaved Africans (178) were incarcerated for life. He acknowledged that prison reform was absolutely necessary, because the enslaved Africans' convictions did not fit the nature of their crimes. However, if he pardoned some of the enslaved Africans they would become free and although their owners would be compensated for their loss, he would set a dangerous precedent for future runaways.[49]

Three months later, Governor Belmore informed the commissioners of legal inquiry in London that the superintendence and inspection of the Jamaican prisons needed maximum attention. The three regional jails, along with the many parish jails across the island, were woefully dilapidated. To make matters worse, the provost marshal, who was the patent sheriff responsible for the jails in the country and a representative of the British Parliament by a patent office, was one of the chief persons who had strongly resisted the badly needed repairs to the infrastructure. Furthermore, the Jamaican assembly was not interested in improving the state of the prisons. In 1818, a previous governor, the Duke of Manchester, appointed a committee to examine the conditions of the jails. The committee reported that the jails were materially inadequate and very poorly managed. However, the assembly rejected the report as insignificant and decided only to spend money for rendering the buildings more secure. Interestingly, it was the provost marshal himself who influenced the planters to take this stance in the assembly.[50]

By November 1831, the Crown again demonstrated its commitment to social reforms by pressuring the Jamaican assembly into introducing new measures for the appointment of judges and assistant judges for both the Supreme Court and the Court of Assize. Parliament made it clear that judges of the court were barred from personally owning slaves or being connected to plantations in any way. They were not even to hold political office because they were to remain "neutral".[51] Governor Belmore, in his attempt to bring the legal institution of Jamaica up to par with that of England, decided to limit capital offences to cases of great delinquency, such as murder, arson, robbery attended with violence, rape, forgeries of an aggravated nature and piracy.[52]

The continued resistance of the Jamaican planters influenced Parliament's 1823 amelioration bill, which in principle was non-negotiable. These 1823 reforms have been correctly described by Mary Turner as the beginning of the end for the British West Indian planters.[53] The Jamaicans' continued resistance along with fellow British colonies after 1823 left Parliament with no other option but to shift its policy from gradual to immediate emancipation.

Political Context

The Jamaican planters had always been rebellious.[54] Governor Nugent, one of the early nineteenth-century governors, expressed frustration to the Colonial Office regarding his inability to influence the Jamaican assembly. In one of his dispatches he wrote, "I must consider the Assembly of Jamaica as decidedly hostile at the present moment to any measure which may be proposed for the natural benefit of the mother country and the colony and actually blind to their own interests. I beg you to take into consideration if a change of government here might not be likely to advantage the public."[55] Nugent came to this conclusion in his second year as governor, when he observed the stubborn resistance of the Jamaican planters to metropolitan initiatives.

The Jamaican planters used their power in the assembly to resist efforts to improve the judicial process and give more privileges to the enslaved Africans, free blacks and the coloured population. This resistance to amelioration continued throughout the early nineteenth century. In 1823, the governor, the Duke of Manchester, embarrassed because of the planters' continuous resistance to metropolitan reform, apologized on the Jamaicans' behalf. He wrote:

> I am grieved to say that the Assembly is composed of such materials that I fear there is more Creole prejudice remaining than ought to be formed amongst them and a greater reluctance to part power over their slave, than might have been expected in the present age, which makes them view with suspicion and dis-satisfaction any measure which is to raise the slave above his personal level. . . . Your lordship may reasonably suppose that there are persons in the Assembly with whom I could confidentially communicate, and whom I might induce to bring forward measures recommended by government. There have been such persons and there are some still, but most of them who were possessed of either talent or influence have left the island and the very few who remain find it in vain to oppose the violence and indiscretion of the great majority of their colleagues.[56]

London's resolve to pressure the Jamaican planters into accepting change can be seen in the kind of governors sent to Jamaica by the 1830s. In 1832, the Earl of Mulgrave was chosen to lead the transition to the new reforms. Governor Mulgrave was viewed as a just, resolute and firm individual who was best suited to control the rebellious Jamaicans.[57] The Earl of Mulgrave lived up to his reputation and was very critical of the planters in his first official communication to the colonial authorities. He realized that many of his civil servants believed that the enslaved Africans were not yet ready for emancipation. They did not believe that the enslaved Africans had developed a responsible work ethic to meet the demands of free labour. Furthermore, they were convinced that the enslaved Africans would only resort to universal idleness when emancipated. Thus, the Earl of Mulgrave decided to test their views by conducting a tour of the island, seeing that the British Parliament's programme of reform was based on the assumption that the enslaved Africans could become excellent wage labourers.[58]

After his tour, Mulgrave realized that he faced other enormous challenges. As governor, he did not have unilateral power to enforce compliance. Thus, he would start by removing magistrates for willful neglect of their duties, since it would serve as a good example to others. Second, he had a real dilemma in finding credible alternatives to the custodes and magistrates in the parishes. He concluded that there was hardly any resident proprietor worthy of being placed in such an office.[59] Although his options were limited, however, he decided to work with what was available and to see how he could engage them to become more responsible.

Lord Goderich highly commended Governor Mulgrave for his wisdom in not firing all of the custodes and magistrates. He applauded him for gently imploring the members of the judicial service to become more consistent as civil servants. Lord Goderich wrote: "You may probably find it convenient to impress upon them that should you be compelled to dispense with their services . . . it may be necessary to fill up their places with persons chosen for their moderate and creditable demeanor and respect for the authority of the crown . . . than with any exclusive reference to pretensions founded upon distinctions of color."[60] Governor Mulgrave's handling of the first assembly over which he presided in 1832 was also commendable. He threatened the assembly with dissolution and then vetoed a bill that sought to influence an election in the parish of Kingston.[61] The assembly fell into line and became compliant. In his assessment of his first assembly, Mulgrave correctly concluded that unless Great Britain continued to interfere in the affairs of Jamaica, the irreconcilable differences between the two worlds would not be repaired. It was obvious that London and Jamaica had different needs and expectations.

Mulgrave further considered supporting publicly the candidacy of some mulattoes or free coloureds in the upcoming elections for seats in the House of Assembly. He wondered if such a move would help the assembly become more civil. He later concluded that it would not work because the mulattoes were only powerful in the parish of Kingston and could not win anywhere else on the island. Even if some won seats in Kingston, their limited presence would not significantly change the tone of the assembly. As a matter of fact, it might encourage more resistance.[62]

Despite the bold attempts of Governor Mulgrave, he could not prevent the rapid growth of an organized political movement by the planters. The Jamaican planters had formed an island-wide organization in 1831 called the Colonial Church Union. This political union had already enacted what the Jamaican authorities called "violent resolutions" in all of its seventeen parishes.[63] Despite assurances from the British authorities to the chief magistrates in all the parishes that the British government was more interested in colonial reforms than in the direct extinction of slavery, the Colonial Church Union continued to argue otherwise.[64] In some parishes, committees of correspondences were even appointed to make linkages with other parishes. Delegates were also nominated in all the parishes to attend an island-wide meeting in Spanish Town, the same town where the assembly also met. Interestingly, this coincided with the time of the regular assembly meetings.[65] The alternative assembly, however, drafted a petition calling not just for economic protection but also to send its own delegation to London to further petition the metropolitan power. They were convinced that their once peaceful colony was under threat of extinction from pro-abolitionists. They felt the delegation to London was necessary because they had doubts as to whether their interests were really being heard and understood.[66] The two delegates who petitioned the colonial authorities in London could not influence the officials, however, as the die was already cast.

The political instability that had been caused by the Colonial Church Union had inflamed even moderate persons who felt that they had to join to remain respected in their communities. This included many free coloureds and other loyal representatives of the Crown. Thus, it became difficult for Governor Mulgrave to bring to justice the perpetrators of crimes.[67]

The Jamaican planters' continued disregard for due process of law and their belief that only the whip and extreme force would serve to control their enslaved Africans contributed to more public and violent slave rebellions. The changing early nineteenth-century context demanded a more conciliatory form of management in order for the planters to meet production targets: far less repressive measures, more leniency and more concessions to the enslaved workers. The fact that concessions were made, however, does not indicate that the enslaved Africans in Jamaica wished to remain as slaves. Nothing short of freedom was their main goal. But in the interim between slavery and freedom, more concessions would have meant that the planters would have had greater control of their labour, which would have likely meant fewer rebellions. The planters would have been better served devoting their time and attention to creating initiatives for better management rather than implementing harsher measures under the guise of procuring better "security of the island". As it was, open and violent resistance was endemic to Jamaican society, starting with the arrival of the Europeans and continuing up to Apprenticeship in 1834.[68]

Mary Turner incorrectly writes that between the 1807 abolition of the slave trade and 1831, the incidence of open slave rebellions diminished in Jamaica. Outside of the 1831 Sam Sharpe Rebellion, she acknowledges only one other uprising, a small-scale attempt in 1824 by the enslaved Africans of three estates in Hanover. She further argues that slave managers as individuals were rarely attacked and that even cases of arson were unusual.[69] She thus conveys the impression that slave rebellions in early nineteenth-century Jamaica were not as frequent as the Maroon rebellions that had occurred in the eighteenth century. This is far from true. Table 1.3 suggests that early nineteenth-century Jamaica was as openly rebellious as it had been in the eighteenth century, including attempts to set up Maroon-style communities. Furthermore, in early nineteenth-century Jamaica, one of the features of resistance on the part of the enslaved was the seeking of legal redress. The enslaved Africans, being more knowledgeable of their "rights" under the slave laws and empowered by discussions in England surrounding their gradual emancipation, reported their abuses directly to the magistrates at their own risk. This move to report abuses was in addition to the open rebellions. Plantation papers further show a kind of militant labour resistance on the part of the enslaved Africans in the early nineteenth century. Whenever they became deeply dissatisfied over changes in their labour conditions, they proceeded to burn down the plantations, run away in mass numbers or flatly refuse to work until their grievances were addressed by management.[70] Furthermore, the records of slave courts in the individual parishes in the early nineteenth century show that the predominant

Table 1.3 Early Nineteenth-Century Rebellions in Jamaica

Year	Parish	Type	Outcome
1806	St George	Small	2 slaves executed, 1 deported
1807	Portland	Small	?
1808	Port Royal	Small	?
1809	Kingston	Medium	2 persons hanged, over 20 deported
1815	St Elizabeth	Medium	2 slaves convicted
1819	St Catherine	Large	Extensive Maroon community destroyed
1823	5 parishes	Very large	25 slaves hanged and total cost of £15,270.12
1831	9 parishes	Extremely large	Thousands of slaves involved

Note: "Small" means the involvement of dozens of slaves; "medium", up to two hundred slaves; "large", over three hundred slaves; "very large", up to one thousand slaves; and "extremely large", many thousands of slaves.

Source: Colonial Office Papers.

convictions were for runaways from enslavement.[71] Turner was correct in writing that approximately twenty-five hundred to three thousand enslaved Africans were reported as running away every year in the last decade of slavery.[72]

What was also interesting about the early nineteenth-century rebellions in Jamaica, as seen in table 1.3, was the relationship between the planters' political agitation and the increasing rebellion of the enslaved Africans. The more the planters sought to control their enslaved population through repressive security measures, the more the enslaved Africans became openly rebellious in asserting their rights. Again, this does not mean that the enslaved were not naturally resistant, as demonstrated by the number of runaways and fires. But all the major rebellions in the early nineteenth century followed periods of intense political turmoil between the Jamaican assembly and the Crown. As can be seen in table 1.3, the agitation surrounding the 1807 Abolition Act was preceded and followed by three rebellions between 1806 and 1809; the discord concerning the Registration Act between 1812 and 1819 was followed by two rebellions in 1815 and 1819; the 1823–24 House of Commons decision was followed by widespread revolts across the island in those two years; and the 1831 formation of the Colonial Church Union and its associated political activity had an effect on the 1831 Sam Sharpe Rebellion. The timing of these rebellions might very well be coincidental, but what makes them seem to be directly related to the planters' political activity is the increasing number of enslaved Africans who were becoming involved. The rebellions moved from small to extremely large in scope between 1806 and 1831, as demonstrated in table 1.3.

While the planters had become agitated, the enslaved Africans had also become militant and had asserted their right to be free either by metropolitan law or by war. No wonder Governor Belmore stated in 1832 that his arrival in Jamaica was greeted with great scepticism by the planters but great excitement by the enslaved Africans. The enslaved Africans thought that he had been given the emancipation proclamation. He was greeted by the largest number of enslaved Africans ever gathered at the Kingston wharf.[73]

Reports submitted by the Jamaican assembly in regard to the two largest early nineteenth-century rebellions, those of 1823–24 and 1831, support the point that the planters' agitation spurred further violent rebellion on the part of the enslaved.[74] Based on his reading of preliminary reports, Lord Goderich stated that it was clear that the 1831 rebellion resulted from a feeling among the enslaved Africans that their masters had denied them the freedom that they had been granted.[75] Lord Goderich then blamed the assembly's intransigence for inciting the enslaved Africans. It took the Jamaican planters in the assembly from 1823 to February 1831 to pass a fair act on religious toleration. Although they passed the 1831 Slave Laws, it was with the understanding that it still needed more revision. Lord Goderich also believed that the Colonial Church Unions' loose talk aided the rebellion. He indicated that the enslaved Africans had been models of decency up to the time of the planters' agitation. In addition, he felt that the removal of the enslaved Africans' Christmas holidays in 1831 had provided further justification for their revolt. Lord Goderich concluded that the enslaved Africans should not be blamed for rebelling if they felt the planters were withholding their freedom. To underscore his message, he sent another proclamation calling on all representatives of the Crown to work harder to bring to justice the perpetrators of crime and to urge the enslaved Africans to remain loyal to their masters, since they were not yet released from slavery.[76]

The most serious indictment of the Jamaican planters, however, came from the Marquess of Sligo, who replaced Mulgrave as governor of Jamaica in 1835. He blamed the planters of St James, not the influence of sectarian preachers, as the main culprits for inciting the enslaved Africans to rebel in 1831. The St James planters, he claimed, had taken advantage of their apprentices and attempted to sabotage Apprenticeship. With a few exceptions, the governor castigated the St James planters for being more severe than the planters in the rest of the island.[77]

The Marquess of Sligo seemed to have been correct, as the period of Apprenticeship (1834–38) further vindicated the enslaved Africans. On numerous occasions, the enslaved Africans were reported as hardworking and industrious human beings who, if treated fairly, were a model workforce. The Jamaican governors and stipendiary magistrates were finally convinced that the planters of Jamaica were to be blamed for their non-interest in plantation reform.[78] The planters were still strategically finding means of coercing African labourers and creating enormous labour difficulties. From the outset, the Jamaican planters sought to hijack and undermine Apprenticeship. Mulgrave indicated clearly that the assembly was still comprised of the same individuals who had shown bitter opposition to reform in the previous years. Mulgrave reprimanded them openly for such bitter opposition as they publicly opposed every plan of government. He then quietly encouraged them to suppress their own opinions in favour of unanimity and to stick with the British Parliament's plan. Although the planters eventually took his advice, it was clear that Apprenticeship would not last. Mulgrave concluded as early as 1833 that the planters' opposition to the plan would ultimately prevail, leading to a shortened version of Apprenticeship, which would in turn lead to the enslaved Africans being set free.[79]

With the dawn of emancipation, it became quite evident that the Jamaican plantation economy faced a problem of management[80] and not a shortage of labour as stated by the planters. The Jamaican planters hastened their own demise with their opposition to amelioration and, in turn, created the myth of the "lazy" black to absolve themselves of their own inadequacies and fears. The following chapter will demonstrate the deepening rut in which early nineteenth-century plantation managers found themselves and will further show that management reform was the plantations' most urgent need if they were to compete in the changing economic environment.

CHAPTER 2

Ambiguous Management

Management Structure

By the dawn of the nineteenth century, two types of plantation managers, residential and absentee, were well entrenched in Jamaica. Higman aptly describes the historical circumstances that led to the birth of these two managerial practices, along with the distinct advantages and disadvantages of each.[1] Higman, unlike many of his colleagues, is of the view that absentee management was productive and efficient, and thus absentee landlords should not be blamed for the decline of the planter class in Jamaica.[2] Despite Higman's revelations, the two-tier management structure of early nineteenth-century Jamaica (absentee and residential) led to a complex management structure and function at a time when the 1807 Abolition Act necessitated managerial reforms.

Despite the collusion of the residential and absentee managers in forcing the enslaved Africans to work to the point of death, in many cases the policies of the absentee owners residing in Great Britain were not necessarily executed by the "stewards" of management at the plantation level.[3] This was because the owners were often intricately connected with a number of steward managers (attorneys, overseers, bookkeepers), most of whom were also attempting to squeeze as much money as they could from the plantations.[4]

To understand better the problems associated with plantation management in early nineteenth-century Jamaica, one has to examine its structure and operations. First, there was the problem of ownership. The owner of the plantation was usually an absentee residing in Great Britain. In some cases the alleged owner of an estate had great difficulty in making serious managerial policies, as there were legal disputes in the Court of Chancery by immediate family members over ownership of the plantation.[5] Second, owners oftentimes were embroiled in serious legal issues with merchants and creditors, who in many cases owned the plantations based on the enormous unpaid loans.[6] In seeking to resolve their conflicts on the matter of ownership, the various parties often ignored the necessary reforms, such as labour procurement, given the imperatives arising from the Abolition Act.

The stewards of management, who were the resident plantation managers in Jamaica, further added to this ambiguity. The plantation owners in Great Britain would often resort to hiring renowned attorneys residing in Jamaica. Most often, these Jamaican attorneys were absentees themselves, since they were being hired to manage many plantations and could not reside on them all. Most of these sought-after attorneys also had their own plantations to manage,[7] and as a result, they had to depend on overseers. These overseers were usually the ones who actually implemented managerial policies on the plantations, since they were usually resident planters. However, in many cases the "resident" overseer was also an absentee, and as such the daily running of the plantation was left either to the plantation clerks or bookkeepers, who usually resided on the plantations.[8]

This hierarchy of owners and stewards in the management structure of the plantation is significant given the realities of the 1807 Abolition Act. The persons responsible for drafting managerial policies in Great Britain often found themselves at variance with those responsible for their implementation in Jamaica. The groups of managers in different geographical locations (Great Britain and Jamaica) were driven by different socio-economic and political realities caused by the perceived attack on the institution of slavery. This partially accounts for the divisions between the West Indian planters in London and the resident Jamaican planters over plantation strategies, despite their mutual interest in accruing wealth through the enslaved Africans. An example of this division was evident in the 1832 Jamaican House of Assembly. The Jamaican assembly was comprised mainly of attorneys or steward managers. They made it clear to the governor that they would not be as conciliatory to the British Parliament's plan of amelioration as the owners in Great Britain.

They stated:

> This House was no party to the measure by which an enquiry was obtained in one House of the British Parliament by the West India Proprietors residing out of the island. . . . As this House never did recognise the resolutions of Parliament in 1823 – as this House never did admit the right of the House of Commons to legislate on the internal affairs of Jamaica, even when the West Indies were indirectly represented in Parliament.[9]

Governor Mulgrave scolded the assembly members, saying that they did not have the right to disassociate themselves from their colleagues in London because their interests were different. Thus, he said, they should fall into line and support their managerial colleagues.[10] Mulgrave further stressed that the assembly's narrow self-interest in sending its own delegation to the imperial legislature in London and not trusting its own representatives to petition on their behalf had backfired. The British Parliament had decided to interfere in the politics of the colonies since they were now convinced that colonies like Jamaica were not serious about socio-economic reform. Lord Goderich cautioned the Jamaican assembly on their shortsightedness. He wrote: "It unhappily forces upon me the conviction that the members of the Assembly are not prepared to meet the present exigency. . . . Instead of a resolution to engage earnestly in the solution of the question how the transition from slavery to freedom can be effected with the least danger to society at large, their Assembly confine themselves to recriminations, which even were they well founded would be un-availing."[11]

Selwyn Carrington, in his latest monograph, has argued that the sugar industry in the British West Indies at the close of the eighteenth century desperately needed restructuring for the planters to remain competitive in the nineteenth century.[12] In fact, Lord Castlereagh frankly told the Jamaican assembly to stop resisting the passing of the 1807 Abolition Act. He gave a number of reasons why they needed to do this. Among these were that the British West Indies were overproducing sugar, that their sugar was too expensive for the British public and, most importantly, that their institution of slavery was too inhumane. Lord Castlereagh enumerated what the planters needed to do to ameliorate these problems. They needed to increase the number of marriages among the enslaved Africans and procure more natural increases of children; investigate why so many children were dying from tetanus; and

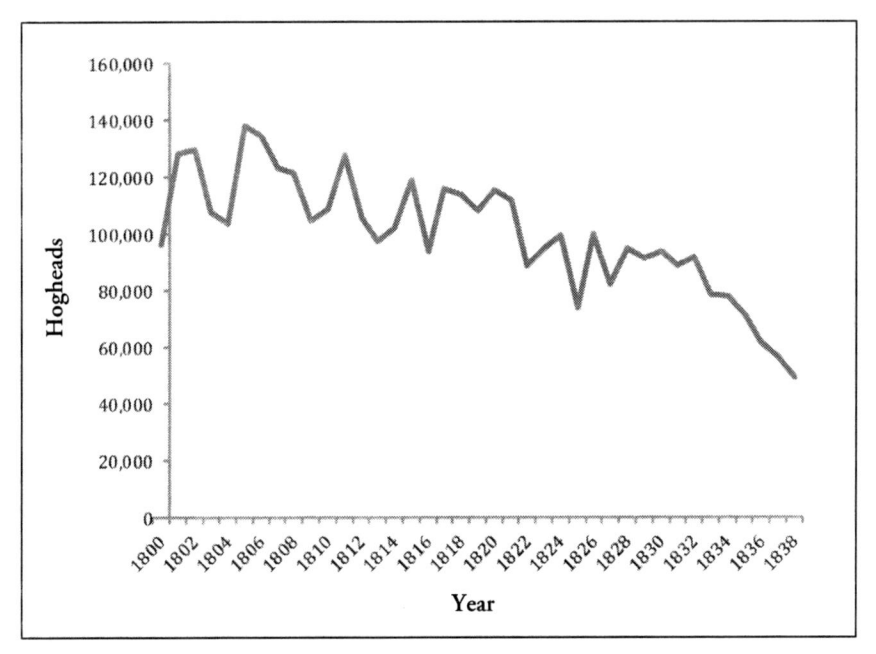

Figure 2.1 Sugar production in Jamaica, 1800–1838

Source: Selwyn H.H. Carrington, "Statistics for the Study of Caribbean History in the Eighteenth and Nineteenth Centuries" (manuscript).

pursue more ameliorative health care, mainly for women and children. In addition, Lord Castlereagh stated, the planters should now follow the models of some of the newer sugar islands such as Tobago and St Vincent.[13]

One restructuring measure that was absolutely necessary for the Jamaican planters was at the level of the plantations' managerial structure. This was complex and not relevant for the new market reality of the early nineteenth century. Plantation management in Jamaica was not properly defined. I will show that this was one of the factors that led to declining production on many Jamaican estates, as seen in figure 2.1.

Absentee Management and Its Effects

One of the reasons that absentee management added to the complexity of plantation management in the early nineteenth century was that many of the plantation owners were sons of absentee Jamaican planters. Unlike their parents, many of them never visited their parents' plantations. Thus, they were not only inexperienced in the techniques of planting but also unfamiliar with the peculiar conditions of British West Indian agriculture. Some of these young managers, such as Henry Goulburn, were even underage and could not make managerial decisions. Thus, they were dependent on an elder member of the family or one of the plantation trustees.[14] Edward Long, a noted Jamaican planter, argued that plantation agriculture in Jamaica could best be learned through trial and error because the conditions were unique. Thus, a significant amount of time was needed for these young British planters to learn successfully the difficult art of plantation management.[15]

To understand better the dilemma many of these absentee planters faced after 1807, the examples of the following planters are instructive. Absentee planter Joseph Foster Barham decided in 1801 that if his plantation was to remain productive, he had to take the daily tasks of management from the hands of clerks and bookkeepers. He ordered William Rodgers, one of his two attorneys at Mesopotamia plantation in Westmoreland, to revive the policy in which the overseer had to live on the estate, as Rodgers had when he was an overseer.[16] Later, Thomas Plummer, one of his attorneys at another plantation, Island in the parish of St Elizabeth, assured Barham that he had followed his instructions and that Mr Ellis, the overseer, had already returned to live at the plantation.[17] Barham's decision is commendable, as other absentee planters paid dearly for allowing junior managers to run the daily affairs of their plantations.

As an example of this, attorney John Shand insisted that his absentee proprietor should not send any gifts to his overseers since they were all useless. His overseers could not make an extraordinary crop without injuring the enslaved Africans or the cattle. Shand wrote that "none of them have any great length of service to plead. The oldest Mr. Cumming at Holland is by no means a manager entirely. . . . You will ask why he is not removed and a better sent there. I regret to add that this is a matter of great difficulty and that it is by no means easy to select or procure a person equal to so important a trust."[18] Shand proceeded to blame one of his overseers as the main culprit for that year's rum not being as strong as in the previous years. He had doubted him for some time and wanted to find somebody better, but he could not.[19]

Two years later, Shand still bemoaned the fact that he had not seen any suitable and available attorneys to manage the estates in the eventuality that he and his brother, William, could not. Jamaican plantations could not be managed as those in England were. In the latter, if the owner did not irritate the tenant, his plantation was certain to bring in an income since the owner or the agent did not have to meddle in the plantation's agricultural management. But in Jamaica, the attorney had to be an excellent farmer, be knowledgeable about managing enslaved Africans and understand the mechanics of employing additional enslaved day labourers (jobbers). Since the owners often lived thousands miles from their plantations, they depended completely on their attorneys to micromanage their plantations. The salvation of the plantation was entirely in the attorney's hands. Furthermore, the overseer could badly tarnish the attorney's reputation.[20]

Shand, who resided in Spanish Town, depended completely on his overseers since he was in charge of many plantations. On one of the plantations owned by Lord Penrhyn in the parish of Clarendon, Shand made it clear that the success of the plantation was completely in the hands of overseer Thomas Graham.[21] John's brother, William Shand, experienced great embarrassment at the hand of the overseer of one of his plantations. It was reported that the overseer, Mr Fairclough, whom he had left in charge, was absent most of the time and that it was thus his plantation clerk who was very much the working overseer. As a result, the great house for the overseer, which was comfortably furnished, had become so dilapidated that it was no better than the other houses on the plantation. Its furniture had decayed immensely and the clothes press, ceiling lumber, tables, chairs and sofas were so badly deteriorated that the new overseer had to make immediate repairs at great expense to the plantation.[22]

Colonel Phillips, the new attorney who succeeded William Shand, castigated Shand for gross mismanagement, specifically for not knowing that overseer Fairclough was always absent from the plantation. This was because Shand himself hardly visited the plantation, since he had so many others to manage. Colonel Phillips even believed that Shand may have been embezzling funds, judging by the many bills drawn for all kinds of jobs for which there was no evidence. In addition, Shand had supplied the plantation with cattle from his own pen at the highest price. Phillps was of the view that if Shand was a better manager, the plantation cattle would not have deteriorated from neglect, improper treatment and inadequate pasture.[23]

It was customary, however, for new attorneys or overseers to paint a bad picture of their predecessors, as Phillips did. Furthermore, the particular plantation that William Shand had managed belonged to John Tharp. Tharp's estates had been embroiled in management controversy since his death in 1804. Thus, many of the arguments on mismanagement were political since his family was desperately trying to gain control of the plantation. This does not diminish the fact that much mudslinging by attorneys and overseers has been associated with plantation management. Even the outstanding Jamaican planter Simon Taylor was accused of dishonesty in not disclosing the amount of land that one of his clients possessed.[24]

Many absentee owners were not given the true picture regarding daily operations on their estates because not all attorneys were as frank as John Shand in stating categorically that they were not impressed with their overseers. These absentee owners were completely at the mercy of the attorneys, who often had their own agendas and on many occasions used the plantations under their care to enhance their private businesses.

What was even more distressing was that most absentee owners seemed to have been completely dependent on their attorneys to draft a plan for management succession. In most cases, the new attorney was chosen by the old attorney. As a result, plantations continued to suffer from neglect as the new attorneys were also busy men running their own businesses along with other plantations far away. Simon Taylor, whom Higman describes as managing twelve properties in 1832, is a good example.[25] Taylor informed one of his owners, Andrew Arcedeckne, that he had been extremely sick for the previous four months and had not been able to conduct any kind of business, not even on his own estate. At seventy-two years of age, he was seriously ailing and was therefore recommending Mr Steward, his overseer at Arcedeckne's property in Golden Grove, to become the attorney. Steward had become the de facto plantation manager, and thus Taylor felt it should be formalized.[26] Steward later received his letter granting him the power of attorney, but he died within a few months. Taylor then recommended the overworked Shand brothers, William and John, as the new attorneys. Taylor also appointed them attorneys for his properties in the event of his sudden death.[27] Taylor was also instrumental in having the Shand brothers employed as attorneys for the Tharp estates in St Thomas after John Tharp died in 1804. As a result, the Shand brothers ended up being attorneys for many estates when it was clear that they could not give much attention to so many plantations at great distances from each other.

Attorney Rowland Fearon provides another example of the difficulties many absentee managers faced as they were primarily dependent on their Jamaican attorneys. These local attorneys had tremendous influence over these absentee planters. In 1806, Fearon took the initiative and informed Lord Penrhyn that in case of any eventuality, he should appoint Fearon's brother to succeed him as attorney. Fearon highly recommended his brother since he had managed Fearon's own plantation very well and resided near Penrhyn's plantations. To persuade Penrhyn, Fearon even reminded him of the importance of plantation managers living on the plantation or near the district where the plantation was located. He had personally witnessed the mismanagement of many plantations as a result of absentee management. Fearon's comments are indeed true that many plantations were ruined because of wrong choices in managers. However, was it true that Fearon's brother was as good a manager as he claimed or was this a case of nepotism?[28]

What made the early nineteenth-century plantation model of management unsuited to the overall economic health of the Jamaican economy was that the model replicated itself. The more it was replicated, the more hardened the resident Jamaican planters became in their resistance to every sinew of colonial reform, since their economic, social and political salvation was wrapped up in slavery. In 1801, David Reid of Great Britain, the father of a young proprietor apprentice under Simon Taylor, enquired about his son's progress. Reid eagerly asked when his son would become a plantation attorney and become distinguished, like other attorneys with much money and social and political influence. Taylor remarked that young Reid was learning the art of management very well and could soon have his own gang of Africans and his own plantation, but he needed to be patient. The best land would only become available when a current proprietor died. Even then, if one got the chance to obtain such land, it would be quite expensive and would cost around twenty-five to thirty pounds per acre. The best strategy for Reid's son to pursue at the moment, said Taylor, was the purchase of enslaved Africans from his current income, to be used as jobbers. In so doing he would further learn the art of plantation management and would be building up his income to buy his own plantation later on as the opportunity presented itself.[29]

For every young white proprietor apprentice in Jamaica learning the art of plantation management, such as Reid, there were scores of white men already working as clerks, skilled artisans or overseers waiting their turn to be appointed attorneys and become rich. Among those already in the system trying to gain promotions were scores of young persons in Great Britain wishing to immigrate to Jamaica to seek their own socio-economic and political glory. The management system thus replicated itself, making the Jamaican planters ever more dependent on the institution of slavery. The planters had much to gain from the cumbersome management structure; it allowed them to provide additional services to the plantation through which they could make money in addition to their regular salaries. Of such services, jobbing was the most profitable.[30] It was not impossible for white personnel to earn two separate wages for two different posts on the same or different estates. In addition, white personnel on plantations could reduce their cost of living by several means. They had few living expenses and could save most of their incomes because the plantations provided accommodation, food and the use of many of their resources. White personnel could also utilize plantation lands, although this oftentimes resulted in major disputes between owners and attorneys.[31] Heather Cateau describes the many ways in which the planters took advantage of the plantations they led to increase their wealth. She contends that the British West Indies still reflected an atmosphere of frontier colonies, with individuals coming to the region to make quick fortunes and to consolidate their positions.[32] With so many personal advantages to be gained from slavery, one can better understand the unwillingness of many of the resident white planters in Jamaica to accept or implement thorough ameliorative measures, as discussed previously.

This dependence on "reliable" attorneys by absentee owners was not only limited to sugar plantations but was also prevalent on coffee plantations. Coffee was the second largest exported staple in early nineteenth-century Jamaica. James Daley, a coffee planter who lived in Spanish Town in eastern Jamaica but managed a western plantation, Hermitage, in St Elizabeth, admitted that in addition to the challenge posed by inadequate labour, the plantation's most current problem was the overseer, Mr McLean. Of late, McLean had become belligerent towards his fellow attorney, William Adlam, and his appearance led Daley to believe that he had become a drunkard. Daley was not convinced that McLean was keeping a correct account of the coffee that was picked. Consequently, the actual quantity of coffee was falling short of the reported

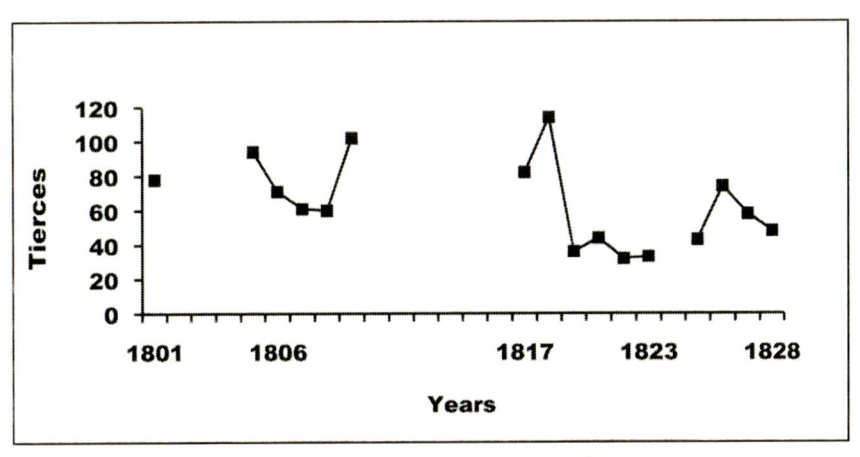

Figure 2.2 Crop accounts on Hermitage estate, 1801–1809 and 1817–1828
Source: Crop Accounts, Jamaica Archives.

amount.³³ It also took McLean a long time to gather the small crops. Furthermore, the coffee fields were generally foul-smelling and the coffee trees were overrun by shrubs, which made it difficult to clean them using the plantation's inadequate labour supply.³⁴ Daley eventually fired McLean and lamented that his careless management had tremendously set back the efficiency of the operations. Figure 2.2 represents the plantation's crop accounts. Although full figures were not available, especially from 1810 to 1816, the constant fluctuations in the plantation's production levels seem to suggest that along with inadequate labour, management instability was a critical factor in the destabilization of the plantation. McLean was the overseer from 1820; the exact time of his appointment as overseer is not known, however.³⁵

One of the reasons poor management has to be blamed for fluctuating production levels at Hermitage estate is that the plantation was much more productive in 1817, when it had fewer enslaved Africans, than in the years 1820 and 1823, when the plantation had more enslaved Africans but produced much less coffee, as seen in table 2.1. McLean was overseer in the years 1820 to 1823.

In addition, slave productivity between the years 1817 and 1828 also shows fluctuations. In 1817, each enslaved African produced around 2.4 tierces of coffee, while this figure dropped to under one tierce from 1820 to 1823. It again rose to 1.15 in 1826 but dropped again to 0.75 by 1828 (table 2.1).

Table 2.1 Slave Productivity on Hermitage Estate, 1817–1828

Year	Tierces of Coffee	Slaves	Average (Tierces)
1817	82	34	2.40
1820	44	60	0.73
1823	33	60	0.55
1826	74	64	1.15
1828	48	64	0.75

Source: Letterbook of John Wemyss, Hermitage Estate, 1819–1824, MS 250.

The Cedar Grove coffee plantation in Manchester also witnessed the effect of absenteeism on its operation. Mrs Boucher, resident in Jamaica and representing her absentee son's interests, had serious problems with the management of the estate. As the mother of the young owner, R. Boucher, she believed that one of the attorneys, John Salmon Jr, wanted to be manager for life. She was convinced that under his management the plantation would never become productive. She warned attorney Herbert James to find ways to dismiss Salmon; otherwise, she threatened, she would carry the entire management team back to the Court of Chancery.[36]

Meanwhile, the Court of Chancery had recently appointed an administrator of the property in the person of Mr Crabb. Unfortunately, he too was an absentee administrator. Crabb was sternly warned by one of the Chancery Court attorneys to return immediately to Jamaica since the estate was being badly managed. The management team in Jamaica was not executing Crabb's management wishes. In addition, the trustees in Great Britain wanted to be paid their annuities before he, Crabb, could pay the other beneficiaries from the remaining profit.

The most pressing problem on the estate, however, was that overseer Saunders had become useless, since he was always drunk and continued to abuse his wife severely. It was further alleged that Saunders enjoyed full luxuries on the estate, as he had nine illegitimate coloured children living with him along with his wife, all of whom lived off the property's expenses. Complicating the issue, Saunders was related to John Salmon Jr, which made it difficult to have Saunders dismissed. Further, Salmon was anxious for one of his other relatives

– Mr Cooper, who managed occasionally – to become part of the permanent management team.[37] Given the complicated management structure, Crabb had to remind the management team that all the proceeds of the last crop should be turned over to him and that he was the only person empowered by the court to pay annuities.[38] To make matters even worse, the other attorney, James, bemoaned the fact that having searched through the parish of Manchester he could not find another suitable overseer to replace Saunders. James recognized that in light of Apprenticeship, when management strategies had to be more conciliatory to the enslaved Africans, they now had to choose overseers who were both amicable with the Negroes and who could gain the maximum cultivation out of the property.[39]

This was a management dilemma of many absentee owners. The many persons pretending to be looking after the owners' interests, from attorneys to overseers, were the same persons strangling them economically. Mrs Boucher implored her son in the strongest language to stop procrastinating and come immediately to Jamaica to save his plantation. She pleaded with him to even come and evaluate his estate before he married. If he did not, Salmon's continued mismanagement would leave him financially bankrupt.[40] As further incentive, she warned him of a story that had allegedly been published recently in the Jamaican newspapers. One absentee planter, Mr Bruce, had left his fine property to the same John Salmon Jr to manage and kept getting only minimal returns from the estate. It was later discovered that Salmon had taken the liberty of lending a friend the horned cattle of the estate, at a value of thirteen hundred pounds, to pay his debts. The friend had died before repaying the money, leaving Salmon with the debt. Bruce had sued him and had been able to recover his damages in the Cornwall Court of Assizes.[41]

Mrs Boucher's other major grouse with the management team was the ridiculous commission along with other fees being charged by the attorneys. With those fees, she felt, the plantation could never become efficient. Furthermore, the plantation would shortly face a severe labour problem, since the apprentices were not willing to work with the current managers when Apprenticeship was over.[42]

The Cedar Grove plantation further demonstrates the complexities surrounding the setting and implementing of managerial policy by absentee planters: in this case, Mrs Boucher; her son, R. Boucher; Crabb; attorneys James and Salmon Jr; and Mr Saunders, the overseer. The interests of absentee owners were oftentimes secondary to the interests of plantation managers, most of whom had their own financial agendas and were also absentees themselves from the plantations under their care.

Higman, in his study of the Montpelier plantation, observed that hired managers, such as attorneys and overseers, viewed the plantation merely as a means of making quick money, as opposed to implementing the necessary measures that would result in long-term development and the maximization of production.[43] This was exactly one of the reasons for the Jamaican planters' resistance to change, as seen previously. The management structure benefited them. Furthermore, on many Jamaican plantations, the planters knew that there was no serious system of evaluation. Hence, no other interest mattered than theirs.

Internal Management Conflicts

The Golden Grove plantation, along with Bachelor's Hall Pen, owned by Andrew Arcedeckne, provide good examples of competing self-interests among management teams. It took a Court of Chancery decision in 1821 to determine a critical management issue: Were these two plantations stocked with an adequate number of enslaved Africans in order to reach their full productive capacity as stated in Andrew's father's will? Andrew Arcedeckne argued that they were not adequately stocked and carried the surviving trustees, Beeston Long and the Reverend George Turner, to court. Andrew argued that his father, who had died on 22 June 1808, had requested that around fifty enslaved Africans were to be purchased every year in small sets of fifteen, for the purposes of better seasoning. These enslaved Africans were to be used on the plantations and made available for hire as income, and he should receive the profits. The surviving trustees rebutted the claim since they already had slaves for hire. They claimed that Andrew Arcedeckne had already been paid three thousand pounds.[44]

The Shand brothers were the attorneys for the plantations and they, along with the overseers in that period, Richard Grant and Thomas McCormack, all supported the trustees.[45] William Shand boasted categorically that he was a very experienced planter, having been working in Jamaica for over thirty years and managing Golden Grove, along with his brother, for the last twenty. Thus, he was confident that the current enslaved Africans on the plantations were more than sufficient for the proper cultivation of eight hundred hogsheads of sugar annually. He argued further that one of the strategies they used to keep the enslaved Africans healthy was to use the plough rather than the hoe to aid cultivation. Despite the lengthy supporting affidavits submitted by the plantation overseers, the trustees lost the case in the Court of Chancery.[46]

The court concluded that evidence of the plough's beneficial effect on the health of the enslaved Africans had not been substantiated. Thus, the court reasoned, the enslaved Africans at Golden Grove were unhealthy.[47] If conditions were as good on the plantation and if the enslaved Africans were as healthy as the trustees argued they were, then a natural increase of the enslaved population should have been obvious. Instead, there had been a natural decrease in births over a period of nine years, from 1 January 1810 to 30 September 1819. In addition, the trend seemed to have continued thereafter. Since the loss over the last four years of the period 1810–19 appeared to have been greater than during the first four years, it could only be concluded that the number and effective strength of the enslaved population had not been equal to all the labours of the plantations. The court also concluded that other reasons contributing to the overall natural population decrease were poor diet, overwork and lack of material care of the enslaved Africans.[48] In summing up, the court stated that "something had to be wrong in the management of the plantations, if 'well-fed' and 'moderately worked' enslaved women who were reported as having no special debility, were not even producing children".[49]

This case clearly shows how different the perspectives of the Jamaican plantation managers and those of the absentee planters were. Most of the Jamaican planters were not interested in serious plantation reform given the realities of the 1807 decision to abolish the slave trade. The Jamaican planters seemed to be more interested in maintaining the status quo, since they benefited immensely from it. Andrew Arcedeckne had to carry his entire management team to court in order to purchase more enslaved Africans on his own plantation. As figure 2.3 shows, Golden Grove's production of sugar began slowly declining around 1807. The yearly average of six hundred hogsheads of sugar that attorney McCormack argued was possible in 1821 was an illusion, as the plantation's production plummeted after that year. Arcedeckne's fight with

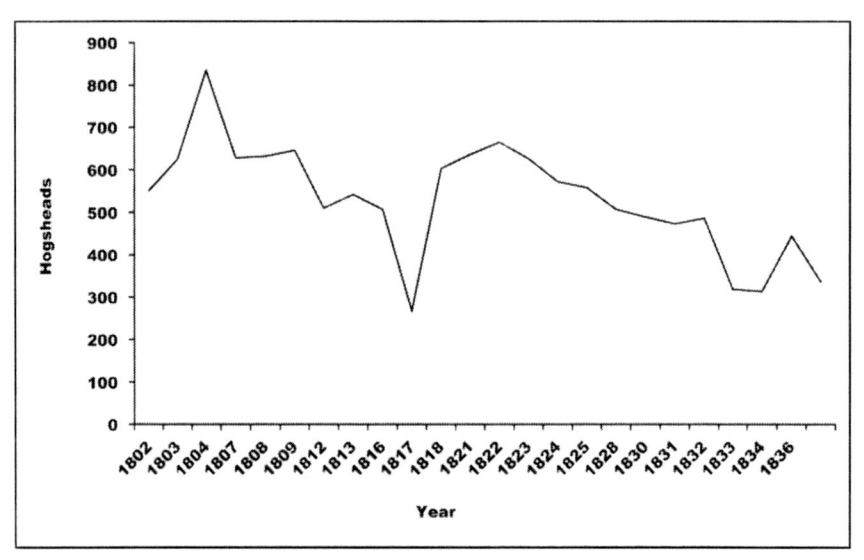

Figure 2.3 Yearly hogsheads of sugar produced at Golden Grove, 1802–1836
Source: Crop Accounts, Jamaica Archives.

his own management team while his yearly production was slowly declining speaks volumes about the ambiguity in plantation management on many Jamaican plantations.

As a result, many plantation owners, especially younger ones, remained constantly in debt from the inadequate system of managerial evaluation. In 1809, for example, a significant error was discovered in the accounts compiled by attorney Rowland Fearon. The computation of Fearon's commission of 6 per cent should have been on the net profits rather than on the gross. Richard Pennant, the young owner of the estate, and his Jamaican attorney John Shand assumed that Fearon would be given the same commission as was given to his predecessor, Mr Falconer. Fearon was told by Shand, on behalf of Pennant, that if he had made other arrangements with the late Lord Penrhyn, then the accounts would be honoured, but the plantation was already in debt for £4,521.12 and they wanted the issue settled before they made out the budget for the usual contingencies.[50] Fearon defended his accounts. He provided a written letter to show that Lord Penrhyn had been in agreement with his commission. Thus, he said, they should adjust the accounts to settle on his debt, as Lord Penrhyn would have done.[51]

What made Fearon's claim most suspicious was that his predecessor Falconer had only been paid 5 per cent on net profits, whether the sugar was shipped to London or sold in Jamaica by Lord Penrhyn. It had been Falconer's recommendation that had led Lord Penrhyn to agree to have Fearon run the estate in case of Falconer's death. Fearon had received the power of attorney from Lord Penrhyn after Falconer's death, on 13 November 1806, but it was not recorded in Jamaica until 15 January 1808, and even then the contract was not specifically drafted. Consequently, Fearon knew that the lack of specificity on commissions gave him a strong ground from which to deceive young Richard Pennant. If Fearon's 1804–7 commissions were calculated on the net profits, he would only have gained £4,182.6.2 sterling, rather than the £11,266.19.5 sterling on gross profit. Most plantation owners would never have agreed to compensate so handsomely a new attorney that had been handpicked by his predecessor with such a vast salary difference. Furthermore, even if one were to use the most exorbitant rate of calculation employed by absentee planters, £32 per hundredweight, to calculate Fearon's commission, it would only have come to £5,000, a drastic difference from the £11,266.19.5. Fearon had also been able to deceive the late Lord Penrhyn because his attorneys did not make up current accounts, which showed the annual charges against his estates; they kept instead what they called a regular set of books and sent copies to Lord Penrhyn. Fearon argued that it was in these books that the charge of a gross commission was made.[52] It appeared as if Lord Penrhyn had made no objections to Fearon's calculations, seeing that he had been misled into believing that the 6 per cent commission was on the net profits. This would have meant a 1 per cent increase over Mr Falconer's commission. Fearon addressed this in a letter to Lord Penrhyn. The letter stated: "as to the commission it formerly used to be at 5 per cent but the present law regulated it at 6 per cent, however, be assured that it shall be altered according to your Lordship's wishes".[53]

The Jamaican absentee planters placed themselves under enormous economic pressure with their inefficient method of evaluating the accounting procedures of their managers in Jamaica. Improper accounting seemed to have been most prevalent, especially after a change of ownership. Patrick White, the bookkeeper for Island estate in St Elizabeth, informed his boss, Joseph Barham, that he was having problems reconciling the estate's accounts after the death of Mr Plummer, the previous attorney. It seemed as if Barham now owed a much larger balance than he had previously thought.[54] On Tharp estates in Trelawny, charges of financial impropriety were widespread under the management of overseer Fairclough. In 1820, it became clear that the Tharp accounts were incorrect and needed serious auditing.[55] In 1816, the plantation merchants Steele and Hardyman, who reportedly owed the Good Hope plantation upwards of £1,400, threatened legal action if the plantation could not show that they had paid the amount. They insisted that the money had been paid to one of the plantation clerks and was recorded in their books.[56] What made the merchants' claim somewhat believable was that Mr Fairclough earlier had been accused of ordering excessive plantation supplies, some of which he had resold by disguising the transactions in the name of his clerks. He had also been accused of supplying himself with seventy pounds of fresh beef weekly at the plantation's expense.[57] Such claims against Fairclough have to be viewed with some scepticism as a result of Tharp's family's case in Chancery to declare Fairclough and William Shand incompetent managers. Yet the point must be stressed that financial irregularities were common on many Jamaican plantations.

All of the plantations I examined seem to have been indebted to their creditors for most of the early nineteenth century. Some of the plantation owners were further financially stressed as their creditors charged them extremely high interest rates, not just on ordinary loans but also on defaulted loans. For example, Andrew Arcedeckne was charged 13.5 per cent on the remainder of an unpaid loan.[58] Local merchants (creditors) were sometimes worse than "loan sharks", according to Edward Long.[59] William Rodgers, the attorney from Mesopotamia, believed that the Jamaican creditors were no better than their English counterparts. Regarding the purchase of local lumber, he wrote: "and should I fall short of cash in the future it will be better to draw a bill for the quantity required than to take it here on credit".[60]

In addition to clashes among estate managers, major conflict was also common among family members. Generally the point of contention was the division of family income, usually triggered by the death of the plantation owner and the awarding of annuities. These family conflicts further detracted from owners' abilities to make long-term decisions to enhance the overall productivity of their estates. The case of young plantation owner Andrew Arcedeckne serves as an example. Arcedeckne decided that his conflict with one of his relatives, Catherine Lambert, who had claimed possession of 500 acres of his land for the previous eighteen years, should finally be resolved. His father had given him the land and a court of law would prove the land was his. As a compromise, he would sell her the land for fifty pounds an acre rather than at the market value of one hundred pounds an acre.[61] Mrs Lambert was ambivalent, since the maps of the land showing ownership were old and varied. She was willing, however, to reach a compromise, as she wanted to leave clear land boundaries with good titles to her children.[62]

One of Arcedeckne's plantation trustees reminded him that, given the complex nature of ownership and management, the issue with Mrs Lambert was not that simple; his father's executors and trustees had to be satisfied with the compromise he was attempting to reach before it could be legally binding. They too, as trustees, had to be paid rent and other costs on the property. Arcedeckne's willingness to accept only half of the value of the land was not sufficient for the trustees and executors. Any sum of money he received brought with it a problem of indemnity to them. His best course of action, they felt, would be to suspend negotiations with Mrs Lambert unless she first offered a specific sum and agreed to other terms in which the rest of the money would be paid, including payment on the use of water, as he had mentioned in his first correspondence.[63]

The conflict between Ann Tharp and the rest of the Tharp family over the correct annuity to be paid to her daughter, Sarah, is another apt example of family conflict in plantation management. This case demonstrates how desperate family members often were to get their hands on plantation proceeds without concern for the plantation's continued profitability. Ann Tharp, the seemingly unfaithful wife of entrepreneur John Tharp, insisted that she needed a correct financial picture of the Jamaican plantations, as her little girl's annual expenses were £200. Attorney William Green, who was the manager for thirty other Jamaican plantations,[64] instructed that she be given only £150 for her daughter's expenses, which was quite sufficient. But she insisted that she needed an additional £100 along with the proceeds from the sale of her enslaved Africans.[65] Seven months later, she demanded more money. When she heard that the Greenfield estate was out of debt, she made it clear that she needed the additional £600 from the sale of the property, and that this was money to which she was entitled.[66] Three months later, it became clear that the main reason she needed the money was to purchase a new home to maintain her circle of upper-class friends. She could not understand why she could not profit from her daughter's income as she perceived the merchants were doing. One merchant, Mr Pope, was paid quarterly while another, Mr Shirley, benefited immensely from plantation money. Mr Shirley, for example, lived ostentatiously, she complained, with "a vanity of ladies in his home: black, brown, shaw color and whites".[67]

In 1804, Ann Tharp encouraged one plantation attorney, Mr Green, to stop wasting money on the plantations' infrastructure and place all the profits in the hands of her daughter, Sarah.[68] The £300 she had received for the sale of her enslaved Africans was too inadequate for her to relocate, and she would have to wait until she could receive another £1,000. Just as her brother had moved to the "Queens", she said, she too would love to relocate to France with her family when the war was over. Furthermore, she was paying £100 for the best teachers to teach her darling Sarah to play the harp, and she wanted the new harp that she had bought for Sarah to be paid for in six months. Thus, she argued, Green should persuade John Tharp to pay an additional £200 a year rather than the inadequate £80 he was currently paying.[69]

Amity Hall

The Amity Hall plantation in the parish of Vere further highlights the conflict of interests among management personnel. In 1803, its young absentee owner, Henry Goulburn, who would later become undersecretary in the Colonial Office, appointed Thomas Samson the new attorney of the plantation. Goulburn informed Samson that he could not make any large investments or changes in infrastructure at that time, since he (Goulburn) was not yet of age to make unilateral decisions regarding the plantation.[70] This was quite unfortunate, in Samson's view, since he was of the opinion that important changes in infrastructure were needed in order for the plantation to remain competitive. For example, he wrote to Goulburn, informing him that the plantation had two good plots of land in Carpenter's Mountain. One could be turned into a coffee estate, as coffee currently enjoyed a high price. The other plot was less useful as it did not have timber, but it could still be used in the estate's long-term development.[71] Goulburn had never visited his own estate, as was the case among many absentee landlords. Although he had a case in Chancery that prevented him from restructuring his estate, he also did not pressure Samson to draft a long-term development plan and to have it presented to his mother or the trustees running the plantation.

Samson was told clearly that the plantation could not afford any new investments at that time, not even the purchasing of new Africans, which he had desperately pleaded for. This did not deter Sampson from constantly begging for more enslaved labour and for the expediting of coffee planting on part of Goulburn's available land. Even when Goulburn came of age, his management policy remained one of contraction, as Samson was told to produce more quality produce than worry over quantity of commodities. Goulburn preferred a smaller crop with less cruelty to his enslaved Africans since they were the lifeblood of his plantation.[72]

Goulburn further wrote to Samson that if he were to reduce the acreage of cane on the plantation, it would reduce the amount of work to be done by each enslaved African. Goulburn was not willing to settle St Jago Pen because he did not have adequate labour for such a task, and he realized that he would need many more enslaved Africans to keep the pen viable. He did not even want Sampson to hire jobbing labour, which had become the norm in order to ensure that crops were reaped on time. The reality was that most Jamaican plantations after 1807 struggled with inadequate labour. Goulburn's plan, in accordance with what he had been taught, was to keep plantation expenses at a minimum and to use the rum proceeds to cover the contingencies.[73] But, as Sampson explained to him, rum prices were falling drastically and other minor crops that had once been helpful, such as corn, were being destroyed on account of the weather. The enslaved population was not only decreasing but was also rebelling through arson and flight, mainly due to Samson's heavy-handed leadership.[74] Although Samson's financial stewardship was highly questionable, adding to the plantation's woes (this will be discussed later), Amity Hall faced genuine problems of inadequate labour. This forced Samson to hire jobbers; thus, he could not effectively reduce the plantation's expenses.

For a sugar plantation such as Amity Hall to increase its production, it had to keep its workforce healthy. This, Samson could not accomplish. Amity Hall also needed technological improvements and changes in infrastructure. Goulburn refused to make such investments. Even a good cattle pen was indispensable, not only as a means of defraying plantation expenses through the sale of cattle, but also through its production of manure for the cane pieces. Thus, when Goulburn refused to develop St Jago Pen, he was aiding the plantation's demise. Samson was aware of this. In 1814, he conveyed to Goulburn that he had missed a great opportunity to diversify, as coffee had taken off and had become the new economic saviour of many plantations. Furthermore, it had aided many plantations as an excellent secondary staple in place of rum or corn. On some plantations it had become the main staple.[75]

Whether Goulburn's strategy of avoiding capital expansion of his operations and emphasizing instead a greater concentration on the quality of staples over quantity was a good policy is debatable. Ward suggests that it was an effective policy as it bore fruit in Barbados.[76] Nevertheless, sugar cultivation was an extremely intensive operation with numerous variables, any of which could seriously affect the plantations' overall production and productivity.[77] Thus, at times, expansion through capital infusion was necessary for the plantation to become more viable. Regardless of the soundness of Goulburn's policies, it was evident that he and Sampson viewed plantation management in early nineteenth-century Jamaica from different perspectives. It is therefore not surprising that Amity Hall shows fluctuating sugar yields from 1802 to 1838, as seen in figure 2.4.

The management team at Amity Hall must take some of the blame for the declining production. The parish of Vere had one of the best soils for sugar

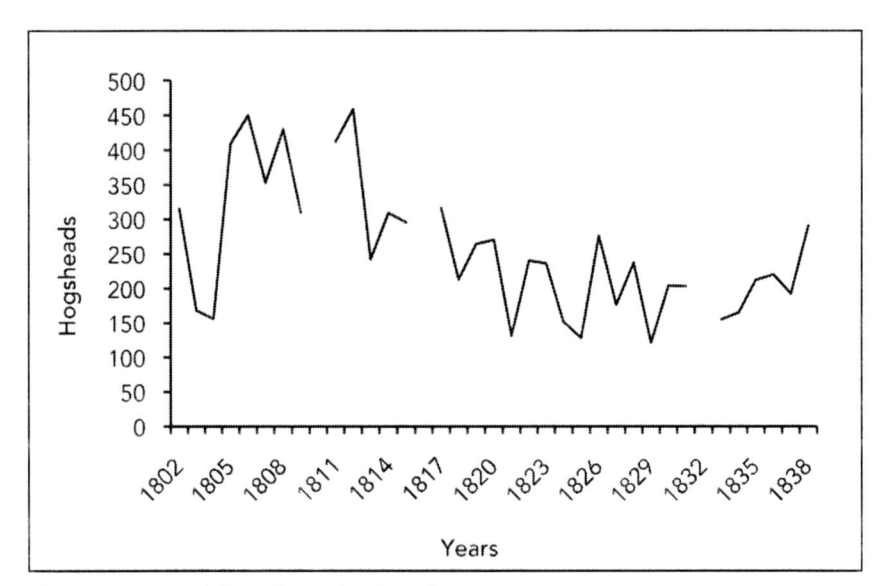

Figure 2.4 Amity Hall yearly production of sugar, 1802–1838
Source: Goulburn Plantation Papers and Crop Accounts.

Table 2.2 Slave Productivity at Amity Hall, Selected Years 1803–1836

Year	Hogsheads	Slaves	Averages
1803	168	254	0.66
1811	410	n/a	
1812	459	n/a	
1813	242	235	1.02
1814	309	n/a	
1815	295	n/a	
1817	316	240	1.32
1818	213	n/a	
1819	264	n/a	
1820	270	238	1.13
1821	131	n/a	
1822	240	n/a	
1823	236	260	0.91
1824	151	n/a	
1825	120	n/a	
1826	276	251	1.09
1827	173	n/a	
1829	121	243	0.49
1831	203	237	0.85
1833	155	241	0.64
1836	220	211	1.04

Source: Goulburn Papers, 304/J/1/21, 6.

cultivation. As will be shown later, Vere was the only Jamaican parish that moved from natural decreases to natural increases from 1817 to 1832.[78] Vere's softer soil meant that it was one of the few parishes in Jamaica where the constant manual work of the enslaved Africans was physically less demanding than elsewhere and easier on their health. Despite the advantages of the soil in Vere, it did not aid the enslaved Africans' levels of productivity at Amity Hall, as seen in table 2.2. Between the years 1803 and 1836, average productivity levels kept fluctuating from under one hogshead per slave to a little above. Slave productivity was unstable and has to be attributed to internal management differences between Goulburn and his Jamaican attorneys.

Samson, with his request for capital expansion, seemed to have had his own plan to fleece Amity Hall. Coming towards the end of his tenure he was accused of committing one of the most glaring cases of financial impropriety in the plantation's history. Samson was promoted as temporary attorney after the previous attorney died, sometime between 1801 and 1802. He was eventually appointed as permanent attorney despite strong opposition from Goulburn's own mother. Susannah Goulburn believed that Samson was an insensitive tyrant who knew only one language of management, the whip.[79] She felt that such a management style was already archaic.

In 1802, Samson hinted that he was having problems settling the accounts of a former clerk, Mr Craggs, but he did not indicate exactly what the problems were. Five months later, he was still having trouble with the accounts. In January of 1803, he kept finding an error of £100 in one of the accounts. In July of 1803, Samson finally admitted that he and his accounting staff did not meet too often and that this was probably the reason the accounts had not been settled.[80] Another two months later, the bookkeeper, Mr Nethersole, still could not reconcile the accounts from Samson.[81] By November 1804, the list of demands against the estate totalled £2,745.2.10. Samson was owed nearly half of the amount, £1,010: £390 for steers and £620 for salary. It seemed as if Samson had sold the plantation some of his personal steers and that his salary of £500 per year had increased.[82] By 1807, the demands against the estate had risen to £3,580.10.0. Of this amount, Samson was owed £677: £87 for jobbing labour, £70 for salary and a mysterious £520, which he charged the estate but did not identify its exact purpose. From information later given, this £520 seems to have been for his jobbing gang, which he did not want to acknowledge to Goulburn.[83]

In 1805, Samson acknowledged that the former clerk to Craggs had sued the plantation for one year's salary. Trying to cover up his poor management of the finances, Samson indicated that he had not made up the account for that year and that it had been contracted out to someone else. Thus, he said, it was best to enter a plea bargain because going to court would be too much of an imposition on the plantation. This legal challenge was in addition to a previous case that Goulburn had in the Court of Chancery.[84] Not only did Samson's financial mismanagement prevent the plantation from detecting that money was still owed to Craggs, but Samson continued to make "mistakes" with the accounts during the entire period of his management. In 1813, when

Goulburn pointed out further financial irregularities with the accounts, Samson found ways of explaining them away. Six months later, he apologized for his bookkeeping mistakes, claiming that they were genuine errors resulting from the charging of incorrect salaries.[85] A year later, in 1814, Goulburn once more castigated Samson for problems with the accounts of 1812; three of the items were excessive payments to Mr Higson, one of the merchants, for lumber and for digging two cane pieces.[86] With regard to the high jobbing bill, Samson argued that he paid the customary price of nine pounds per acre, which was standard for his parish.[87] Samson never indicated, however, that the charges were to himself for his own jobbing gang.[88]

Samson's inability to tender correct accounts was not from a genuine ignorance of accounting procedures but from a deliberate attempt to milk the plantation by charging the highest available prices for his jobbing gangs and by squeezing as much money from the plantation as he could. In 1816, after Goulburn again castigated him for continuing to make mistakes with the accounts, Samson again apologized for his errors. He was at a loss to explain how the errors had been made. Furthermore, he could not reconcile the mistakes in his recording of the crop for 1814.[89]

Of all the suspicious incidents under Samson's management, one that most clearly exposes his wrongdoing took place in 1818. Samson left for England as he was suffering from rheumatism in his right hand, and one Mr Richards, who had a neighbouring estate, took over the management of Amity Hall. Prior to his leaving, Samson informed Goulburn that the land at Carpenter's Mountain could be sold for £7 per acre, which would be equivalent to around £3,000. But Richards later estimated that the land was actually worth £8 per acre. Even then, Richards said he would go higher, up to £4,000, which was still a conservative figure. This was £1,000 more than the amount Samson had calculated.[90] It seems most likely that Samson had been planning to pocket the additional £1,000.

Goulburn eventually fired Samson in favour of Richards, after he observed the positive changes in his plantation under the management of the latter. Goulburn later learned that Samson had consistently ordered excessive amounts of supplies and helped himself to the extras. He had done this so often that he had lost the respect of some of his junior staff on the plantation; they, along with the enslaved Africans, had suffered immensely from inadequate food supplies.[91] Clearly, Samson's financial dishonesty had a ripple effect on his lower management staff. Richards had to dismiss one of these junior managers who not only was absent from work because of his drinking habits but who had stolen a significant amount of sugar and corn for his horses. Along with other white plantation employees and overseers, this manager had carried on a smuggling operation at night, using the plantation's enslaved Africans, cattle and wagons to steal three to four hundred barrels of flour, gin and other items from the storehouses. The employees involved were all convicted at the Admiralty Court in the parish of Vere.[92]

The enslaved Africans on the plantation were also happy with Samson's dismissal. Natural increases occurred among them for the first time in many years, and many runaways returned. The enslaved workers complained of Samson's brutality and his severe exploitation of them.[93]

Another dubious financial occurrence from the period under Samson's management was also discovered. In 1811, he had employed a new bookkeeper and reported that he was going to pay the individual £160 a year. Samson had not given the person's name or stated his reason for employing a new bookkeeper. It was unusual to hire a bookkeeper at such a high salary. Samson had justified his decision by stating that the individual was extremely trustworthy and that his high salary was a result of his being such a rare find. Persons of this calibre, he had argued, were not paid less than £100 per annum. Samson had further indicated that if Goulburn was still unhappy with the arrangement, Samson would pay the £60 himself and charge the plantation only £100.[94] As late as 1835, an account of all salaries at Amity Hall showed that the bookkeeper had been paid only £60 per year. Even in 1835, the overseer made only £200; the closest figure to his salary was the carpenter, who made £160.[95] Samson had made this hire in 1811, but up to 1810, most bookkeepers didn't make more than £60 annually and the average for most overseers ranged from £100 to £150.[96]

Goulburn received confirmation that Samson and his junior managers had been fleecing the estate upon his brother Frederick Goulburn's visit to Amity Hall while he was on a temporary break from the army, which was stationed briefly in Jamaica. After Frederick's tour of the plantation, he commended Richards's management and comforted his brother that he had made the right choice in dismissing Samson. His assessment was that Samson had become wealthy to the point that he was able to purchase his own property, which had become his priority.[97]

Tharp's Estates

The Tharp estates in the parish of Trelawny also illustrate the impact of plantation management on productivity, especially after 1807. Since at that time new enslaved Africans were not readily available for sale on the market, those being sold were scarce and thus more expensive. As a result, plantation managers had to implement new labour strategies, such as task work, rather than forcing the enslaved Africans to work by way of the whip, as they had before. Thus, plantation managers post-1807 had to be concerned with maintaining the health of their main labour force in order to enhance productivity. An examination of the plantation managers on the Tharp estates shows how difficult it was for many of them to be creative and to offer a new kind of management.

In the 1820s, after a long Court of Chancery battle over the management of the Tharp estate, John Tharp Jr (1769–1851) gained the management of the estate over the trustees. The battle had been intense, as the plantations were indebted to trustees such as George Hibbert, who was owed £54,000, and P.J. Miles, who was owed £2,000. John Tharp Jr was given control of the plantations since he was able to prove that the trustees had mismanaged them. He had to agree, however, to a compromise with the trustees, since he didn't have the financial capital required to repay the enormous debt owed to merchants Miles and Hibbert. Both merchants and John Tharp Jr agreed, however, on management initiatives to save the plantations. First, they decided to terminate the services of the Jamaican managers: the attorney William Shand and the overseer William Fairclough. They appointed Colonel F.J. Phillips as attorney and W.M. Kerr as overseer. Colonel Phillips, interestingly, was the brother-in-law of John Tharp Jr.

The new managers were expected to maintain tight fiscal discipline to ensure the profitability of the estates. In part, this meant eliminating the heavy loans to the merchants and paying the annuities to the various members of the Tharp family. Phillips and Kerr were able to reduce the yearly cost of plantation supplies from over £10,000 to £7,000 between 1823 and 1828.[98] But by 1830, when another relative of the Tharp family, William Tharp, a cousin of the heir, was unanimously appointed the new attorney, the plantations' debts had increased. Hibbert's debt had decreased slightly, to £52,112, but Miles's had increased significantly, to £42,171. Despite Phillips and Kerr's bold attempts, they were unable to reduce the overall expenses of the plantations.

A look at the years 1830–34 provides more interesting detail on management policies of that time, specifically in the interaction between Hibbert and the new attorney William Tharp. Hibbert argued on behalf of the trustees that the debt due to the trustees was so enormous and the prospect of the sugar market was so discouraging that every expedient measure had to be adopted for a reduction of plantation expenses. The trustees, however, were willing to pay William Tharp an annual net salary of one thousand pounds along with other commissions and emoluments, which far exceeded the salaries of other attorneys, to bring their objectives to fruition.[99] A year later, Hibbert expressed his frustration at the continued effect of the weather on their efforts, writing to Tharp that he wished that they could just enjoy a good season of very successful production to begin to climb out of their dilemma. The prices of both sugar and rum had declined drastically in their respective markets. Hibbert wrote: "These ill-fated properties seemed doomed never to experience one entirely favorable season. . . . Mr Tharp's estates are now become a fearful burden upon the consignees as we can now look with hope to those active measures of economy."[100] Hibbert then congratulated Tharp for reducing medical expenses, an item that should have been increased rather than reduced, since it was necessary for the health of the enslaved Africans. Hibbert also encouraged Tharp to find a way to amend the Deficiency Laws or to make a reduction in the amount of money they paid, because it was impossible to maintain an adequate number of white personnel on their estates.[101] Hibbert further congratulated Tharp for hiring out some of the enslaved Africans for jobbing and encouraged him to reduce the expenses on the wharf, since on 31 December 1829 they had paid £1,298, which was much too high.

Hibbert was, however, much more critical when it came to Tharp's initiative to use more of the plantation's own native lumber for staves, over using imported lumber. It had already been tried before and it had failed, he wrote, as there had been numerous complaints that the lumber was too heavy and created other problems.[102] But by 1832, despite Tharp's "good management practices", the plantation's debt to the trustees was increasing and the forecast looked gloomier. Sir Thomas Buxton's 1832 proposal in the British Parliament to examine the efficiency of slavery itself left many planters and merchants fearing that the enslaved Africans would no longer work unless they were forced to do so by the whip or by soldiers.[103] In 1833, despite congratulating

Tharp for his continued attempts at reducing his overhead expenses, along with increasing both the quality and the quantity of his sugar, Hibbert admitted that unless the price of sugar increased dramatically very shortly, they were economically doomed from the intense competition from other countries that were producing sugar more cheaply.[104]

Although the price of sugar was declining precipitously, the real problem on Tharp's estates was that overall productivity was low (figure 2.5 and table 2.3). Hibbert was not concerned with initiating new programmes that would improve the plantations' long-term development and, by extension, increase productivity. Based on Hibbert's past record and his description of the enslaved Africans' refusal to work unless forced, it seems clear that Hibbert would never consent to necessary initiatives such as task work, even if they were to be recommended by Tharp in order to turn around the fortunes of the plantations. Hibbert wanted tight fiscal discipline and encouraged Tharp to continue to reduce expenditure at a time when enslaved Africans throughout Jamaica lived in unhealthy conditions and needed more material resources to be healthier. Plantation managers wanted increased productivity but never saw a relationship between improved health for the workers and greater production. More significant for the Tharp plantations was that their management policy of tight fiscal prudence without concern for the socio-economic and material needs of the enslaved Africans did not take them out of their

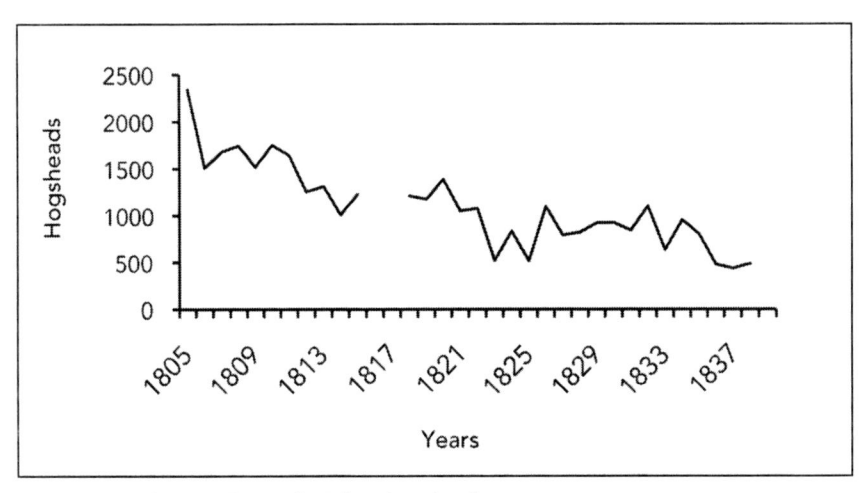

Figure 2.5 Production figures for Tharp's eight plantations, 1805–1837
Source: Tharp Papers and Crop Accounts.

Table 2.3 Slave Productivity at Tharp's Sugar Plantations, 1795–1837

Year	Hogsheads	Slaves	Averages
1795	1,500	2,551	0.6
1800	1,569	n.a.	
1802	1,830	n/a	
1803	n/a	2,786	
1805	2,345	n/a	
1806	1,507	n/a	
1807	1,678	n/a	
1816	1,239	n/a	
1817	1,094	2,542	0.43
1818	1,210	n/a	
1819	1,175	n/a	
1820	1,385	n/a	
1821	1,051	2,546	0.41
1822	1,078	n/a	
1823	518	n/a	
1824	837	2,496	0.33
1825	514	n/a	
1826	1,100	2,558	0.43
1827	792	n/a	
1828	823	2,291	0.36
1829	923	n/a	
1830	926	n/a	
1831	843	2,193	0.38
1836	478	n/a	
1837	435	1,675	0.26

Source: Adapted from Tharp's plantation papers.

financial dilemma, but instead led to a serious decline in crude production and productivity, as seen in figure 2.5 and table 2.3.

Table 2.3 confirms the deteriorating levels of productivity on Tharp's estates. In 1817, each enslaved African produced less than half of a hogshead of sugar. By 1837, slave productivity had reached its lowest ebb with each slave producing 0.26 hogsheads of sugar, a significant drop from the 0.48 produced per slave in 1817. In 1795, the rate of productivity on Tharp's plantations was around 0.6 hogsheads of sugar per slave.[105] Although I could not substantiate the levels of productivity between 1801 and 1816, it seems as if the rate of productivity continually decreased, reaching its lowest level in 1837. It is clear that by then, Tharp's plantations had become uncompetitive, despite the efforts of Hibbert and Miles.

One of the interesting features of Apprenticeship (1834–38) is that some of the plantations that encouraged the apprentices to remain productive labourers by paying them for their own time were also the ones that boasted of dramatically improved production and productivity. Amity Hall is an example of this. As seen in table 2.2, slave productivity returned to over one hogshead per slave after ten years. In 1826, Amity Hall had a productivity ratio of 1.09. After that, it declined to under one hogshead until 1836, when it increased to 1.04 hogsheads per apprentice. Amity Hall paid ten pence per day to their apprentices and even entered into contract with other apprentices to pay four shillings and two pence per week.[106] The management recognized that the enslaved Africans were willing to work if they were paid reasonably well.

Golden Grove estate is another example. In 1803, it produced around 720 hogsheads of sugar.[107] Between the years 1810 and 1819, it produced around 504 hogsheads,[108] but this had declined significantly to 313 by 1833. However, in 1835, during Apprenticeship, crude production increased to 446 hogsheads. It continued to increase in 1838, when the plantation produced 452 hogsheads of sugar. One of the factors accounting for this increase in crude production during Apprenticeship was the willingness of the plantation management to pay their apprentices. In 1835, the managers paid around £253.11.8 to the apprentices, and they also paid additional medical costs, both for the apprentices and for the free children living on the plantation. In July of 1838, the plantation had already surpassed the 1835 wage total, having paid around £340 to the apprentices.[109]

Many of the white stipendiary magistrates during Apprenticeship were impressed with the work ethic of the apprentices, especially when their managers did not attempt to rob them of the opportunity to work for good wages. One particular magistrate praised the apprentices and highlighted how they had done the same amount of work in nine hours as they formerly did in twelve hours when they were enslaved. Furthermore, he observed, more apprentices were more willing to dig cane holes, which was one of the most arduous tasks on the plantation. Overall, this magistrate believed that among the apprentices who were encouraged to work, the rate of productivity increased by around 50 per cent.[110] Another magistrate even noted that the health of the apprentices was better on many of the plantations that rewarded them with reasonable pay. During slavery, numerous enslaved Africans had been sent to the hospital, ill from working long days and late nights. Under Apprenticeship, however, the formerly enslaved Africans kept in better health since they completed their tasks before nightfall.[111]

Conclusion

There are several internal and external factors that account for the decline of the planter class in Jamaica and, by extension, the British West Indies. Historians have not highlighted the critical role played by plantation management in profitability and productivity. I have shown in this chapter how many of the plantation managers of Jamaica, through their own failures, contributed to the declining production and productivity on their plantations. In contrast to the views of eminent Caribbean historian Higman, who believes that absentee management was not destructive to plantation management in Jamaica, I have shown that absentee management contributed to some extent to a cumbersome management structure.[112] As a result, managerial systems of evaluation and accountability were most difficult for absentee proprietors to implement in an era of free trade and withdrawal of economic protection. The kind of plantation restructuring that was called for by Carrington at the close of the eighteenth century was not executed in the early nineteenth century.[113] Consequently, declining production and productivity continued on many Jamaican estates. In the next chapter, I will examine the Worthy Park plantation, which underwent such restructuring in the late eighteenth century. To its credit, it never experienced the severe kinds of decline that many other nineteenth-century Jamaican plantations did. I will examine the role of its managers to determine how critical they were to the plantation's buoyancy.

CHAPTER 3

Worthy Park
Example of Management for Survival

AS EARLY AS 1914, U.B. PHILLIPS highlighted the significant role that humane management played in the success of the Worthy Park plantation between the years 1792 and 1796.[1] Although Phillips acknowledges that the enslaved Africans were disproportionately fed corn and herring, unlike whites, who were given salt-pork, beef and other delicacies, he believed that the former still had sufficient food. They ate adequate amounts of ground provisions, such as yams and plantains, along with an ample amount of vegetables and meat proteins, such as pigs and poultry.[2] Phillips conveys the impression that the average African at Worthy Park was reasonably fed and sufficiently clothed, although he admits that they were never given shoes.[3] Phillips does not indicate, however, that whatever proteins the Africans ate were procured by themselves during their limited free time. The enslaved Africans saw this as necessary to prevent starvation and to provide themselves with petty cash. What is even more troubling in Phillips's analysis is his belief that the high infant mortality and low fertility rates at Worthy Park were due to the absence of white mistresses on the plantation.[4] He does not show that these rates were the result of the Africans being overworked along with their unhygienic work and living environments.

Michael Craton and James Walvin seem to have borrowed from Phillips in their work on Worthy Park. They make a similar argument that humane management, born out of practical necessity, contributed to the productive success of Worthy Park in the early nineteenth century, when many other plantations in Jamaica and the British West Indies were experiencing declining production. Although they list other reasons for the plantation's success, their work does not depart significantly from that of Phillips regarding the caring and considerate role of the plantation managers. Craton and Walvin believe that the humane policies of Rose Price, who managed Worthy Park beginning in 1792, resulted in improved health for the enslaved Africans. One reason for this was the plantation's policy to give the enslaved Africans more land and more opportunity to feed themselves.[5] Another was that Worthy Park created a fourth work gang in addition to the traditional three gangs,[6] which eased the workload of the Africans and in turn improved their health. These humane factors, Craton and Walvin explain, resulted in a lower death rate and a higher fertility rate for the first twenty years of the nineteenth century, a rare feat on Jamaican plantations. Furthermore, they point to the benevolent manumissions adopted by Rose Price, which benefited the overall health of the Africans. Craton and Walvin offer three other reasons for the success of Worthy Park: the increased development of infrastructure, access to finance and better management. It is in these three latter areas that Craton and Walvin help us to understand better the managerial strategies of young Rose Price.

In a later work on Worthy Park, Michael Craton clarifies much of his earlier assessment of Price's humane form of management, arguing that in fact from 1792 to 1838, the level of the slaves' health at Worthy Park was low. Nevertheless, he holds on to the view that health on the plantation in the later period (1792–1838) was still comparatively better than its earlier period (1760–91).[7] His most significant statement remains that the social and living conditions of the enslaved Africans at Worthy Park contributed immensely to their poor health. Furthermore, he believes that ameliorative legislation by planters was mere window-dressing because the Africans, towards the end of formal slavery, had to grow their own food and provide material necessities from their own efforts.[8]

Craton, however, does not clarify from his earlier work whether Worthy Park was successful in establishing a natural increase in their enslaved population for the first twenty years of the nineteenth century. From my examination of the plantation books and journals of Worthy Park, I have concluded that Worthy Park maintained a level of stability in its sugar production independently of any natural population increases that may have occurred. Worthy Park maintained stability because of the development of its infrastructure, available access to financing that its managers utilized to obtain a constant supply of enslaved Africans, and better management.

Worthy Park was no more humane in their treatment of their enslaved population than other Jamaican plantations. The records do show that their rates of infant mortality were high, a fact obscured by the plantation's constant purchasing of additional enslaved Africans. Worthy Park was better able to disguise the unhealthy state of their enslaved population until the 1820s. Apart from health, however, Rose Price's leadership in other areas of plantation life was superior to that of many other absentee managers in Jamaica. In addition, the management practices at Worthy Park in the latter eighteenth and early nineteenth centuries provide an excellent comparative analysis regarding the reasons for the productive failures and successes of Jamaican plantations leading up to emancipation. This chapter will thus demonstrate the critical relationship between management and productivity.

Worthy Park's sugar production (figure 3.1) in the early 1900s was superior to that of many other Jamaican plantations. It seems to have been more stable than the Jamaican average, as seen in figure 2.1 in the previous chapter. Worthy Park scarcely showed signs of declining sugar production, although in reality it declined slightly. In the difficult 1820s, the plantation was able to maintain an average of around four hundred hogsheads of sugar, compared to its previous high of six hundred hogsheads between 1800 and 1810. From available figures spanning from 1812 to 1837 (table 3.1), its level of productivity per slave also declined slightly below one hogshead of sugar between 1821 and 1824, but remained over one hogshead for the remaining years (table 3.1). In that period of time, Worthy Park's levels of productivity also seem to have been better than the plantations examined in the previous chapter, Amity Hall and the Tharp plantations. Worthy Park seemed to have even exceeded the Jamaican average (figure 3.1), as the latter showed steadily declining sugar production, similar to some of the sugar plantations in the previous chapter.

To understand better the buoyancy of Worthy Park, the involvement of young Rose Price in the management of the plantation has to be understood. Rose Price was sent by his father John Price to Jamaica in 1792, at the young age of twenty-three, to restore efficient management to Worthy Park. The plantation was mismanaged and heavily indebted after a century of operations.[9] Although Rose Price spent only three years in Jamaica, these were three fundamental years that sowed the seeds of recovery for the plantation and brought about massive improvements in infrastructure.[10] Price, unlike many other Jamaican planters, experienced little difficulty in obtaining

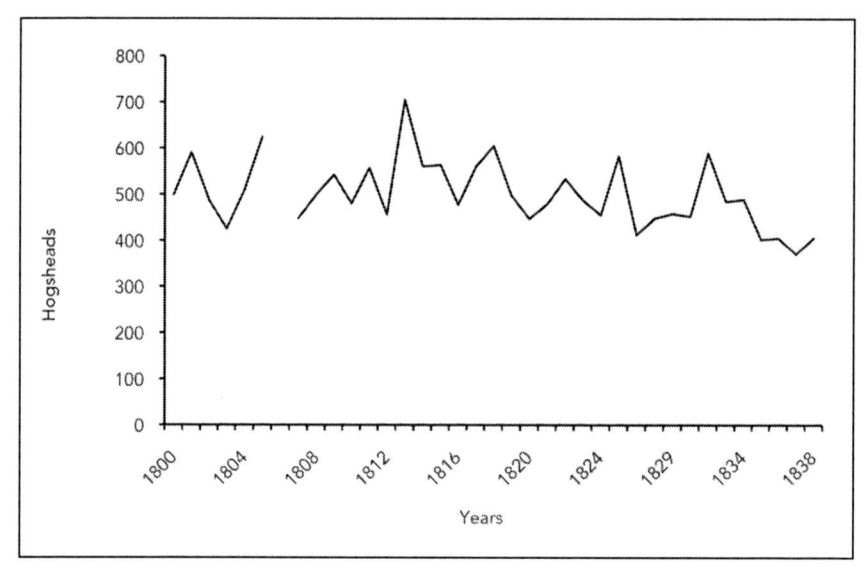

Figure 3.1 Worthy Park sugar production, 1800–1838
Source: Crop Accounts, Jamaica Archives.

finances. From the outset in 1792 through the 1830s, Price spent much money on the plantation to improve its production. He seems to have possessed the skills of a salesman, which he used to influence his merchants to keep investing in Worthy Park, even when it was heavily indebted. Furthermore, Price was fortunate in gaining accounting write-offs, as he had become well connected through marriage to a wealthy family, the Talbots.[11] The main funding that he received, however, was not through the liberal generosity of his merchants, even though they were willing to shower him with finances at his request. He received it largely out of his own sacrifice, mortgaging most of his estates to obtain funding. For example, on 14 October 1812, Price, saddled with a £17,935.14.10 debt from his father, agreed to a new ninety-nine-year lease to his main merchant, Thomas Smith. He agreed to give Smith all the staples of his estates. Like other planters, he could not send the estates' production to other metropolitan areas where he could obtain a better price. In making such an arrangement, he had secured his financial security by ensuring that he received from Smith an annual annuity of £6,000 along with an annuity to his mother of £300 to £600 until she died. Price also ensured that there was financial support for his twelve children.[12] Price then continued his financial

Table 3.1 Rate of Productivity at Worthy Park, 1812–1837

Year	Hogsheads (hhds)	Slaves	Productivity	Averages
1812	456	505	0.90 hhds	
1813	705	503	1.40 hhds	
1814	560	511	1.09 hhds	1.07 hhds (1812–17)
1815	563	514	1.09 hhds	
1816	477	527	0.90 hhds	
1817	560	525	1.06 hhds	
1818	604			
1819	497			
1820	447			
1821	479	509	0.94 hhds	
1822	533	503	1.06 hhds	0.97 hhds (1821–24)
1823	487	494	0.98 hhds	
1824	455	495	0.92 hhds	
1826	583			
1827	412			
1828	448			
1829	458			
1830		420		
1831	452	334	1.35 hhds	1.56 hhds (1831–37)
1832	589	316	1.86 hhds	
1833	484	309	1.56 hhds	
1834	489	295	1.65 hhds	
1835	402	266	1.51 hhds	
1836	405	260	1.55 hhds	
1837	371	248	1.50 hhds	

Source: Worthy Park Plantation Books.

juggling by later transferring his debts to his brother-in-law, Charles, the Earl of Talbot. This was significant, as Price owed Thomas Smith £30,987.15.1 in 1805, when Smith died and his will was read. Thus, he was able to transfer his debts to his own family.[13] As was indicated in Rose Price's will of 1817, the only plantation in Jamaica that Price still owned by the 1830s was Spring Gardens. Price had successfully mortgaged all his father's plantations to gain the finances he needed to continue the improvements at Worthy Park.[14] The Lists of Apprentices for the years 1836 to 1838 lend support to this claim, as they were divided into three different groups: Worthy Park, Arthur's Seat and those under Rose Price. In 1836, it seems as if Price only had compensation claims for 45 apprentices out of a total of 407; in 1837, he had 42 out of 389, and 60 out of 389 in 1838.[15] Price's last will and testament, made on 28 November 1834, conveys a similar impression of his significantly declining assets. In it, he stated that all of his assets in diverse dioceses were to be granted to his three executors: the Right Honorable Charles, the Earl of Talbot, the Honorable John Talbot and the Right Honorable John Lord Sherborne, Baron Sherborne. A fourth executor, the Right Honorable Henry Lord Viscount, was also to be given his share when he applied for it at a certain time.[16]

The records reveal that Price was also quite fortunate in having inside information to help him access further financial support, other than from members of his own family. Despite the brevity of his stay in Jamaica, he was nominated as one of three executors of the property of James Lyons of St Thomas in the Vale. When Lyons died, the executors released the legacy to those who had been appointed.[17] But Rose Price was able to capitalize on Lyons's property in 1815 and 1816, buying his 150 enslaved Africans for £12,360 and his stock of seventy-five from Russell and Derry pens for £16,702.[18] He paid an average of £82.4 for each enslaved African, which was an excellent bargain in the context of the early 1800s, when the cost of an average healthy enslaved African seems to have been between £150 and £200, as seen in the slave lists. After that purchase, Rose Price had a total enslaved population of 783 and a total stock of 1,031 on all of his plantations: Worthy Park, Spring Gardens, Mickleton Pen and Derry and Russell pens, which he had just purchased.[19]

Price's ability to persuade property owners to sell him their lands under various arrangements which did not necessarily involve direct cash can also be observed in the following two accounts. His two fellow executors in the administration of the property of James Lyons were James Seaton Lane of St

Thomas in the Vale and John Hanson of the parish of St Catherine. It is not clear why Seaton Lane did not acquire Lyons's property, but the other executor, Hanson, owned a 300-acre property adjacent to Price's. Later, Hanson sold it to Price for a mere ten shillings, Jamaican currency. For Price to be purchasing Hanson's land in 1826 speaks volumes of Price's continuous plan to expand Worthy Park and its adjacent plantations and to improve on its infrastructure. Hanson's sale of land to Price, despite the land being of poor quality for fertile production, also signals Hanson's desire not to continue expanding. It also might explain the possible reason that Price purchased the Lyons's property instead of Hanson. Even more intriguing is the other 600 acres of land that Price also purchased in 1826 from neighbours John Blair and William Bullock, 300 acres each. Both men sold Rose Price their land for ten shillings each, as Hanson had done. Interestingly, both Blair and Bullock were former employees of Price. John Blair was one of Price's bookkeepers in 1792[20] and later became his resident manager and attorney in the 1820s.[21] William Bullock, on the other hand, was Price's new overseer in 1822. Although the 900 acres of land that Price bought from his neighbours for thirty shillings was described as un-surveyed marshland, it enlarged the area of Cocoree, a section of Price's land; the purchase shows how Price seemed to be well positioned to gain access to financial preferences. Craton and Walvin show that Price's purchases of land around Cocoree brought his total land acreage from 3,200 to 4,000 acres. Furthermore, in 1830, he purchased another plantation, Arthur Seat, with its complement of 127 Africans, which he preferentially gained for £6,100, an average of around £48 per African.[22] This, again, was an excellent bargain in 1830.

The contrast between Price and some of the plantation owners described in the previous chapter is clear. Price never hesitated to enlarge his stock, land and labour supply, unlike Goulburn, who never wanted to spend a pound to purchase Africans or diversify into coffee with his available land at Carpenter's Mountain. At some of the other plantations, such as Hermitage, planters faced serious labour shortages, triggered mainly by their inability to procure labour. Other planters, such as Andrew Arcedeckne, had to fight their management staff to increase the number of Africans because their plantations could not maintain an adequate supply.

Price's access to cash was only the first step in his management plans to restructure his plantation. Not only did he invest heavily in the infrastructure of his plantation by purchasing extra land but he also developed Spring Gardens and Mickleton, which were Worthy Park's adjunct pens, located miles away from the plantation.[23] Spring Gardens, the larger and probably the more important of the two pens, was responsible for the breeding of new stock for Worthy Park. It purchased old steers and spayed heifers from Worthy Park at a minimal cost of eight to ten pounds, thus helping Worthy Park to dispose of their undesirable cattle. The profits helped Worthy Park to purchase new cattle. Mickleton Pen, on the other hand, seems to have concentrated more on the resting, servicing and fattening of Worthy Park's working stock, rather than on breeding, because they had more fattening stock than breeding stock. Because both pens were miles away from the estate, Price also built three manure pens strategically located on different areas of the estate, next to newly grown cane fields. He installed these manure pens to ensure that their rich dung would help in fertilizing the cane fields.[24] Also significant is that the plantation's amount of stock never declined significantly; this was in part due to Price's purchase of the two additional pens, Russell and Derry. In 1812, Price had a total stock of 1,075: 395 at Worthy Park, 471 at Spring Gardens and 209 at Mickleton Pen. In 1817, he had a total stock of 1,046, and by 1831 it had only declined to 937: 303 at Worthy Park, 500 at Spring Gardens and 134 at Mickleton.[25] With effective pens, Worthy Park's fortune was greatly enhanced.

The plantation book for 1792 to 1795 further shows how Price developed his plantation by increasing both its acreage and its labour supply. In 1792, Price purchased ninety enslaved Africans: twenty-five men, twenty-seven women, sixteen boys, sixteen girls and six children.[26] In addition, he embarked on the heavy use of hired labour for the next three years (1792–95) to maintain the health of his enslaved Africans. As a sign of his commitment to developing his plantation, he paid higher prices for jobbing labour: two shillings and six pence to two shillings and eleven pence per day,[27] when the average price during that time period (1792–95) seems to have been between one shilling and eight pence to two shillings and one pence, as seen in table 3.2.

Price's liberal wages for hired labour in the context of the 1790s are significant, showing his desire to augment his infrastructure. During the Apprenticeship period (1834–38), many planters still had difficulty paying as much as three shillings per day for jobbing labour, as seen in both the magistrates' reports and the plantation papers. Even as late as 1836, one of Price's attorneys

Table 3.2 Jobbing Charges in Jamaica, 1793–1799

Year	Jobbing Charges
1793	1s. 8d.
1794	2s. 1d.
1795	2s. 1d.
1796	2s. 1d.
1797	2s. 11d.
1798	3s. 4d.
1799	3s. 4d.

Source: Jamaica House of Assembly Minutes, 1B/5/12/1, 451.

was still paying two shillings and six pence for hired labour.[28] This attorney was still using the same pay structure that Price had used forty years previously. Price's generosity in paying much more for labour than his contemporaries is an important point. Many of the Jamaican plantation papers show the limitations of attorneys in obtaining funding from absentee owners to do the necessary infrastructure work. Such work was critical for maximizing estate production and enhancing profits. This puts into context the extent to which Price was willing to lay the necessary infrastructure by making the financial investments required to increase his production. Some of the hired labour contracts that he negotiated can be seen in the following accounts (figure 3.2).

Worthy Park seems to have been way ahead of many other Jamaican plantations in terms of the availability of finances to develop the infrastructure of both land and labour. Another significant point that Craton and Walvin make is that in essence, Price was not an absentee planter in the way that other young plantation owners, such as Henry Goulburn, were. The three years Price spent in Jamaica gave him first-hand knowledge of plantation agriculture, which meant that he was not easily deceived by his managers and overseers. Being intimately involved in the restructuring of his own estate, he was able to better evaluate his managers. He left detailed instructions before his departure from Jamaica in 1795. As a result of his close supervision, in 1820 he fired one of his managers, John Blair, for mismanagement.[29]

Mr McFarlane's Account
- [n.d.]: The jobbing gang holed and moulded the Negro Grounds and dug cane holes for 802 days at 2s. 6d. per day.
- January 1793: The jobbing gang worked for 721½ days making cattle pens and doing other tasks for 2s. 11d. per day for a total cost of £105.4.4½. They also dug 31.2.20 acres of land for planting nursery stock and making fences for £8 per acre at a total cost of £253.53. Members of the jobbing gang assisted the plantation's enslaved Africans in making bricks, for which they were paid 2s. 11d. per day. In the same year, 1793, they also cleaned and planted in Guinea grass 50 acres of land at the "Mountain" and another 18 acres of Guinea grass behind the "Works".

Peter Douglas's Account
- 14 July 1795: Rose Price signed a contract with Peter Douglas to clean the canes that he had previously planted three times a year, on the direction of the overseer. The cleaning was to be done for £4 an acre, in addition to the £4 that he had been paid for planting the canes.
- March 1795: Douglas was paid £590.7.1 for the following work: 525½ days' hire of Negro labour at 2s. 11d. per day; building 72 chains and 59 feet of stonewall at £3.18 per chain; and building an additional 57½ chains of stonewall.
- Peter Douglas's jobbers were paid 30d. per acre for cleaning 269.3.35 acres of cane.

Other Accounts
1793–1794:
- Mr Richard Barnes' jobbers were paid 2s. 11d. per day for cutting wood, hoeing and performing other tasks, such as cleaning 40 acres of cane.
- John Anderson's gang was paid 30d. per acre for cleaning 32 acres of cane. He was also paid £220.19.3 for making fences and ditches along with holing and ratooning of canes.
- James Grant was also paid for making fences and ditches, holing and ratooning.

Figure 3.2 Individual jobbing contracts at Worthy Park, 1793–1795
Source: Worthy Park Plantation Book, AC 4035.

Table 3.3 Mortality and Fertility Rates of Africans at Worthy Park, 1792–1834

Years	Increases	Decreases	Results
1792–96	38	119	-81
1813–17	90	64	+26
1821–24	39	64	-25
1830–34	26	90	-64

Source: Worthy Park Plantation Papers.

The most disappointing aspect of Worthy Park's operations was its failure to maintain a healthy enslaved population. One of the reasons the plantation's production of sugar did not decline as did that of many other Jamaican plantations was that Worthy Park had a much larger pool of enslaved workers whom they overworked, despite their use of occasional hired slave labour. Worthy Park's success in maintaining enslaved labourers for most of the early nineteenth century, unlike many Jamaican plantations, worked to their advantage. The material conditions at Worthy Park were as horrible as on any other Jamaican plantation. In fact, health care there got progressively worse in the early 1800s, leading up to emancipation. For example, the fertility rate in comparison to the mortality rate declined in this period, except for one brief moment, 1813–17 (table 3.3).

Comparing all four periods from which data is available in table 3.3, it is clear that the earlier years, 1813–17, depict much better fertility and less mortality in the enslaved population than the latter periods, 1821–24 and 1830–34. The years 1813–17 were the only ones in which the increases surpassed the decreases. The latter periods saw a reverse, as the fertility rates after 1817 dropped by over 50 per cent and the mortality rates increased. By the 1820s, the decreasing fertility and increasing mortality at Worthy Park brought the rates back to where they had been in the 1790s, thus wiping out the gains that the plantation had made between 1813 and 1817. Even more significant, the high mortality rate in the 1790s seems to have been a result of the seasoning process, based on the large number of new captive Africans that Rose Price purchased in 1792.

Experienced Jamaican planters, such as Edward Long, warned that the more captive Africans that were purchased on any one occasion, the higher the mortality rate would be. Long contended that, ideally, no more than eight to ten captive Africans were to be purchased at any time, as in such numbers it would be much easier to provide them with greater attention and care.[30] The higher mortality rate after the 1820s cannot be explained by Rose Price's continuous purchase of Africans, since he was no longer buying unseasoned or "salt-water" Africans. He purchased seasoned or Creole Africans from plantations that were in receivership. Thus, the management of the plantation has to be singled out as one of the main contributors to the high mortality rate. If one compares the mortality and fertility rates from the periods 1821–24 and 1830–34, it is evident that the management of the plantation was not able to halt the trends of decreasing fertility and increasing mortality. The fertility rates decreased from thirty-nine to twenty-six and the mortality rates increased from sixty-four to ninety.

It should be further noted that for the same period (1800–38), the strength of the enslaved labour force at Worthy Park dwindled. Four separate slave lists – those of 1813, 1824, 1830 and 1836 – reveal an increase in the number of persons listed as "unhealthy" (table 3.4). In 1813, there were forty-four persons in this category, and by 1824, the numbers had increased to seventy-nine. The figure remained in the seventies until 1836. What seems to have helped the plantation, however, were the two large purchases of additional labour that it procured (150 in 1815–16 from the property of James Lyons, and 127 in 1830 from the Arthur Seat plantation). It seems as if these two purchases prevented the plantation from a disastrous decrease in their African population. As long as Worthy Park was able to make such large purchases of additional Africans, their decreasing enslaved population would not have a serious effect on their

Table 3.4 Health Indicators of Worthy Park's Enslaved Africans, 1813–1836

Year	Slave Population	Unhealthy	Percentage	% Increase/ Decrease of Health
1813	512	44	8.6	
1824	355	79	22.3	-13.7% over 1813
1830	414	76	18.4	+3.9% over 1824
1836	248	74	29.8	-11.4% over 1830

Source: Worthy Park Plantation Papers.

levels of productivity. This is significant, as I will further show in the following chapters that having an adequate number of enslaved Africans on a plantation was critical to experiencing increased production.

One could further argue that one of the reasons for the declining health of the African population at Worthy Park was that the plantation had purchased many unhealthy enslaved Africans. This was a reality in the purchasing of additional Africans from fellow planters in the early 1800s. However, upon examination of the mortality figures in table 3.4, this does not seem to have been the case with Worthy Park. The increasing mortality and dwindling fertility seem to have been a continuous trend at Worthy Park. This suggests that the plantation was losing its labour strength leading to emancipation and that the health index was declining from both overwork and inadequate material conditions.

The mortality rates shown in table 3.5 and figure 3.3 demonstrate that the large number of individuals dying on the Worthy Park plantation were young enslaved Africans under thirty, and not the older Africans who may have been considered weak and sickly. Mortality was highest in the one-to-ten age group, followed by ages twenty-one to thirty, the plantation's leading gang, and then by one of the older age groups, fifty-one to sixty.[31] This runs counter to the claims of Craton and other historians who argue that the predominant work-

Table 3.5 Analysis of Mortality Rates at Worthy Park, 1813–1834

Years	1813–17	1821–24	1830–34	Total
1–10	28	13	17	58
11–20	3	4	11	18
21–30	11	1	14	26
31–40	6	5	2	13
41–50	4	5	13	22
51–60	2	11	10	23
61–70	5	5	11	21
71–80	4	1	8	13
81–90	3	1	3	7
91–100	0	1	0	1

Source: Worthy Park Plantation Papers.

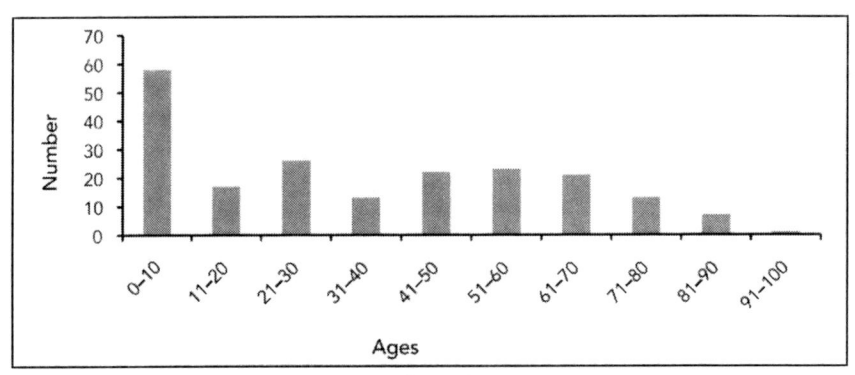

Figure 3.3 Mortality by age group at Worthy Park, 1813–1834
Source: Crop Accounts, Jamaica Archives.

force deaths on most plantations were the very young and the very old together.[32]

If infants accounted for most deaths, followed by the strongest workers from the first gang on the plantation, then the conclusion has to be drawn that the plantation was far from healthy and that the enslaved Africans were being overworked in order to satisfy production targets.

This is significant for two reasons. First, post-1807 plantation management was supposed to have been different from its earlier period. One of the purposes of the 1807 Abolition Act was the prevention of more enslaved Africans being brought to the Caribbean. Plantation managers throughout the British West Indies would be forced to initiate ameliorative and other necessary measures to procure their labour supply through natural means. The management at Worthy Park did not make such a readjustment, choosing instead to continue the same eighteenth-century paradigm by overworking their enslaved Africans and replacing them with new labour.

Second, the mortality rates of Worthy Park further demonstrate that one of the keys to successful plantation management in the early nineteenth century was to find a way to keep one's enslaved labour force healthy. This issue will be examined in more detail in the following chapters. This is significant for Worthy Park because on the surface, their production levels seemed stable, but in reality the volume of sugar production was gradually declining. For example, the average volume of sugar that Worthy Park produced for the following time periods is shown in table 3.6.

Table 3.6 Average Volume of Sugar at Worthy Park, 1800–1838

Years	Hogsheads of Sugar
1800–10	657.0
1811–20	542.6
1821–30	482.0
1831–38	463.0

Source: Worthy Park Plantation Papers.

Given the decreasing health of the main enslaved labour force at Worthy Park during the early nineteenth century, it comes as no surprise that production levels declined as well. Although Worthy Park's production of sugar was far better than that of many Jamaican plantations, it could not be considered a model for other Jamaican planters. The managers at Worthy Park, like other Jamaican managers, did not see the necessity of implementing ameliorative and other necessary measures to maintain their labour force. For a Jamaican plantation to remain productive in the early nineteenth century, it had to institute the necessary measures to keep its African labourers healthy.

It was in the maintenance of its labourers' health that Worthy Park did a poor job. It is not clear whether the planters were aware that infants and children up to the age of ten years accounted for most plantation deaths, and if they were, what measures they implemented to solve the problem, no longer having access to new supplies of captive Africans. Planters were well aware of and were insured financially against high infant mortality. Thus, the need to institute safer health measures was not a driving concern. Carrington cites Joseph Foster Barham as an example. Barham, one of the leading Jamaican planters in the late eighteenth century, had insured both mothers and children up to the age of fourteen.[33] In addition, the renowned Jamaican planter and historian Edward Long highlights the insurance of enslaved Africans as a regular practice among planters in eighteenth-century Jamaica, as can be seen in table 3.7. One can only assume that the practice extended into the early nineteenth century. On several Jamaican plantations, both the planters and the medical practitioners largely blamed the African women for the high levels of infant mortality from their "primitive" African habits.[34] Planters would have concluded that it was best to insure the lives of mothers and children, as the "unsafe" habits of African women would not change.

Table 3.7 Cost of Maintaining Africans Annually

	Pounds	Shillings	
Food	6	10	
Clothing	1	3	
Physic/doctor	0	5	
Poll tax on each	0	2	
Total	**8**	**0**	
Insurance @ 10% (value of an enslaved worker being £80)	8	0	
Grand total	**16**	**0**	= £16 sterling

Source: Edward Long Papers, Add. MS 12404, fo. 406d.

This attitude underscores one of the failures of many managers in early nineteenth-century Jamaica. Most managers were not convinced that preventative health measures could stem the volumes of natural population decreases or that a healthy African labour force was necessary to healthy production. As far as they were concerned, the Africans' natural habits of self-destruction could not be prevented, at least not in the short term. The management team at Worthy Park was not exempt from such a view.

Dr John Quier, the distinguished medical practitioner for Worthy Park, of whom Craton has spoken highly, is an excellent example of this perspective. Dr Quier practised medicine in the parish of St John for twenty-one years. In his testimony to the Jamaican House of Assembly in 1778 concerning the care and treatment of Africans, he lays blame for the high infant mortality at Worthy Park squarely at the feet of the Negro women. He wrote:

> The known want of cleanliness arising from the obstinate attachment of Negro women to their own old customs, particularly, to one so evidently mischievous, in a warm climate, as that of not shifting the child's clothes for the first three days after its birth; and sometimes from the deficiency of linen and other necessaries proper for a new-born infant. Secondly, the nature of their habitations, sometimes suffocating with heat and smoke, at others, when the fires subsides especially by night, admitting the cold damp air through innumerable crevices and holes of the walls, which are seldom kept in proper repair; which sudden transition from heat to cold

by occasioning peripneumonic fevers . . . [is] the most general cause of deaths of new-born infants. Lastly, the injudicious custom of suckling a new-born child for the first week after its birth, or longer with the milk of a woman who often has a child at her breast a year old, or perhaps older.[35]

Although Dr Quier held the plantation responsible for not having proper material comforts for the Africans, he concluded his testimony by blaming the African women as the chief cause of the high infant mortality rate in comparison with that of poor white women in Great Britain. He further claimed that the African women's lack of morality and their promiscuity were the underlying causes and that they resorted frequently to abortion. Among all cases of abortions or miscarriages that he knew, he stated, none could be fairly imputed to ill usage or excessive labour.[36] In addition, he indicated that many children died through neglect and the want of maternal affection, which the African mothers seldom retained for their offspring because they were promiscuous.[37]

The truth, however, was that the plantation managers accused the enslaved Africans for their own inadequacies. Without the whip to force the Africans to conform, the managers were not trained to lead them. The three reasons given by Dr Quier for the high infant mortality were unfair to the African women. Improper housing, the planters' refusal to allow the African women to bond with their children and the improper use or unavailability of proper baby linens were all failures of the plantation. The managers had themselves to blame for not instituting the necessary initiatives to improve the health of their enslaved women.

If the opinion of Dr Quier was synonymous with those of fellow planters and fellow whites, which in most cases it was, then it would have been easy for planters to assume that maternal care of their infants was a losing battle. As a result, they factored in high mortality as an expense of their businesses or provided insurance for African mothers and children to reclaim their expenses. My findings show clearly that infant mortality could have been prevented on Worthy Park plantation. A careful examination shows that the deaths recorded were among children who had already lived beyond the first few days. Foetuses that were believed to have been aborted were never listed as such in the plantation records and thus were not included in the high figure of deaths in the one- to ten-year age range.

Craton, in his study of the mortality figures on the Worthy Park estate, examined the causes rather than the ages of death.[38] Although it is helpful to know the chief causes behind the high mortality rates at Worthy Park, the reasons given by its plantation doctors could be misleading. What they described as particular symptoms then, in some cases may be better understood today as belonging to other categories of illnesses. Furthermore, plantation doctors were part of plantation management and as such were not immune from ascribing certain causes for mortality to fit their agenda or their particular racial ideology. The recorded ages of death in groups of ten years I believe, is a better assessment to determine what categories of persons were frequently dying on the plantation.

Of the total of fifty-eight deaths listed of children up to age ten during the years 1813 to 1834, as recorded in table 3.5 and figure 3.3, only sixteen were of children under a year old. The other forty-two deaths were of children over a year. Of the sixteen deaths of children under a year old, only six were recorded as occurring less than a month after birth. On only one occasion, the exact age at death was not known: Cretta's child was listed in 1813 as dying of pleurisy when she was less than a month old. For the other deaths under a month, the exact time of death was listed. For example, in 1815, two children were listed as dying sixteen and twenty-three days after birth, respectively. In 1822, two additional children were listed as dying twenty-four and twenty-five days after birth, and in 1833 another child was listed as dying after one month.

The important point here is that of the sixteen deaths recorded among children under a year old, only one child's record was ambiguous regarding the time of death. All the others are shown to have been fully developed children who were never listed as having serious complications at birth. Thus, it is only reasonable to conclude that one of the possible reasons for the high rate of mortality in the one-to-ten age group was the poor state of medical assistance, poor diet and the diseased environment in which these children lived. At Worthy Park, children entered the children's gang at age eight and served there for a year or two.[39] At age ten, they were transferred to a third gang. At Spring Gardens Pen, an adjunct plantation to Worthy Park, children were put in a special gang at age seven, not age eight. Thus, on the same plantation, the practice varied. This is significant because at Worthy Park, children seem to have been transferred to one of the regular working gangs at a much earlier age than the average eleven to twelve years on other Jamaican plantations.

As shown in table 3.5, a few Africans at Worthy Park lived up to age 90, which was unusual in plantation life. Between the years 1813 and 1834, Worthy Park recorded 13 deaths between the ages of 71 and 80 years, 7 between 81 and 90 years, and 1 between the ages of 91 and 100 years. Of the 202 recorded deaths from 1813 to 1834, 21 of those deaths (10 per cent) were of individuals who lived over the age of 71. In the age group of 61 and up, there were 42 deaths between the years 1813 and 1834 (21 per cent). There is thus ample evidence to support the argument of longevity of some of the enslaved at Worthy Park. This should not be interpreted as a sign of humane management but one of plain common sense; the slave lists indicate that the managers reclassified older enslaved Africans over the age of 35 to different labour tasks that would be less physically demanding than fieldwork. Rose Price's financial ability to keep purchasing Africans from other plantations after 1807 further made this transferral of worn-out Africans possible. As a result, Worthy Park was always able to keep its "great gang", or first gang, which comprised the strongest workers, predominantly young. For example, in the 1824 slave list, only 40 of the 124 members of the great gang were over 35 years old, while the remaining 84 were between ages 19 and 35.[40] In the four available slave lists, the majority of Africans over the age of 35 were not listed as healthy. One plantation role to which many such Africans were transferred was that of watchmen. An example of this transferral can be seen in the following examples.

On 1 January 1792, Worthy Park had an enslaved population of 357. Of these, 42.1 per cent (150 enslaved workers) were active in the field and 57.01 per cent were non-fieldworkers. The plantation had eighteen different categories in which older enslaved Africans were working. In 1793, when the plantation's enslaved African population grew to 542 by way of purchase, management was able to place more labourers in the field. Thus, 318 persons (58.7 per cent) were fieldworkers. By 1813, out of an enslaved population of 512, 213 (41.6 per cent) were doing fieldwork. Interestingly, the plantation by then had around thirty-one different categories for older Africans to work in. This was an increase of non-fieldwork areas from the eighteen categories there had been in 1792. This indicates that Worthy Park was able to increase the number of younger Africans doing fieldwork, since they had the luxury of moving their older fieldworkers to other work categories.

The longevity evident at Worthy Park was a result of the plantation transferring most of their enslaved Africans over thirty-five to other areas, since they could afford to. As a result, a few of these older Africans were able to enjoy greater longevity than on other plantations where fresh supplies of Africans were harder to obtain after 1807. This explains why there was an increasing number of Africans recorded as "unhealthy" by age thirty-five, as seen in the 1836 slave lists.[41] This could also explain in part why around 40 per cent of the deaths at Worthy Park were enslaved Africans under thirty years of age who were being severely overworked. It could also account for the need for the "fourth gang" that was created by Worthy Park's management; this was comprised primarily of the weaker Africans, ranging in age from their twenties up to their sixties. As a weak gang, they were responsible for cutting grass, a task normally reserved for the children's gang.[42]

Craton and Walvin mention this fourth gang, but they are incorrect in suggesting that it was created to make work easier for the "general" enslaved population. Its essential purpose was to find lighter work for the large unhealthy enslaved population. For example, one of the persons assigned to this fourth gang was Eleanor Burrel, who had only one leg and was thirty-two years old. Also interesting was that the group labelled as "invalids" in the 1836 slave list comprised persons from ages thirty to seventy.[43] The managers at Worthy Park had found a way to redirect worn-out enslaved Africans into a more supporting role, thus giving them greater longevity.

On the issue of diet and health, there is also no evidence that Worthy Park had an abundance of fresh ground provisions, which would have benefited the Africans. It remains unclear what exactly was the consistent diet of the Africans at Worthy Park, unlike that of the white managerial class. From the limited evidence presented, it could be concluded that the plantation only fed consistently a limited number of Africans, such as the sick and the weak, while the others who had their own provision grounds and were healthy were left to fend for themselves.

In 1792, the same year that Rose Price took over the management of Worthy Park, an account was given regarding the food and clothes expended on Africans. The clothes were recorded strictly for new Africans, while the diet records were much more inclusive of all enslaved persons. The emphasis seems to have been on new enslaved persons. These new Africans were being seasoned, as they were given one tierce of rice in December, and they shared one other tierce and one barrel of beef with the residents of the "main house" in November. In November, one barrel of herring was also shared with the "weak" enslaved Africans. In December, these "weak" Africans were given two barrels of herring. Seven additional barrels seem to have been given to the general enslaved population, for both general use and Christmas allowances.

Judging from the records of other plantations, it was customary to increase food supplies and other incentives for enslaved Africans during the month of December for Christmas celebrations.[44] Based on records from the month of November, it seems that approximately two barrels of herring were given monthly to the "weak" enslaved Africans. How nutritious this herring was is another topic of discussion. It has been argued that in most instances, the herring was of poor quality and rotted by the time it reached Jamaica.[45] Based on another invoice from 1822, for ninety barrels of excellent white herring from a London merchant for Worthy Park, it seems possible that herring was one of the food items given to Worthy Park slaves or sections of the enslaved population. The regularity of this habit is unclear.[46]

Watchmen and invalids as a collective group were also given one barrel of herring in November and one in December. On the slave list of 1 January, there were twenty-six watchmen and thirty-three invalids listed with the superannuated.[47] This meant that around fifty-nine Africans shared one barrel of herring in November and another in December. The disparity in food items becomes clear when one compares what was reserved for "house use" to what was given to the enslaved Africans. For the month of November (November being more typical of the other months than December), the list of goods for house use included: two barrels of flour, one barrel of pork, one box of candles, and one tierce of rice and one barrel of beef to be shared with the "New Negroes".[48]

This vast inequality in food distribution is evident in figure 3.4, which shows two inventories for Storeroom One at Worthy Park in 1813, one from May and one from October. The food items listed are similar to those reserved for house use in the 1792 list. We can thus conclude that the commodities on this list were not given to the general enslaved population but were reserved for the use of the white planter class. If they had been given to the large African population, which numbered 511 in 1813, then the items listed in the month of May would have completely disappeared by October. It would appear that, except for flour, all the items listed in October were the remains of the commodities from May. There is no mention of herring in the storeroom, which seems to indicate that it was not a popular staple of the white planter class.

Quantity for May 1813	Quantity for October 1813
3 puncheons of 1811 rum	2 puncheons of 1811 rum
3 puncheons of 1812 rum	3 puncheons of 1812 rum
6½ barrels of beef	4½ barrels of beef
3 barrels of pork	2½ barrels of pork
6 barrels of pig cheeks	1½ barrels of pig cheeks
2½ barrels of tongues	2 half barrels of tongues
5 firkins of butter	3 firkins of butter
3 barrels of flour	4 barrels of flour

Figure 3.4 Inventory of food items at Worthy Park, 1813
Source: Worthy Park Plantation Book, 4/23/4.

A similar inventory of food items in Storeroom One from 3 April 1815 also supports the view that items intended for the enslaved population were labelled accordingly (figure 3.5).

The specific labelling of "Negro rum" in contrast to the other rum listed seems to suggest that the other items were for the white planter class and not for the enslaved population.

The 1792 plantation journal gives the impression that management placed much emphasis on the feeding of the new slaves in the seasoning process. In October 1792, Rose Price purchased ninety new captive Africans. Immediately after their purchase, the journal shows the various articles that were bought by Price for their use. This included 1,200 pounds of plantains from Robert Reid, 600 pounds of yams from Nelly Price, and 1,855 pounds of coco-heads

1 puncheon of rum from 1812
1 puncheon of rum from 1813
1 puncheon of Negro rum
3 lb of beef
3 lb of pork
3 lb of pig cheeks
3½ lb of tongues

Figure 3.5 Inventory of food items at Worthy Park, 1815
Source: Worthy Park Plantation Book, 4/23/4, 169.

> 3 puncheons of Virginia corn
>
> 1 puncheon of peas
>
> 2 puncheons of saltfish
>
> 11 puncheons of shads
>
> 4 tons of split peas
>
> 15 barrels of corn flour

Figure 3.6 Food items received from Spring Gardens Pen, 1792
Source: Worthy Park Plantation Book, AC 4035, 42.

from Tydixton Park, along with another 2,000 pounds from James Reed. Interestingly, Worthy Park kept obtaining the same items from the same persons from August to December of 1792.[49] Figure 3.6 shows the ground provisions that Worthy Park received from Spring Gardens Pen, one of their auxiliary estates, in November and December of 1792, as listed in the journal for that year.

The journal indicates that these food items were expended on the inhabitants of the great house and on the new Africans.[50] From all indications, the only two items other than herring that appear to have been given to the enslaved Africans, except under unusual circumstances such as severe drought or intense hurricane, were corn and peas. A record from 1795 (table 3.8) shows the quantity of corn and peas given to enslaved Africans over a period of one to two months.

From table 3.8, it appears that not all Africans received food provisions at the same time. It could also be concluded that the entire African population was not consistently fed. The 271 Africans listed as receiving corn along with the 151 listed as receiving beans do not necessarily signify individual Africans, as the figures could also apply to select groups of Africans, such as parents receiving weekly rations.

While it is unclear what these figures refer to, it could be argued that corn, beans and sometimes herring were given to a select group of enslaved Africans on a weekly basis. This group appears to have included vulnerable Africans such as the weak and disabled, the watchmen and the newly arrived enslaved Africans. They seem to have been fed consistently. The evidence available does not suggest that the healthy enslaved Africans were fed consistently. They seem to have had to rely on their provision grounds to complement their diet.

Table 3.8 Additional Food Items Given to Africans at Worthy Park, 1795

Date	Quarts of Corn	Number of Africans
June 1–7	508	72
June 8–13	242	48
June 13–23	711	71
June 23–July 6	1,120	80

Date	Quarts of Beans	Number of Africans
June 1–7	150	50
June 8–13	225	45
June 13–20	168	56

Source: Edward Long Papers, Add. MS 12404, fo. 406d.

This selective distribution of food to the Africans seems to also apply to the allocation of rum. The plantation book that covers the years 1791–1811 shows that rum was given to the various enslaved gang leaders on a weekly basis.[51] This can also be seen in the crop accounts from 1799 onwards. There was a radical yearly increase in the amount of rum given. This could explain why a puncheon of 1813 rum would have still been in the storeroom in 1815. Rum was not given generally to the enslaved Africans – only to the gang leaders under what seem like special circumstances.

It is likely that the majority of healthy Africans had to provide for themselves. Hence, they were given more land on which to do so. Craton and Walvin argue that Rose Price, in a manner far in advance of his own times, gathered vital statistics concerning the Africans he owned at Worthy Park with the aim of improving their health and morale and reducing their awful mortality rate.[52] The records show that Rose Price made massive improvements to his plantation's infrastructure, including the increase of the overall acreage under cultivation from 2,922 in 1792 to 3,250 in 1813 and 4,450 in 1830.[53] The Worthy Park maps, however, do not give any conclusive evidence that this increase in land utilization included a significant increase in land to grow provisions for the enslaved Africans.[54] This was despite the amelioration laws that the Jamaican planters had been passing since 1792, which granted more land to the Africans for provisions. The planters were never committed to enforcing their own laws. Furthermore, no government agency policed the plantations to ensure that the laws were adhered to. In addition, the planters devised other laws to ensure that any law that was reasonably favourable to the enslaved Africans could be easily evaded.

Although Price nominally devoted the section of 577 acres of his land called Cocoree to the Africans, this did not mean that it was actually used for that purpose.[55] Craton and Walvin show that much of Cocoree was swampy and inaccessible.[56] Instead of increasing available land in favour of their provision grounds, Price further marginalized the Africans in relegating them to inaccessible land that even the very surveyors could not precisely define. In his rush to increase land for cane, Price had taken away the best 20 acres of provision land at "Plantain Walk". Of the 577 acres of land at Cocoree, 51.13 acres were described as mountain land, and this was the only area given to the Africans for provision grounds. The remaining approximately 525 acres were described as abounding in copperwood, not to mention inaccessible and swampy. The Africans had a further 8 acres of mountain land for provision grounds up in an area called "Mountain", as well as some land in Dry Gully. Of the latter's 689 acres, only 33 acres could be planted in cane since the rest of the land was described as being in ruinate, overgrown with woodlawn and timbers. Providing adequate provision grounds for the enslaved Africans was not a priority for Price. The Worthy Park maps show Price's entire infrastructure improvements in precise measures. The enslaved Africans' provision grounds were always described in these maps as mountain land that abounded with timbers to the point of being inaccessible. Thus, we can conclude that the Africans at Worthy Park would have grown limited provisions due to the inaccessibility of the land they were given. We can also conclude that the enslaved people used their creativity and resilience to put the land to productive use despite the difficult topography and terrain.

The year 1813 was the only year in which the plantation acreages for Worthy Park, Spring Gardens and Mickleton were listed to show how the land was utilized. This can be seen in table 3.9. As these were the only figures provided, it is hard to evaluate the precise percentages of land given to the Africans for "Negro grounds". But when these figures are compared with those from other plantations, then the percentages given to the Africans at Worthy Park seem standard and do not support the claims of Craton and Walvin that plantation policy was to give the Africans more land to feed themselves.

Table 3.9 Land Utilization on Rose Price's Plantations, 1813

Land	Worthy Park Acreage	%	Spring Gardens Pen Acreage	%	Mickleton Pen Acreage	%
Canes and ratoons	433.1.10	13.00	–	–	–	–
Guinea grass	429.2.4	13.20	185.0.0	–	–	–
Common grass	700.0.0	21.50	400.0.0	20.23	548.0.0	91.3
Plantain walk, whites	40.0.0	1.23	–	–	–	
Woodlawn and Negro grounds	1647.0.0	50.70	200.0.0	10.10	40.0.0	6.6
Woodlawn	1192.0.0	60.20	–	–	–	–
Corn and provision grounds					12.0.0	2.0

Notes:
% = Percentage of plantation.
Worthy Park had a slave population of 511 and a stock of 375 with 3250.0.0 acres.
Spring Gardens Pen had a slave population of 70 and a stock of 491 with 1977.0.0 acres.
Mickleton Pen had a slave population of 33 and a stock of 197 with 600.0.0 acres.

Source: Worthy Park Plantation Book, 4/23/4.

David Ryden, in his dissertation on Jamaica, indicates that although sugar estates were centred on a single crop, only a small portion of their fields was cultivated for that purpose. Based on the known distribution of land, around 25 per cent was used for the growing of sugar cane, 10 per cent for provisions, 32 per cent for cattle and the remaining 33 per cent remained in wooded land.[57] Ryden further argues that most of the efficient estates had fewer Africans per acre of sugar and a higher ratio of provisions to Africans.[58] B.W. Higman's cartometric study of thirty-seven estate maps in Jamaica from the eighteenth century also lends support to Ryden's thesis on land distribution from the eighteenth to the nineteenth century.[59] It is extremely important to note that on most plantations in Jamaica, around 10 per cent of land was committed to provisions. This meant that the 6.6 per cent at Mickleton Pen and the 10.1 per cent at Spring Gardens committed to African provision grounds was around average. It must be remembered that much of the provision grounds (50.7 per cent) at Worthy Park were covered in woodlawn and were inaccessible for farming. Thus, the percentage being used for African provisions could not have been significantly over 10 per cent.

Last, in the area of manumissions, Craton and Walvin are also guilty of falsely conveying planter benevolence. They write: "The startling rise in the number of manumissions after 1825 was evidence . . . of the liberalization of the manumission and property laws . . . so that slaves now owned money and could buy their freedom more easily."[60] Furthermore, "the Negro population of the estate rose steadily, even without purchases, to a peak in 1817, maintaining itself roughly at this level until the increasing number of manumissions in the 1820s and 1830s brought about a steady decline . . . as up to a dozen slaves were manumitted in each year".

The plantation estate books and manumission records of the early nineteenth century do not support either claim. In fact, there were only twenty-five recorded manumissions from 1792 to 1833. The twelve manumissions a year that Craton and Walvin claim occurred in the 1820s and 1830s do not exist.[61] The year 1834 is the only year in which there were twenty-five manumissions recorded, in addition to three enslaved Africans who purchased their apprenticeships.[62] It must be stated that manumissions at Worthy Park were characteristic of Jamaican plantations in the early nineteenth century. They were predominantly for economic and social purposes. Price, like other Jamaican planters, granted manumissions mainly to the coloured children of white estate workers. Even then, they took on an economic role, as these white personnel usually provided their coloured children in exchange for healthy enslaved Africans. Of the twenty-five manumissions up to 1833 at Worthy Park, nineteen were for coloured children. In some cases, the fathers of these children worked on the plantation and provided alternate healthy enslaved Africans in return.[63] Furthermore, these twenty-five manumissions were done as favours to former white employees and not to appease the enslaved Africans.

In 1811, Rose Price manumitted two coloured Africans, a quadroon by the name of Beddy and a male mulatto by the name of Jack, for £280, Jamaican currency, in exchange for an enslaved boy named Harry and an enslaved girl named Jenny.⁶⁴ In 1816, Price manumitted Thomas James, the mulatto son of one of his faithful white carpenters, Charles James, for the sum of £100, Jamaican currency. James did not pay the £100 but provided a healthy African male named Martin to Price.⁶⁵ In 1824, of the twelve children listed as being born in the plantation book for that year, four were given to Rose Price for the manumission of five coloured children. Susannah Cummings, who was listed in the January 1824 slave list as a healthy thirty-five-year-old mulatto woman who worked in the overseer's house as a washer, was manumitted along with her three children. In exchange, a woman named Delia and her two children, Moses and Susannah, were given to Rose Price.⁶⁶ The attorney for Worthy Park, Thomas Braitsford, also obtained manumission for what appears to be his enslaved child, James, a healthy nineteen-year-old who worked with the head African carpenter, another mulatto on the plantation.⁶⁷ James Braitsford was manumitted and the plantation received another African male, Edward, who was purchased for £100.⁶⁸ These examples show that Africans who were owned by other members of the management staff or fellow whites in the community, or who had some other relation to whites, were most often manumitted. Even then, there was an economic advantage for Rose Price, who was given young and healthy enslaved Africans instead.

The evidence also seems to indicate that even during Apprenticeship, manumissions were primarily aimed at coloured children and were done gratuitously for nominal considerations. For example, in 1837, two African females, Ann Douglas, twenty years old, and Ann Peirce, nineteen years old, both domestic servants, were manumitted for £20 each. Interestingly, their purchase was described as "non-praedial", which implies a gratuitous act based on their privileged status.⁶⁹ This was in keeping with the majority of manumissions granted in Jamaica from 1817 to 1830. In a report given by the secretary's office in Jamaica, sanctioned by the governor of Jamaica and sent to the Colonial Office in England, the amount of gratuitous manumissions outweighed those for valuable considerations: 4,129 to 3,216.⁷⁰ In only five of the years between 1817 and 1830 did valuable considerations outnumber nominal considerations, 1825 and 1827–30. In 1838, two other female Africans also purchased their apprenticeships: Bessy Price, aged nineteen, and Susana Dale, aged seventeen. The women paid a combined total of £53.13.4, which appears again in the records as gratuitous manumissions.⁷¹

It has to be concluded that the Worthy Park plantation was more successful in both its sugar production and its productivity levels than many Jamaican plantations in the early nineteenth century. Rose Price as a young plantation owner restructured his plantation in many more ways than did his contemporaries. He enlarged his acreage of cane and built the necessary infrastructure, such as roads and manure pens. He increased his stock, purchased enslaved Africans and made the necessary financial connections, which was helpful in his continual quest to expand his enslaved labour pool. He also made technological changes, such as the purchase of a mill to grind corn along with a cane top cutter worked by mules, both in 1825.[72] With such improvements, Price ensured that when he returned to Great Britain he would be better able to evaluate his managers and to have them follow his vision for his plantation. As such, his proactive management paid handsomely in stable production levels, despite the plantation's gradual decline prior to emancipation.

Where Price failed, and failed miserably, was in maintaining a healthy enslaved labour force. He, like many fellow Jamaican planters, did not institute the necessary health measures to maintain his labour force, especially their infants and the prime members of the first gang. Because Worthy Park had the financial access to purchase Africans constantly, the declining health of its enslaved labourers did not seriously affect the plantation's production. In the following chapters, I will show that other plantations that could not procure the same amount of Africans as Worthy Park, and who had not instituted ameliorative and other necessary measures to procure labour, paid dearly with plummeting levels of production and productivity.

Most likely, Worthy Park's production would have steadily increased rather than declined if its management had been able to maintain healthier Africans. They would not have had to spend so much money increasing their labour force. Craton and Walvin state that by 1815, Price's income had dwindled substantially, to the point where he made a mere sixteen thousand pounds gross and an almost negligible net profit. This was largely due to external factors, such as rapid decreases in the price of sugar in the international market, the reduction of the drawback and the failure of protective duties.[73] With such external realities, one has to ask if Worthy Park would not have experienced increased production if the plantation had spent more of its income improving the material conditions of the Africans and implementing labour initiatives such as task work. This important relationship between the increased health of labourers and increased production is the focus of the next chapters.

CHAPTER 4

The Impact of Abolition on Labour Procurement

NEWLY APPOINTED PLANTATION ATTORNEYS customarily evaluated their predecessors' management at the beginning of their terms. Two such attorneys, James Wedderburn and J.C. Grant, were no exceptions. In 1806, they made a most critical observation that was to be quite common on many post-1807 Jamaican plantations. The Mesopotamia plantation in Westmoreland, they observed, had the required number of enslaved Africans to perform labour tasks. However, much of the enslaved workforce consisted of physically weak Africans. Thus, the strength of the enslaved labourers was inadequate to meet the hard demands of estate work. If the plantation was to reap an early crop, have it processed and cope with the other tedious labour demands on the estate, it had to hire jobbers.[1] Most important, if Mesopotamia was to increase its levels of productivity, a healthy gang of enslaved Africans would have to be purchased.[2]

The importance of procuring new enslaved labourers after 1807, either by hire or purchase, was one of the most important recommendations made by Jamaican managers to plantation owners. Many Jamaican plantations after 1807 seem to have suffered from either a reduced number of enslaved labourers or a physically deficient workforce, as was the case at Mesopotamia. Some Jamaican managers, despite having a strong enslaved workforce, still hired "jobbers" or were in possession of jobbing gangs to fatten their pockets. As a result of both a genuine demand for labour and what could be described as unnecessary requests, many absentee owners paid a heavy price for labour costs as they had to depend largely on the assessment or judgement of their local managers. For example, Thomas Samson from Amity Hall made constant appeals to owner Henry Goulburn for additional Africans. The corn crop for 1802 was plentiful, he wrote, and he needed extra workers to have it harvested and sold before the plantation could pay its contingencies.[3] Samson purchased twenty Africans in two installments: first, eight men and two women for ninety pounds each, and later five men and five women at one hundred pounds each.[4] In 1803, however, Samson told Goulburn that he could not purchase new Africans that year because the corn crop had been destroyed by a drought and he did not have the provisions to feed the Africans. He recommended that he be allowed to hire more jobbers.[5] In early 1804, Samson returned to his initial preference to buy new enslaved Africans, making a purchase of ten. The island had had good rainfall and consequently, he would have enough provisions for at least two years.[6] He nevertheless waited until 1805 to purchase an additional twenty enslaved Africans. While he waited, he employed jobbing labour, stating that regular plantation labour was inadequate.[7] Goulburn was upset with Samson's use of jobbers, but Samson assured him that they were most critical to maintain production on the estate.[8] Samson's decision not to buy more enslaved Africans and to use jobbing labour was deliberate. He created work for his own jobbing gang and thus exploited Goulburn's ignorance. This shows the difficulty that absentee planters such as Goulburn faced. They had to decide either to use the existing African labour force and run the risk of decline in productivity and production or accept increased labour costs with the hope of increasing these.[9] In most cases, the plantation owners preferred the former option, while the local managers usually preferred the latter, either to augment their incomes or to increase their levels of production to impress the owners. In addition, some managers such as Samson preferred the use of jobbing gangs, since they could not spare the time to nurse the relatively weak enslaved labour force back to health.

On Joseph Foster Barham's estates, there was never a large enough labour force to perform all the necessary plantation work. In 1801, the attorney of Mesopotamia, William Rodgers, insisted on the need for jobbers. Although his contingencies were already high, he had to invest in hired labour if the plantation was to reap a crop of three hundred hogsheads of sugar and keep adequate guinea grass for the pen.[10] In 1805, the managers asked for an annual expenditure of two to three hundred pounds for jobbing labour. Most of this would be expended on digging cane holes; they wanted to save the Africans from this demanding job, as it was injurious to their health. This was of critical importance, as the gangs at Mesopotamia were completely worn out and were far from adequate.[11] At Island estate, Barham's other Jamaican plantation in St Elizabeth, the attorney, Mr Webb, argued that the 32 acres of cane for the fall plant was insufficient and that it should be increased to 40 acres if Barham was to reap an excellent crop. Hired labour, on which many estates were completely dependent, would be required.[12]

As more and more plantations turned to hired workers to meet their labour requirements, jobbing gangs became difficult to obtain. Demand was exceeding availability and the owners of these jobbing gangs began stipulating that their jobbers would not dig cane holes. This was considered one of the hardest jobs on the plantations and it contributed significantly to the deteriorating health of the enslaved Africans. Nevertheless, Webb at Island estate continued to seek such a gang for the preparation of the estate's cane holes. This would allow him to use the plantation labour force for the spring season to fence and plant guinea grass for the stock.[13] The regular use of jobbers continued at Island estate up until 1816, since the continued poor physical condition of the enslaved Africans made the job of fencing too arduous for them. Thus, jobbers again had to be employed to construct fencing for the plantation's pastures.[14] The high cost of jobbing had increased Barham's plantation expenses; holing cane pieces had now reached ten to eleven pounds per acre. Yet he had to accept this cost in the interest of relieving his worn-out enslaved labourers.[15]

Similarly, Lord Penrhyn's plantations in Clarendon could not operate without employing jobbing labour. In 1804, attorney Rowland Fearon employed enslaved jobbers in digging cane holes on the mountain estates. This, he wrote to Penrhyn, would assist his enslaved Africans significantly.[16] In response to Penrhyn's objections to the excessive cost of jobbing, Fearon stressed that the fall crop was late and that he would use the estate's labour to do other essential work such as draining the gutters and cleaning the ratoons. Fearon assured Lord Penrhyn that he would ensure that the new overseer paid special attention to both the stock and the enslaved Africans because they were the nerves of the estate. Furthermore, he would strive to maintain the strength of the enslaved Africans, even to gain a population increase through natural birth since this was the sign of a good planter.[17]

Even before the 1807 Abolition Act, many of the plantations in Jamaica suffered from inadequate labour.[18] This fact was not always reflected in the slave lists. The relative strength of the African labour force was what was most significant, not necessarily the numerical figure, but the latter appears to have often been sufficient to satisfy absentee owners. With the passing of the 1807 Abolition Act, however, the plantations' labour woes were exacerbated; they faced a decline not only in the number of enslaved Africans but also in the labour force's relative strength. They could not purchase the regular yearly number of enslaved Africans that were needed to maintain stability. Although many tried, they could not procure it through natural means either. Thus, the strength of their African populations decreased.

Many plantation owners still did not understand that numerical strength on a plantation was not necessarily enough to increase productivity. It was the relative physical strength of the enslaved population that was more critical. Rodgers emphasized this point to Barham despite his uneasiness with the practice of hired labour. Yet Barham had little choice. The Africans on his estate were ill, and inclement weather had set in just after they had finished planting the guinea grass. Thus, it was not in Barham's best interest to have them dig cane holes.[19] It was of great concern to absentee planters to resolve the dilemma of paying hired labour when they already had large numbers of enslaved people on their estates. It was very difficult for them to accept that many of their own labourers were unfit for demanding tasks. At Mesopotamia, the fieldworkers and some of the artisans were very ill. In particular, the head driver had been extremely ill for a long time and the head boiler had "violent" rheumatic pains.[20]

Relative Strength versus Numerical Strength

Many plantation lists, when analysed carefully, reveal that even if a plantation listed a satisfactory number of Africans, only a small percentage of them was healthy and suited for rigorous labour. For example, in an 1806 slave list from Penrhyn's King's Valley estate, the enslaved Africans were divided into four categories: "healthy", "able", "weak" and "invalid". In December 1806, out of an enslaved population of 295, 31.5 per cent were listed as "weak" and "invalid" (seventy "weak" and twenty-three "invalid"). What is even more interesting is that a distinction was made between those who were listed as "able" and those who were listed as "healthy", which was rather rare on plantation lists. Only seventy persons, or 23.8 per cent, were listed as "healthy", predominantly young men and women of ages seventeen and younger. Only a very small number of adults, around five, over seventeen years of age were listed as "healthy". The other adults over seventeen, if they were not described as "weak" with diseases, were listed as "able". This meant then that the real strength of the enslaved population was only 23.8 per cent, as 44.7 per cent (132 labourers) played a supporting role as "able" individuals and the remaining 31.5 per cent was classified as "weak" and "invalids".

This does not mean that the seventy persons described as weak were discarded from plantation life; they were simply taken from the field gangs and placed in other useful occupations on the plantation. For example, fifteen such persons were employed as watchmen. It must also be noted that labourers in the "weak" category ranged from ages twenty-five to fifty-six. Thus, it is not surprising that most of those listed as "healthy" were less than twenty years of age. Another interesting feature of the list is that young women were placed in the first or main gang at age fifteen, which was much earlier than the young men, who started at age eighteen. This had consequences for the health of the African women, as seen in table 4.1. In addition, their ability or willingness to produce children naturally was also affected.[21]

The 1808 slave list for King's Valley, which has similar categorizations to the 1806 list, is shown in table 4.1. From an enslaved population of 295, only

Table 4.1 Division of Africans at King's Valley Estate, 1 February 1808

Category	Total	Weak	Invalid	Healthy	Able
Men	84	29	9	2	44
Women	113	33	23	8	49
Young men, 11–18	22	2	0	20	0
Young women, 11–16	21	1	0	20	0
Male children, 0–10	25	2	0	23	0
Female children, 0–10	30	5	0	25	0
Total	295	72	32	98	93

Source: Penrhyn Papers, 1495.

33.2 per cent (98 individuals) were described as "healthy". Those listed as "able" accounted for 31.5 per cent, while 35.3 per cent were classified as "weak" or "invalid". The number of persons described as "healthy" was almost equal to the number of those described as "able". This again implies that only one-third of the African population was healthy; meanwhile, one-third bordered between being healthy and weak. The healthiest enslaved workers were 40 young men and women (aged eleven to eighteen), along with 10 adults and a number of individuals under ten years old from the children's gang. If most plantations had a similar composition of Africans around that period (1806–8), which seems to have been the case, then one can understand how the African population classified as healthy would never have been strong enough to perform the varied and hard tasks on most plantations without hired labour or fresh supplies of enslaved Africans.

Also evident in table 4.1 is the deteriorating health of the enslaved women, who had to enter the demanding tasks of fieldwork at the early age of fifteen to sixteen. Female invalids outnumbered male invalids by twenty-three to nine. More women than men were also classified as weak. Necessity may well have been the reason for which women entered the first gang at a younger age, as there were more women than men in both the young children and adult populations. This, however, had disastrous effects on the health and productivity of the enslaved population.

The limited number of labourers who constituted the main gangs in proportion to the total enslaved population can also be seen on two of Penrhyn's other plantations in 1807. The enslaved population of Thomas River and Kupius were combined for the month of October. The population of 421 Africans was composed generally as follows: 116 of the first two gangs (together called the great gang); 156 artisans and skilled workers (tradesmen, stock keepers, domestics, watchmen and boilers); 54 infants; 54 listed as weak and invalids; 28 sick persons in the hospital; 9 persons attending to the ill; and 4 constant runaways. The great gang made up only 27.5 per cent of the African population. The 156 skilled artisans were traditionally older persons who had been transferred from more physically demanding roles to more specific responsibilities.[22] It is thus not surprising that jobbing labour had to be sought on most estates, as the labourers' relative strength was small in comparison to the numerical figures portrayed on the plantation lists. Plantation managers had to implement labour management techniques to transfer older adults, often in their thirties, who were losing strength to other avenues of service. For example, attorney David Ewart conveyed to George Pennant that he had transferred most of the older men on the plantation to watchmen positions because they were incapable of performing any other duty.[23]

An 1825 list for the Amity Hall plantation shows that out of an enslaved population of 254, there were 26 different categories in the estate's division of labour (table 4.2). In this list, 18 Africans were classified as "weakly", and another 19 were listed as "invalids". The professions assigned to the "weakly" included head cooper, oil boiler, nurse, house woman, second gang cook, third gang cook, sheep man, hog man and watchman. All were positions that were not as laborious as fieldwork. The task of grass cutter, for example, was often assigned to young children who were being weaned into plantation life; this shows the extent to which the grass cutter could be physically weak.

The number of unhealthy members of the plantation, totaling 47 (19 invalids and 28 young children), seems rather low at only 18.5 per cent. But interestingly, the plantation's chief workforce was not necessarily the 143 members of the three work gangs (56.3 per cent), but rather the 106 members of the first gang (41.7 per cent). The second and third gangs in this particular case were weaker in terms of relative strength and were most likely composed of weaker teenagers and older adults.

The formation of a great gang was a management initiative for better control of labour and was practised not only on sugar plantations, but on coffee plantations as well. Radnor coffee plantation, which had a population of 225 Africans in 1821, had four traditional gangs. On an average Monday, the first gang would be hoeing grass on one coffee piece, while the second gang would be picking coffee on another. The third gang would be weeding grass to plant corn and the fourth would be weeding grass in the garden and filling it with dung. On most Fridays, the first two gangs, which were the strongest, would combine and form the great gang, to pick coffee.[24] The great gang would be composed of 60 to 70 Africans.[25] Table 4.3 shows the division of labour at Radnor.

Again, the relative strength of the Radnor plantation was not necessarily in the first three gangs, which comprised 60.5 per cent of the population. Its strength was really in the great gang, which comprised only 40 per cent of the population. The second and third gangs provided support, but the great gang was the one on which the estate depended to perform the hardest fieldwork

Table 4.2 Division of Africans at Amity Hall Plantation, 1 January 1825

Category	Number of Africans	
Drivers	3	
Dreweses	2	
Carpenters	5	
Coopers	6	
Masons	1	
Blacksmiths	1	
Cattlemen	1	
Great gang	106	
Second gang	22	
Third gang	15	
Young children	28	
Fish carriers	1	
Wainboys	1	
Carpenter boys	1	
Invalids	19	
Stock menders	9	
Washers	2	
Fishermen	1	
Grass cutters	1	
Doctresses	1	
Midwives	1	
Nurses	2	W
Field cooks & water carriers	5	W
Domestics	8	W
Oil boilers	1	W
Watchmen	11	4 W

Note: "W" signifies that the individual or some individuals in the group were transferred to that category because they were classified as "weak".

Source: Goulburn Papers, 304/J/1/21, 5.

Table 4.3 Division of Africans at Radnor Plantation, 1824

Category	Numbers of Africans
Great gang	85
Second gang	23
Third gang	22
Carpenters	7
Masons	3
Doctors	1
Boatswains	1
Domestics	6
Saddlers	1
Mule men	2
Sheep boys	2
Watchmen	7
Invalids	7
Midwives	1
Nurses	3
Sawyers	5
Children	38
Great house	1
Total	215

Source: Radnor Plantation Journal, 250.

on the plantation. At Christmas, members were compensated based on their levels of performance.[26] Following are the amounts of provisions that the different categories received by way of compensation:

Head personnel:	12 lb fish, 2 bottles of rum, 2 cups of sugar
Great gang:	6 lb fish, 1 bottle of rum, 1 cup of sugar
Second gang:	4 lb fish, 1/2 bottle of rum, 1/2 cup of sugar
Third gang:	2 lb fish, 1/2 cup of sugar
Children:	1 lb fish, 1/3 cup of sugar

The third gang seems to have been comprised of children on the verge of becoming teenagers; this is probably the reason they were not given any rum. The second gang appears to have been the weak and elderly persons on the plantation. This again underscores the point that the relative strength of the plantation was in the great gang.

The same observation could also be made regarding pens. A summary of the 245 apprentices at the Pepper and Bona Vista pens, at the beginning of 1838, can be seen in table 4.4. The three classes listed are work gangs composed according to age and strength, in the manner of gangs on sugar plantations. In an 1826 list, the third class was the children's gang, ranging from ages six to fourteen, with the other two classes described as fieldworkers. We can extrapolate, then, that in the list shown in table 4.4, the first class was the pen's great gang. This consisted of only forty-six persons, 18.8 per cent of the plantation.

The first class was ably supported by the other two classes; all three, added together, amounted to 48.6 per cent of the total (119 persons). It is also inter-

Table 4.4 Apprentices at Pepper and Bona Vista Pens in 1838

Categories	Males	Females	Total
Tradesmen	8	0	8
Breakers, stablemen and boys	21	0	21
Pen keepers and boys	13	0	13
Domestics, cooks and washers	4	12	16
Small-stock attendants	2	2	4
Doctors and midwives	1	1	2
Rangers, gardeners and cart-men	3	0	3
Breadnut and grass cutters	2	9	11
Hired out	1	1	2
Watchmen and invalids	16	30	46
First class	23	23	46
Second class	8	33	41
Third class	14	18	32
Total	116	129	245

Source: 1838 List of Africans at Pepper and Bona Vista, 57. From Pepper and Bona Vista Estate Books, University of the West Indies Library.

esting to note that the number of individuals listed as watchmen and invalids (forty-six, or 18.8 per cent of the total) is equal to the number in the first class. Most of these plantation lists do not carry the category of "able" persons, as did Lord Penrhyn's plantation. One then has to assume that the "able" persons were those listed in other supporting roles on the plantation, apart from those in the first two gangs. They were only able to perform limited fieldwork.

Enslaved Africans working in pens performed hard backbreaking labour just as those on sugar plantations did. They had to prepare fields of guinea grass, which involved hoeing, for the plantation stock to graze on. They had to collect the manure from the stock to fertilize other fields for planting. They constructed fences and planted provisions for the plantation and for themselves. In 1826, the enslaved Africans at Pepper and Bona Vista pens had to provide adequate fields for their 862 stock, 640 horned stock and 222 horses of all kinds, to graze. Furthermore, they had to prepare around eighty acres in plantation corn and "Negro grounds", where the enslaved planted food for their own sustenance, some of which could also be sold in the market on weekends. The volume of labour that had to be done severely affected the Africans' relative strength, especially as there was an unusual number of weak persons on the plantation, as seen in table 4.5.

Table 4.5 Enslaved Africans at Pepper and Bona Vista Pens in 1826

Categories	Number of Africans
Great gang	98
Small gang (ages 6–14)	31
Weak and invalids (watchmen came from this group)	76
Unemployed children (ages 0–6)	41
Pen keepers	13
Stablemen	13
Skilled artisans	10
Grass cutters and breadnut cutters	5
Doctors and midwives	2
House workers	6
Washer women	3

Source: Pepper and Bona Vista Papers.

Of the 298 enslaved Africans at Pepper and Bona Vista, the real strength of the population was in the 98 members of the great gang. This made up 32.8 per cent of the population, which corresponds to averages on other plantations. The approximately 76 persons classified as "weak" comprised around 25.6 per cent of the population. This is a high figure. Of these approximate 76 persons, 17 were aged 30 and under; 25 were between 31 and 50 years of age and 34 were over age 50. The number of weak persons on the plantation was thus not limited to persons over 50 but was spread throughout all the age groups. The backbreaking manual work performed by the Africans, due in part to the lack of adequate technology on many Jamaican plantations, resulted in a decline in strength and left the plantations in desperate need of labour.

Labour and Diversification

The deterioration of labour strength led to a host of other problems. Planters were caught in a vicious cycle of decline that extended into other areas of plantation life. At Mesopotamia, William Rodgers indicated that the Africans on the plantation worked very well, but because only a few of them were really healthy, he was unable to devote much attention to the plantation's pen. This explained the long neglect of the plantation's pastures. Rodgers did not have the enslaved labour force required to control the weeds and to develop proper pastures while continuing the plantation's work at the same time.[27] John Blyth, who had preceded Rodgers as manager, had gone further and made the link between an unproductive pen and its effect on declining sugar production. In 1819, Blyth wrote to Joseph Foster Barham, the plantation's owner that in 1798, the pen had been adequately stocked with 700 head and adequate enslaved labour. By 1805, however, when he took over the management, the stock had been reduced to 460, along with an unaccounted 78 head. As of the last quarter of 1818, the pen was still far from recovery, with its stock at only 394. His current problem, he wrote, was that the pen's guinea grass was almost exhausted and the two fallow pieces at the Cornwall line being prepared for the next season were not showing any significant growth. As a result, the cane land was poor, unable to benefit from the necessary manure from the stock. Furthermore, the plantation's ailing stock was failing to procure the natural increases that would have occurred in an effectively managed pen. The plantation could only afford to fatten the old cattle and occasionally sell a steer or two, given the inadequate strength of their enslaved labour force. Blyth stressed that for the pen to become productive and have a positive effect on the quality of the estate's sugar production, an increased enslaved workforce was urgently needed.[28]

The relationship between inadequate labour and diversification can be further illuminated by looking at the example of Mesopotamia. In 1818, in order to acquire more enslaved labour, Mesopotamia's managers had to purchase the entire Springfield plantation, containing 104 enslaved Africans, in Hanover, one of the parishes adjoining Westmoreland. The purchase of this additional plantation and the consequent increase in the workforce meant that the managers had the chance to improve the efficiency of their operations and to diversify. The Springfield enslaved Africans were, however, described as "trifling" as well as unhealthy. After 1807, it had become difficult to purchase healthy enslaved Africans without taking the weak ones as well.[29] Since Mesopotamia only wanted the enslaved Africans and not Springfield's entire infrastructure, the managers removed the enslaved labourers to Mesopotamia as soon as they were finished building the necessary houses for them. The Springfield property was also too far away to be annexed to any of Barham's properties. Springfield had no timber and the soil was unsuitable for coffee, but it was excellent for other crops, such as ginger and arrowroot. The land in that part of Hanover was also excellent for growing ground provisions, and Mesopotamia's managers saw in it the potential for enormous economic benefit. With inadequate labour at both locations, the managers decided that the best decision would be to divide the Springfield property into lots, reserving the Africans' provision ground until sufficient provision grounds were established at Mesopotamia.[30] Relocating the Springfield Africans to Mesopotamia was on the one hand essential to lessen the cost of jobbing labour and to make the pen more productive. Unfortunately, the plantation could not capitalize on the opportunity to use the land at Springfield to diversify their operations and develop the necessary staples. Inadequate labour also placed much undue stress upon the entire enslaved population, which continued to be overworked. At Mesopotamia, this resulted in the older enslaved Africans, of whom there were many, experiencing declining health. Rodgers wrote to Barham:

> We have such a number of them in the three different gangs, which in all humane probability cannot hold out much longer. I begin to think something is wrong when

the hothouse attendant keeps coming to me. . . . Last week we lost old Eve, an invalid, who died immediately, several have come into the hothouse these last two days with violent colds and pain in their sides, which I hope, will soon wear away.[31]

Rodgers assured Barham that he was indeed taking good care of his enslaved Africans. The reality, however, was that around two-thirds of them were old and invalids, and he was sure that if they were to be thoroughly examined medically, most of them would be found to be diseased and ulcerated as well. He provided a further example of four young African men and women who were still in the hospital with serious diseases and who he did not believe would survive.[32]

The decision by owners such as Henry Goulburn and Joseph Barham to enforce stringent economies on their plantations also created additional labour problems. The planters' resistance to continued investment in the human resources of their plantations placed undue pressure on the overworked Africans and contributed to the shortage of labour on their estates. This was one way in which Rose Price of Worthy Park differed from many of his contemporaries, despite the fact that he too was an absentee planter. Price invested liberally in his estate.

Further compounding these labour shortages was the planters' failure to increase their enslaved populations through natural means. Tables 4.6 and 4.7 demonstrate the low birth rate at Amity Hall in 1827 among the thirty-nine enslaved women of childbearing age. This example seems to typify the reality on many Jamaican plantations.

Further demonstrating the difficulty of procuring healthy enslaved Africans in early nineteenth-century Jamaica, attorney John Shand, representing planter Andrew Arcedeckne, paid as much as 20 per cent higher than the market value just to obtain some. In addition, Shand took the risk of removing a large number of enslaved Africans from a great distance to his plantation. Enslaved Africans who were settled on a plantation and who had planted ample ground provisions both for consumption and for sale tended to rebel violently if they had to change location. Shand wrote to Arcedeckne that he had to take the chance of removing them because such a fine group of enslaved Africans could not be easily procured. He further argued that the high cost he had paid for the enslaved Africans was justified since such an investment would lead to increased production and productivity for the next five years.[33]

Table 4.6 African Women under Forty Years at Amity Hall: Number of Children, 1827

Number	Names	Age	Condition	Alive	Dead	Total
1	Nelly	32	Healthy	1	–	1
2	Bessy Burnes	37	Healthy	2	3	5
3	Bessy Anderson	32	Healthy	1	1	2
4	Catherine Walters	25	Healthy	1	–	1
5	Big Judy	34	Healthy	1	–	1
6	Candis	33	Healthy	4	1	5
7	Mary Mckenzie	23	Healthy	1	–	1
8	Diana Reid	29	Healthy	1	1	2
9	Mary Alsood	34	Healthy	2	–	2
10	Marva Williams	25	Healthy	2	–	2
11	Little Salina	28	Healthy	1	–	1
12	Peggy	23	Healthy	1	–	1
13	Little Kitty	18	Healthy	1	–	1
14	Rosanna	39	Sickly	1	1	2
15	Prudence	20	Sickly	2	–	2
16	Mahiny Molly	18	Healthy	2	–	2
17	Rebecca Lindsay	33	Healthy	1	–	1
18	Manemia	33	Healthy	3	–	3
19	Nancy Booth	30	Healthy	3	–	3
20	Betty	19	Healthy	2	–	2
21	Grace	34	Healthy	1	–	1
22	Ellen Reid	28	Healthy	3	–	3
23	Pliza Mahony	27	Healthy	1	–	1
24	Bonny	29	Healthy	2	–	2
Total				40	7	47

Source: Goulburn Papers, 304/J/1/21.

Table 4.7 African Women under Forty Years at Amity Hall without Children in 1827

Number	Name	Age	Condition
1	Ann Roberts	30	Healthy
2	Eliza Williams	30	Healthy
3	Sue	22	Healthy
4	Sarey	37	Healthy
5	Christmas	20	Healthy
6	Phoebe	18	Subject to sores
7	Ann Williams	17	Healthy
8	Diana	30	Healthy
9	Rosey	24	Subject to sores
10	Antonio	22	Healthy
11	Big Mary	36	Healthy
12	Mimba	17	Healthy
13	Molly Mae	36	Healthy
14	Cook Molly	25	Healthy
15	Abby	35	Healthy

Source: Goulburn Papers, 304/J/1/21.

In 1805, attorney Rowland Fearon reported to his boss, George Pennant, that the enslaved Africans belonging to his previous attorney, Mr Falconer, were being sold. Fearon recommended that Pennant purchase them because they had already worked on the plantation as jobbers and they were an excellent group. In order to convince Pennant to purchase the Africans, Fearon stated that he had previously purchased twenty-five healthy young African women, aged seventeen to eighteen, at a remarkably high price. This was due to the intense market competition for such enslaved Africans.[34]

Labour and Coffee

The coffee boom on the island from the late eighteenth to the early nineteenth century also contributed to the shortage of healthy enslaved Africans on the sugar plantations. The coffee planters were spending large amounts of money on new female enslaved Africans. Amity Hall's attorney, Thomas Samson, confirmed the impact of the coffee expansion in Jamaica when he complained in 1814 that he was having difficulty finding available enslaved Africans to purchase because of the increase that had taken place in coffee production.[35]

It was only after the decline of the coffee industry in Jamaica, mainly in the 1820s, that a few enslaved Africans seem to have been released from some of the coffee plantations in receivership. Despite this, some plantations, depending on their geographical location, still had problems locating adequate enslaved Africans to purchase, much less to hire. Hermitage coffee estate in the parish of St Elizabeth was one such example. Attorney William Adlam lamented in 1819 that coffee on his plantation was plentiful, but he did not have adequate enslaved labour to pick it. Jobbing gangs were scarce, and those available charged a high price of three shillings and two pence to pick a barrel of coffee. As a result, he was extremely fearful that much of his coffee would fall off the trees before it could be picked. It would become even more difficult for his enslaved Africans to retrieve the crop, he wrote, once the hard rains came and washed the seeds away. Furthermore, nine of his enslaved Africans were extremely sick with fevers, and had been left in the hothouse by the plantation doctor.[36] Although Adlam did not indicate the relative strength of his enslaved population, an evaluation carried out in 1824 shows that only a few of his sixty-one Africans were under the age of twenty; most were between ages thirty-one and forty, as seen in figure 4.1. Thus, he too had an aging labour population.

After his initial report in February, a shortage of labour prevented Adlam from reaping the coffee crop until late March. Even then, hired labour remained scarce. In order to gain additional enslaved workers, he offered Mr Bonthorn's mulatto daughter in exchange for a healthy enslaved man or woman. Bonthorn, who was a member of the management team, opposed the idea, but the estate no longer had a choice. The plantation had reached this state because the enslaved women on Hermitage, many of whom were extremely attractive, had not become pregnant, a fact that Adlam could not understand.[37] By the middle of April, Adlam still had not finished picking the coffee and he forecasted that there was still another two to three weeks' work left. The labour shortage was obviously devastating for Hermitage. The delay of the harvest resulted in the coffee reaching the British market late and receiv-

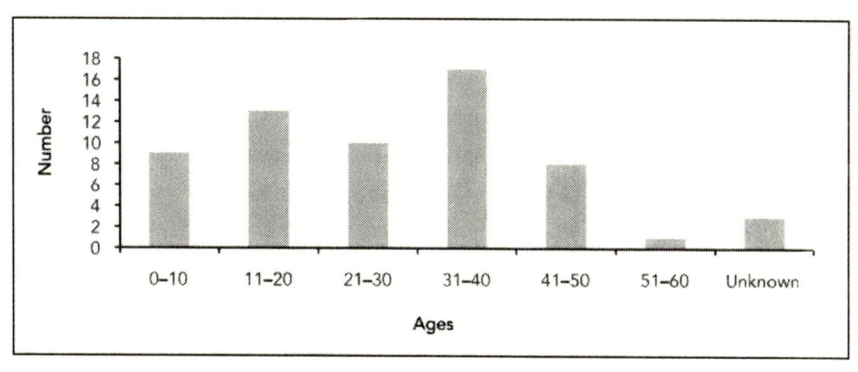

[Figure: bar chart showing ages of Africans]

Figure 4.1 Summary of ages of Africans at Hermitage estate in 1824
Source: Hermitage Estate Book, National Library of Jamaica.

ing poor prices. Furthermore, Adlam could not procure ten to fifteen tons of ebony lumber at one guinea per ton for Captain Wilson, as he had promised. He could not take any of his enslaved Africans away from picking coffee in order to prepare the lumber.[38]

In a later correspondence, Adlam commented on the sale of Bonthorn's daughter. She was expected to fetch between £140 and £160 because of her colour, but no more than that since she had no marketable skills. Such a price for a non-fieldworker was very good; it reflected the dire need in the market for healthy fieldworkers. Hermitage, like other estates discussed earlier, had an enslaved population that was weak and sickly. Adding to their poor condition, many had recently contracted measles. Adlam's efforts to purchase ten to fifteen enslaved Africans did not seem very promising. The Abolition Act had given the advantage to the owners of labourers rather than the purchasers. The owners took the scarcity in the market into account and often attached all kinds of conditions to ensure that all of their enslaved Africans would be sold, even the weakest ones. Furthermore, they preferred cash or good bills of exchange as down payments. The purchasers had to take the entire gang of Africans, both young and old, at an appraised value of £110 to £140 each, based on appearance and ability.[39]

Labour problems at Hermitage estate, furthermore, led to a reduction in the quality of its coffee beans. Since there were not enough labourers to prune the trees, the berries were generally small. In order to restore the quality of the berries for the future, jobbers or new enslaved Africans would have to be procured.[40] With such a scarcity of labour, some owners of jobbing gangs started to prevent their enslaved Africans from doing the extremely hard plantation work, such as holing (digging cane holes).[41] Other owners of labour charged higher prices for the use of their jobbers based on higher calculation of the risks. With the intense competition for jobbers, many poorer planters were priced out of the market, in favour of rich proprietors.[42] This affected the average price of jobbing per acre, which ranged from around £9 to £14. For example, Mesopotamia paid between £10 and £11 per acre for holing in 1816.[43] By 1818, the managers were paying as much as £14 per acre to a jobbing gang to clean and plant food provisions on 4 acres of land.[44] Hired labour became so significant to Mesopotamia that the estate's Current Accounts for 1816 show it as the second largest item of expense, next to salaries. The plantation managers paid at least £930.9.9 for hired labour, in comparison to the £958.10.3 for the salaries of white workers.[45] Lord Penrhyn's plantations, around the same time, 1815–18, also reflected the high cost of jobbing labour. Denbigh in 1815 spent at least £478.3.4 for jobbers, which increased in 1816 to at least £542.18.6.[46]

Kupius, another of Lord Penrhyn's plantations, spent in 1815 approximately £436.10 for jobbing labour. Interestingly, the manager at Kupius paid as much as 5 shillings per slave per day for jobbing work.[47] This was extremely high for a day's work, as the average seems to have been around 3 shillings and 4 pence per slave per day. Thomas River, another of Lord Penrhyn's plantations, spent at least £456 for jobbing around 45 acres of cane holes at the regular price of £9 per acre.

Table 4.8 Average Prices of Captive Africans, 1793–1799

Year	Pounds Sterling
1793	45.16.10
1794	46.09.09
1795	42.17.11
1796	51.06.03
1797	51.01.05
1798	58.11.08
1799	72.04.10

Source: House of Assembly Journals, 1B/5/1/45.

Jobbing was not the only expensive cost in the period between 1792 and 1807. The cost of purchasing well-experienced enslaved Africans who were knowledgeable of Jamaican plantation life was also rising. Table 4.8 highlights the average prices from 1793 to 1799. Between 1800 and 1807, the price of an imported African seems to have jumped from around £72 to around £110–£115. Meanwhile, the market value of an experienced enslaved African who was accustomed to Jamaican plantation life ranged between £160 and £180.[48] Enslaved Africans in post-1807 Jamaica were rarely sold individually. They were sold in groups, and terms and conditions were usually attached.

The difficulty in procuring adequate enslaved labour resulted from both external and internal factors. The planters had little control over the external factors. Internally, however, the planters' ineffective management contributed immensely to their own catastrophe. This was due to a number of reasons, including a cluttered management structure and the racist and sexist stereotyping of the enslaved Africans. By the early nineteenth century, most plantations had predominantly female labour forces working in the fields. Most of the planters did very little to facilitate their health or to draw upon their entrepreneurial spirit.

One clear example of this ineffective management can be seen in the interaction between Henry Goulburn and Thomas Samson regarding labour at Amity Hall plantation. Not only was Samson unwilling to purchase labour, as cited previously, but Goulburn's method of evaluating Samson was inadequate. Samson complained to Goulburn in 1814 that he found it most difficult to obtain additional enslaved Africans for purchase.[49] By January 1815, he was blaming an inadequate supply of enslaved labour as the reason for not producing more sugar.[50] Nevertheless, he wrote that he had lost the opportunity to buy the group of enslaved Africans that he had earlier recommended, as they had already been purchased. In addition, he said that he did not know of other available enslaved Africans being sold.[51] Six months later, in August, Samson continued to complain that he still could not find any healthy Africans to purchase and that he would very shortly start to make new homes to house any that he might find. It is clear, however, that Samson was not serious about purchasing more enslaved Africans; if he were, he would have already built those homes and made the necessary provisions.

In October 1815, Samson continued to express his ambivalence regarding purchasing enslaved Africans. He stated again, as he had in 1803, that even if he purchased more Africans, he would still have the problem of insufficient corn. Its quality was rather poor, he wrote, because of sparse showers.[52] In March 1816, Samson's actions again trigger doubts that he really wanted to purchase additional Africans. He wrote that he was busy planting and reaping since the weather was good.[53] In October 1817, he stated with disappointment that the enslaved Africans that he had wanted to purchase had already been sold along with the land.[54] Samson's failure the second time around to purchase enslaved Africans seems to have been deliberate. It was not until 1818, four years after he had first written of his plans to do so, that he purchased forty-two enslaved Africans for £3,289. He swore that it was a good gang.[55]

Mr Richards, who succeeded Samson as attorney of Amity Hall, disagreed. He stated that the enslaved Africans were inadequate and predominantly old. More significant, Goulburn in London did not have the least idea how his plantation was truly being managed until his brother visited Jamaica and gave him an honest evaluation. Goulburn's shock upon learning of Samson's illegal schemes, including his procurement of his own plantation without informing Goulburn of this possible conflict of interest and the complete mismanagement of the estate, resulted in Samson being fired immediately.[56]

Goulburn, along with many other absentee planters in Great Britain, had unrealistic expectations. The planters wanted their Jamaican managers to perform economic miracles without any realistic management safeguards to ensure that this was not done at the expense of the estate. With their ambiguous management structure, oftentimes the overseers and the plantation clerks were the de facto managers, as the designated attorneys were usually absentees themselves. In addition, with a labour force declining in both quality and quantity, how could the plantations have adequate levels of production and productivity? Deteriorating infrastructure and local managers with their own personal agendas also contributed to this problem. The plantation owners ignored the fact that the attorneys, managers, overseers and clerks all had their own economic dreams and targets. If they could not be held accountable, what would prevent them from overworking their African population to achieve their own personal economic goals rather than those of the plantations?

Governor Nugent of Jamaica articulated the problem as early as 1804. He stated that the declining enslaved population was under immense stress from overwork because too many small planters with limited numbers of enslaved labourers were hustling them to make quick financial returns.[57] This was exactly the case with Samson at Amity Hall. In 1802, Samson defended his overworking of the enslaved Africans, writing to Goulburn that he had no other choice but to drive them harder to meet his production targets and to increase his commission. He rationalized the enslaved labourers' resistance by arguing that their work ethic was poor and that the actual figure of twelve to fifteen runaways was less than what had been reported. Furthermore, he wrote, this was below the national average for a small plantation such as Amity Hall.[58] This was untrue. Many plantations the size of Amity Hall had only about four to five constant runaways in a given year. When Samson was pressed to give his reasons for using small gangs as opposed to larger ones, he admitted that it was not only to prevent the flight of enslaved labourers but to increase the overall work rate of each labourer.[59] It seems unsurprising, then, that the level of resistance at Amity Hall was extremely high under Samson's management.

Mr Mair, who was the bookkeeper and former overseer at Amity Hall in the late 1800s, and who later became the attorney of an estate about a mile from Amity Hall, stated that one of the interesting features of the enslaved Africans there was their disposition to sabotage the plantation when they became unhappy with working conditions. Burning down the plantation and withdrawing their labour were two strategies they pursued to remind their managers that although they were enslaved and were expected to acquiesce, they would not cooperate if certain minimum conditions were not met.

Enslaved Africans were overworked on coffee plantations as well. The daily work schedule of the four gangs on Radnor coffee plantation, as indicated previously, was hard. The enslaved Africans seem to have even worked on alternate weekends, as indicated in the plantation's daily log for the first few months of 1822. This seems to have been a violation of the Consolidated Slave Act of 1817, which stated that only in crop season should the enslaved Africans work on alternate Saturdays. On Saturdays and even Sundays, some of the enslaved Africans could not go to their provision grounds until they had finished picking coffee for sale in the market and attending to the coffee on the barbecue. Forcing some of the enslaved Africans to work on Sundays, even for limited hours, was a violation of the 1817 Jamaican law, which stipulated that Sunday was given entirely to the slaves to do whatever they wished. Even the demands of a hectic crop season should not interfere with their Sundays.[60]

Labour and Race

As mentioned previously, the planters' attitudes towards the enslaved Africans were additional reasons for their failure to procure adequate labour. They racially stereotyped the Africans and berated them as uncivilized and lazy individuals who would not work unless forced. One example of this was the planters' constant mantra that the Africans' failure to produce children naturally, unlike British women, stemmed largely from their high levels of promiscuity.[61] The planters also blamed the Africans' bad work ethic and their crudeness for their failure to reproduce, rather than looking at the poor conditions that might have been contributing to the problem. The planters sought to remove "these bad traits" from the enslaved people through a process of civilization or Europeanization.[62] Most of the planters firmly believed that severe discipline was necessary to correct their enslaved Africans' many defects. Thus, they were critical of amelioration since it would remove the whip and, they believed, make their enslaved Africans more lazy and rebellious. Some of the planters failed to realize that a new paradigm was needed given the abolition of the slave trade and its implications for labour. They stifled the entrepreneurial spirit of their labour force through their insistence on the whip. Ironically, when the enslaved Africans worked for themselves, providing their own provisions, they were highly industrious and created much from the little marginalized plots of land that they were given.[63]

As an indication of some of the planters' contempt for their enslaved Africans, they even rated Chinese workers over the Africans. In 1806, some of the planters, including Joseph Foster Barham, sought to cash in on the opportunity offered by the impending Abolition Act. They sought to import Chinese workers into Jamaica as plantation workers to replace the enslaved Africans. Barham argued fervently that the Chinese were far more responsible labourers. A merchant from Bogue in St Elizabeth, near Island estate where the experiment of Chinese labourers was to be carried out, even argued that the Chinese would become the saviour of Jamaican agriculture. Obviously, the merchant wanted the trade and strongly supported Barham. He, like Barham and others, had probably never done agricultural labour. Yet he bemoaned the fact that the enslaved Africans in Jamaica were lazy and said that he was continually astonished at how little labour they performed. He was certain that the Chin-ese would do twice the amount of work that the enslaved Africans at Island estate did. Furthermore, the Chinese would easily adapt to the swampy conditions at Island estate because they were conducive to the growing of rice. The Chinese labourers would also rear fish in the pond and thus procure a complete diet from the plantation environment.[64]

Another white planter, Colonel Mc Cawley, in support of the merchant, stated:

> The simplest and shortest mode of trying the experiment would be to procure a sugar estate under cultivation; to remove the Negroes and place upon it an adequate number of Chinese laborers with their wives and families and to interest them in the produce of the soil. With a people so industrious, ingenuous and eager of gain more is not requisite. The delay of forming a new settlement will thus be avoided and the beginning rendered easy. The expensive and uncertain inclination of management will be unnecessary and the result of the plan will speedily be obvious. The experiment, tho limited will be complete; should it fail no ill consequence can ensue but a slight pecuniary loss. Should it succeed the example will be quickly and generally extended.[65]

In his opinion, there would be numerous positive consequences if they were successful. First, the motive for continuing with the slave trade would cease because the Chinese would populate the British Caribbean and halt the importation of enslaved Africans. Second, the African population would learn "voluntary industry" by example, resulting in a vast improvement of their moral and civil character. Only then would the present system of slavery be gradually eliminated. Third, the colony would be booming with more white planters, and new enterprises would be introduced to the colonies, some of which could be of great importance to their prosperity and to the general balance of British trade with foreign countries. Last, with labour being hired instead of bought, it would reduce the volume capital being borrowed from overseas merchants for overhead expenses.[66]

If Jamaican planters were prepared to experiment with paid Chinese labour over African slavery, one has to conclude that the ability to pay for labour was not in doubt. Thus, it would follow that racial stereotyping of the enslaved Africans played a critical role in deterring sugar planters from experimenting with paid slave labour. The growth in hired labour after 1807 throughout Jamaica to meet production targets should have been a signal to the sugar planters that they could get better production through initiatives such as task work (paying the Africans for allotted tasks). Noted Jamaican planter Bryan Edwards observed in the late eighteenth century that task work among the enslaved Africans was the route towards greater productivity.[67]

Even planters such as Rose Price, Henry Goulburn and Joseph Barham who boasted of their humanity towards their enslaved Africans never once suggested to their attorneys (except during Apprenticeship) the viability of experimenting with task work, despite the fact that this had become the preferred labour strategy on most Jamaican coffee plantations.[68] The fact that planters did not even consider task work can be largely attributed to their stereo-typing of the enslaved Africans as inferior beings who needed to be taught the virtues of industry.

Barham, for example, realized after much calculation that he could pay each Chinese worker as much as seven shillings and six pence per hundred-weight in Jamaica to produce sugar.[69] He stood to make a profit of at least 10 to 15 per cent on his capital.[70] This could be achieved through a corporation made up of subscribers and investors who would be answerable to their shareholders (appendix 3). However, he never thought about the wisdom of paying the enslaved Africans on his estate even half of that amount as an incentive to work harder. If Barham had implemented such a scheme, it probably would have had a significant impact on his plantations' level of productivity. When one compares the detailed plans drawn up for the importation of Chinese labour in Jamaica to the general disdain of the planters for their enslaved Africans, it is clear that the planters' attitudes had a significant bearing on their labourers' levels of productivity. The following comments about the enslaved Africans support this point:

> They all take the extra day [for worship] but it has done nothing to their morals.[71]

> It is not in the character of the Negro to be grateful as these certainly are considering their present comforts.[72]

> They are a race of beings who cannot bear prosperity. . . . It will be a lapse of ages before the Negro can even participate of the blessings of freedom, the very name of the African must cease to exist in their memories before their customs are obliterated.[73]

The Jamaican planters missed the opportunity to entice the enslaved Africans to work freely on their own initiative, without the use of the whip.

Ironically, the enslaved Africans were much more productive when executing their own forms of entrepreneurship. There are myriad examples of slave entrepreneurship on Jamaican plantations. Enslaved Africans not only carved out a mode of survival within their limited confines, but their agricultural pursuits were so impressive that at times even planters had to comment on their entrepreneurial spirit. In 1774, noted Jamaican planter Edward Long wrote that the enslaved population controlled at least 20 per cent of the coins in circulation.[74] At Mesopotamia in 1825, when Barham was having problems finding an alternative to sugar for cultivation, he was told that all the extra land in the mountains for miles around was covered in Negro provision grounds. This was apart from the few fruit trees that belonged to the plantation.[75] Earlier, in 1804, Barham's attorneys were shocked at the increase in African provisions going to market and commented that these were the greatest quantities they had seen in years.[76] By 1809, the attorneys confessed that the enslaved Africans had very good heifers among the plantation stock and that they owned as many as one hundred head of stock in the names of free people. Free Africans held the cattle for enslaved Africans because it was still illegal under the Consolidated Slave Laws for enslaved labourers to legally own cattle.[77] Barham's attorneys went so far as to suggest to Barham that in their search for heifers to replace the plantation's worn-out stock, a good many could be purchased from the enslaved Africans. They warned that if they did not make such a purchase as quickly as possible, the plantation would not have many young steers for sale in the future. Within a year, the attorneys at Mesopotamia thanked Barham for his permission to purchase stock from his own enslaved Africans, since it could be obtained at reduced prices and "they certainly had too large a proportion of horned stock among them".[78] Furthermore, in 1813, when Mesopotamia experienced a severe drought and the plantation had to order large importations of provisions from North America, it was discovered that the enslaved Africans normally had a large amount of plantains, cassava and potatoes, but the drought had affected them.[79]

At Lord Penrhyn's plantations, African entrepreneurship was also prevalent. In 1807, the enslaved Africans had an abundance of potatoes, cassava and corn from their provision grounds.[80] At Penrhyn's King's Valley estate in Westmoreland, the attorney David Ewart reiterated their remarkable success with stock and encouraged Lord Penrhyn to purchase stock from his own enslaved Africans. Ewart wrote:

He had the Negro stock shown to him and he proposed to buy several bulkins and heifers, which the Negroes readily agreed to and I paid them in cash about 140 pounds. Money is more acceptable to them at this period of the year as they wish to lay it out in little matters of finery for Christmas. I proposed to the Negroes the regulation which I have adopted on other properties and which I mentioned in a former letter to your Lordship. That is, to purchase their calves at a doubloon each when they are 12 months old, which they readily agreed to. I found several Negroes having four or five heads of stock and I expressed a wish that each Negro should have but one, meaning that they should distribute them among their children or relations or sell them to the estate at which they readily agreed and several were transferred from one Negro to another.[81]

The enslaved Africans had so much stock at King's Valley that it became quite difficult to sort from the plantation's own stock, resulting in confusion.[82] These strides of self-empowerment by the enslaved Africans were their own initiative, which they fought vigorously to maintain and which I believe kept many on the plantations. Some historians have interpreted such self-empowerment initiatives to indicate that the enslaved Africans were happy with slavery.[83] They all wanted to be free. In the meantime, however, while they were still enslaved, the best they could do was to carve out a measure of freedom and limited prosperity. Such enterprises kept them working on the plantations until they could earn their freedom.

The period of Apprenticeship in Jamaica (1834–38) further encouraged the entrepreneurial spirit of the Africans and showed that they could work well without the whip. On the Pepper and Bona Vista pens in 1837, eighteen of the enslaved Africans planted and sold the plantation 139 acres of guinea corn at seven shillings and six pence per acre.[84] More important, at R. Boucher's coffee plantations in Manchester, Salmon, one of the managers, drew the owner's attention to the difficulty they would soon face when enslaved labour could no longer be forced to work.[85] Salmon indicated that the formerly enslaved labourers, now apprentices, had all stated that they would buy land when they were fully free. They could then choose carefully the persons for whom they wanted to work. Salmon concluded that the apprentices should not be underestimated, as land was being sold for two to four pounds per acre, which they could easily find. He wrote: "And where is the Negro good for anything who has not that money or has not something or other to dispose of, that will bring this – and show me a Negro so attached to a particular house spot who would agree to remain and work merely to retain what less labour will procure elsewhere, without a master to control and encourage him."[86]

Salmon realized that the apprentices, when finally free, would control the labour market by working two to three days for themselves on their mountain lands and hold the plantation hostage by charging a high fee for their labour. The enslaved Africans knew how vital their labour was. They could easily say in negotiations, "You must come to my terms . . . very well Massa, me wi go to mi mountain."[87] What is significant is that Salmon also realized that the apprentices were most productive and entrepreneurial. They already knew how to produce sugar cane, coffee, ginger, cotton, tobacco and other staples. They were the ones who kept the plantations afloat. After their emancipation, they would continue to produce the same agricultural items, even to the point of controlling sugar production. Hence, Salmon observed that he "would not be surprised if they do not start making sugar as well, with quantities to sell".[88]

CHAPTER 5

Health and Reproduction

THE JAMAICAN PLANTERS OF THE early nineteenth century failed in their bid to procure natural population increases among their enslaved Africans, especially in comparison to their Barbadian colleagues.[1] From 1817 to 1832, Jamaica experienced a natural decrease in the enslaved population from −0.7 to −4.8 per thousand. In contrast, Barbados had reached natural increases by 1810. Between 1817 and 1832, the enslaved Africans in Barbados experienced a natural increase rising from 4.8 to 14.4 per thousand.[2] B.W. Higman has characterized Jamaica as having the highest rates of natural decreases among the older sugar islands. Demerara-Essequibo and Berbice, newer sugar colonies, had similar rates to Jamaica's; however, they were rated more positively than Jamaica since they began from much lower levels of decrease and showed a greater tendency towards improvement.[3]

The contrast between Jamaica and Barbados in terms of levels of reproduction and natural increases is most significant in explaining the health of enslaved Africans during this period. Both were older sugar colonies primarily involved in sugar production. Some scholars have acknowledged that sugar production, unlike the production of other staples, had a unique disadvantage. It was extremely hazardous to its enslaved people, whether in the Caribbean, Brazil or North America.[4] Despite their climatic differences, Barbados and Jamaica, as older sugar colonies with similar social, economic and political realities and similar histories, should never have shown such stark differences in the health of their enslaved populations. I will not attempt to answer this mystery but will nevertheless attempt to explain the unusually high levels of morbidity on Jamaican plantations in the early nineteenth century.

One of the main reasons for the vast differences in health between the enslaved Africans of Barbados and Jamaica seems to be in their respective work rates. Richard Sheridan believes that the enslaved Africans of Barbados worked far less than those of Jamaica. The former worked only thirty-two hundred hours per year, while the latter worked four thousand hours.[5] Furthermore, the enslaved Africans of Jamaica had the additional burden of having to walk long distances over mountainous terrain to care for their provision grounds. These marginal grounds were usually rocky and difficult to work.[6] The enslaved Africans of Barbados, on the other hand, planted their provisions in the cane fields, as they had less mountainous land. Thus, they never had to toil as hard to provide for themselves as did the enslaved Africans of Jamaica.[7]

Mary Turner agrees that Jamaican enslaved workers toiled harder. She believes, however, that the ration-allotment system was the main cause for the differences between Jamaica and Barbados.[8] In the ration-allotment system, the enslaved Africans planted food provisions on sugar lands under the regular supervision of the plantation managers. The food provisions were reaped in the regular time allotted for plantation work and each enslaved family was provided with an allotment of food, administered by the planters. The ration-allotment system became prevalent in Barbados, as the Barbadian planters were dependent on food provisions from their fellow planters in North America.[9] It was also used in around 30 per cent of the British West Indies. These islands had limited marginal lands, but territories such as Jamaica with sufficient marginal lands were able to allocate provision grounds to their enslaved Africans. The ration-allotment system had a major disadvantage, however. It created the potential for greater conflict between managers and enslaved Africans over provisions. The planters had greater control over imported supplies than they did over provision grounds such as those kept in Jamaica.[10]

B.W. Higman concurs with the view that the enslaved Africans of Barbados seem to have worked far less than those of Jamaica and he adds that they had improved housing, along with growing Creole and female populations. He sees the essential difference, however, in the fertility rates of the two colonies. The mortality rates in Barbados and Jamaica were similar, but the Barbadian fertility rate was far better than that of Jamaica. Some Barbadian managers, as early as 1798, paid as much as six shillings and three pence to enslaved mothers as pro-natal strategies to spur population growth. Such strategies also included shorter hours of work and lighter levels of night work for mothers. By 1805, these incentives had become widespread.[11]

J.R. Ward has also made two very important observations. He agrees with Turner that geographical differences should not be underestimated because they were critical to the economic policies of both Jamaica and Barbados. The economic crisis that the British West Indies faced in the 1780s as a result of the American Revolution led Barbados to reduce their cane lands in order to become more efficient, concentrating more on quality than quantity. It was this drive for efficiency that led to the birth of the ration-allotment system. Jamaican planters, on the other hand, sought economic growth by expanding their operations in the 1790s, purchasing additional enslaved Africans, planting more cane lands and opening up more land for plantation pens. This led them into great debt. Thus, in an era calling for efficiency over expansion, the Jamaican planters paid a high price for choosing to expand their operations.[12] What further sunk them into financial ruin were the many notable absentee planters in Jamaica who left their property to "hired hands", men who had their own economic agendas. Barbados had a much greater percentage of residential proprietors and was able to establish successful agricultural societies as early as 1812. In addition, they were better able to discuss and implement various planting innovations.[13]

Health Care and the Weather

While these arguments are all valid, the fundamental issue of effective plantation management has not been stressed in the literature. Poor management was a significant contributor to the morbidity of the early nineteenth-century enslaved Africans of Jamaica. A large part of this was the failure on the part of many plantation managers to initiate safer health practices for their enslaved Africans based on the vicissitudes of the weather. Changes in weather placed the plantation infrastructure and stock under enormous stress; worst of all, the overburdened enslaved Africans were the most vulnerable. The ineffective management of many hired attorneys in Jamaica further aggravated the problem. The managers did not successfully negotiate the effects of the weather on the Africans' health and on the plantations' infrastructure.

Two kinds of bad weather patterns largely dominated the Jamaican landscape: constant droughts and heavy rainfall, often leading to severe flooding. Thus, in many plantation reports, the complaint was either that they had been experiencing droughts for several months, which were seriously affecting plantation production, or that there were devastating floods from the heavy rains, which destroyed the plantations' infrastructure and stock. On relatively few occasions, hurricanes destroyed everything. While it is true that the weather patterns were often catastrophic, there were nevertheless times in which the residential planters were not honest with their bosses in Great Britain. They used the bad weather conditions as excuses for many of their shortcomings.[14] Amity Hall under the management of Samson had such numerous weather-related complaints that one might be inclined to question their authenticity. Although some of the complaints may have been used to cover the shortfalls in Samson's levels of productivity, the constant complaints by other attorneys (those who succeeded Samson and those who served in other geographical areas of Jamaica) indicate that, even if exaggerated at times, they were all genuine. For a clearer understanding of the effect of the weather on the general public health, the plantations' production, the Africans and the stock, the following examples are illustrative.

In 1804, Rowland Fearon apologized to Lord Penrhyn that poor weather had led to unfinished harvests on two of his plantations during the previous few weeks. The weather, he wrote, had been highly detrimental to the Negroes, the stock and the quality of the canes.[15] Four years later, in 1808, Fearon again blamed the low production figures on a severe drought.[16] In 1814, another attorney, John Shand, also blamed his estate's poor production on a severe drought, which had stunted the growth of the crops.[17]

At Island estate in 1802, the exceptionally dry weather was so severe that the estate lost roughly one-third of its fall crop. Other plantations surrounding Island estate fared even worse; some lost everything.[18] The continued dry weather created numerous cane fires, which led to the loss of the still house at Island estate. Consequently, Barham lost 2,040 gallons of rum. He was fortunate that the rest of the estate buildings did not burn down. As a temporary measure, carpenters erected a shade over the cistern.[19] The dry weather continued into January 1803, and Island estate lost another 14 acres of cane.[20] In spite of the intermittent rain, the drought still prevailed until July 1803.[21] The drought conditions had lasted for well over a year. Several years later, in 1807, after Island estate produced a mere 100 hogsheads of sugar, one of the attorneys blamed another exceptional drought, which had followed the unusual one in 1802–3.[22] At Mesopotamia, the 1802–3 droughts were also blamed for the deaths of several plantation cows.[23]

The consequences of the weather on the Africans were even more disastrous than on the plantations' production. At Amity Hall, as a result of the 1802–3 droughts, approximately half of the enslaved Africans suffered from violent sickness for over three weeks; in excess of eighty persons were sent every day to the hothouse. There were no reports of deaths at Amity Hall, but the droughts had caused many casualties in the towns and plantations around the parish of Vere.[24] At Mesopotamia, the 1802–3 droughts caused a near famine among the enslaved Africans. Because they were hungry, they became restive and inattentive to their work. They were constantly in search of food, to the extent that at times they ate green and unripe vegetables and fruits. Many managers established illegal trade with the Americans for provisions in the hope that their corn crops would soon be available to be reaped and that their unripe plantains, which were their last hope of survival, would not be too diminished.[25]

By 1817, conditions seemed to be improving for the enslaved Africans at Mesopotamia. They worked well on their plantain walks and small cocoa pieces and they had completed the cleaning of the cane fields. However, extremely dry weather appeared in August. This was followed by heavy rains, which did further damage. The volume of rainfall was estimated at an excess of two years' normal rain. The consequence was the overcrowding of the hothouse and the sudden deaths of at least four enslaved Africans.[26]

Many managers followed the example of Amity Hall and purchased food staples from the Americans in spite of British restrictions. At Island estate, the managers decided that portions of the animals slaughtered for sale were to be given to the enslaved Africans. In addition, they decided to start rearing sheep as protein to reduce the high levels of contingencies.[27] In spite of these adjustments, the enslaved Africans still continued to be most affected by the weather. In 1826, after severe floods, influenza attacked Island estate and between 115 and 135 persons were hospitalized. The plantation was only able to muster between thirty-six and forty workers, mainly children, for the fields. On this occasion, the estate killed a steer and purchased additional American foods, such as flour and oatmeal, to help the enslaved Africans recover.[28]

In 1807, at Lord Penrhyn's King's Valley plantation in the parish of Westmoreland, the enslaved Africans' ground provisions, which were planted in the mountains, went up in flames from the intense dry weather. Their crops burned for several days. This resulted in a serious scarcity of provisions, not only in the parish of Westmoreland but all over the island.

The planters' worst fear, however, was of hurricanes and their impact on the Africans. When hurricanes struck, they completely devastated the houses that had been built for the enslaved workers. These were cheaply constructed and were easily blown away. The managers were always fearful that such events would affect their labour force immensely and that it would take an exceptionally long time for their plantations to recover.[29]

The 1815 hurricane, for example, which devastated Jamaica, was described by Shand as "the most violent that the country had seen". In the county of Middlesex, where most of Lord Penrhyn's plantations were located, the damage was not as severe as in other places. As usual, the buildings were spared except for the Negro houses, which were destroyed. Although lives were not lost, the animal stock was severely damaged. The owners were asked to make special expenditures to assist the enslaved Africans with food and extra allowances of fish.[30]

The county of Surrey, where Simon Taylor's properties were established, experienced heavier damage. Many roads were impassable and travelling was virtually impossible. Several of the mountain estates, which had some of the finest coffee plantations, were entirely ruined; the banks of hillsides fell into rivers and the fertile soils were swept away, along with the works and buildings of all kinds. Great sections of properties in the mountains of St David, Port Royal and St Andrew were ruined. Plantain Garden plantation was flooded for nearly three days. At Holland estate, the water rose so high that many feared that all the children, the weak and the crippled would be lost; they were surrounded by water on every side. No lives were lost, although the houses of the enslaved Africans were more affected than the stock and the buildings. Even the canes suffered less than the enslaved Africans, a sign of their true vulnerability. At Lyssons plantation, the Africans' provisions were also destroyed, although no lives were lost. Twenty-eight houses belonging to enslaved workers were levelled and many of them were injured. The works were also damaged, two trash houses were blown down, the mill was gutted and still houses were carried away. At Burrowfield Pen, the enslaved Africans' houses were partly blown down and damaged.[31]

The extent to which many plantation managers in Jamaica failed to keep their enslaved workers healthy can be seen in their overall failure to initiate safer public health policies. Jamaica in the early nineteenth century remained a public health hazard. Both whites and blacks died at alarming rates. The rate of mortality in the British regiment stationed in Jamaica was astonishing. The morbidity and death rate among these troops in the British West Indies from 1817 to 1834 was six times greater than among similar white troops in West Africa in the same time period. Black troops in the British West Indies also died and were hospitalized three times more than their counterparts in West Africa.[32] Given the environmental and ecological context of early nineteenth-century Jamaica, the plantation managers failed to give better health practices the attention they warranted, especially in light of the 1807 prohibition against the importation of enslaved Africans.

Health and Management

The European-trained doctors on many of the Jamaican plantations also shared responsibility for the breakdown in public health. The question of these doctors' culpability is still a major debate among several Caribbean historians, including Michael Craton, Kenneth and Virginia Kiple, Richard Sheridan and B.W. Higman.[33] Higman and Craton believe that these white doctors in the British West Indies had some success in public health initiatives, and that their apparent failures should be attributed more to the kinds of medical theories that they learned.[34] Sheridan disagrees and argues that even health care was indicative of the racist and exploitative tendencies of the white planter class. By the early nineteenth century, he argues, good medical knowledge and practice were declining along with the economy. He writes that throughout the eighteenth century, several white doctor-authors such as Collins, Grainger, Williamson, Thompson and Dancer had become sceptical of the conventional wisdom of European medicine. They had developed theories of disease causation and cures based on empirical studies of British West Indian life and knowledge of African folk medicine. Thus, they stressed in their medical manuals the need to improve health through improved material conditions, sanitation, lighter labour and better attention to women and children. Successive European-trained doctors, however, did not act on this information in the early nineteenth century. They failed to develop a medical culture of professional schools, hospitals, societies and journals concerned with developing an indigenous Caribbean approach to medical science.[35]

Sheridan further believes that a major reason for the failure of these European-trained doctors was that a large percentage of the medical personnel who came to the colonies did so primarily to acquire wealth and to establish their careers with the hope of returning home to Great Britain to become members of the landed gentry or to work in more prestigious services of the Crown. Therefore, they catered more to the needs of the white planters and merchants.[36] This was unfortunate for early nineteenth-century Jamaica, which was struggling with an unhealthy environment, a problem further exacerbated by the changing weather patterns.

Tables 5.1 and 5.2 describe the nature and causes of morbidity and their effects on some plantations. Although the tables represent only a small percentage of Jamaican plantations, it is important to note that the three prevalent complaints, as seen in table 5.3, were fevers, smallpox, and dysentery or bowel complaints. These were predominantly caused by the constant changes in the weather and the plantations' failure to improve the environmental and dietary provisions for their enslaved Africans. The absence of proper nutrition as the weather devastated the Africans' provisions left many of them sick and destitute. At times, they had no other choice but to eat unripe foods. Although it would be difficult to prove a direct relationship between morbidity and mortality from these tables, Craton, Higman, Ward and Sheridan all found indirect links between the two.[37] Many of the problems surrounding the lack of natural population increases among fieldworkers in the British West Indies were caused by their unsanitary living and working conditions, along with the seasonal stress placed on their food supplies. These deficiencies in turn may have led to increased resistance by African women to give birth.[38]

Shand, in his justification to Lord Penrhyn for the continuous decline of the enslaved population, acknowledged that the level of decline on his plantations was indicative of the national trend. He wrote that the main contributor to mortality of the enslaved workers was influenza, which was fatal to the African population. The effects of scanty subsistence and the severe drought that had prevailed for the greater part of the year contributed further to the Africans' ill health. Shand further confessed that he found it hard to guard against the onslaught of disease and death among the enslaved Africans.[39]

Table 5.1 Sickness and Mortality on Mesopotamia and Island Plantations, 1801–1826

Sickness	Estate	Date	Season	Reason/Result
Smallpox	Mesopotamia	1801	June	Smallpox causes natural decreases
Dropsy (chest)	Mesopotamia	1801	December	Most valuable Africans die
Influenza	Mesopotamia	1802	September	Flu and pleurisy kill many Africans on estate
Fever	Mesopotamia	1802	September	Overseer dies from fever
Dysentery	Mesopotamia	1802	May	Caused by the drought
Dysentery	Island	1802	July	Many hospitalized and one dies
Dysentery	Island	1802	October	Caused by eating unripe provisions
Smallpox	Mesopotamia	1802	September	Africans had been vaccinated against smallpox, however, it was ineffective
Cold/fevers	Mesopotamia	1803	April	Caused by the changes in the weather
Fevers	Mesopotamia	1803	November	Changes in the weather; 19 whites die
Fevers	Mesopotamia	1803	April	Plantation doctor dies
Whooping cough	Island	1805	October	Africans are sickly; 3 enslaved children die
Dysentery	Mesopotamia	1809	July	Eating green corn – many Africans are hospitalized
Smallpox	Island	1815	September	Around 13 Africans are sick
Smallpox	Island	1816	November	Around 42 enslaved children affected with smallpox
Whooping cough	Mesopotamia	1816	March	5 Africans die and many others affected

Table 5.1 continues

Table 5.1 Sickness and Mortality on Mesopotamia and Island Plantations, 1801–1826 (*cont'd*)

Sickness	Estate	Date	Season	Reason/Result
Dysentery	Mesopotamia	1817	April	Eating unripe provisions
Lockjaw	Mesopotamia	1818	June	Missionary dies from a draft in his garden
Fevers	Mesopotamia	1818	June	2 months flood, many sick and 2 Africans die
Fevers	Mesopotamia	1819	October	Continuous rains and many Africans are sick
?	Island	1820	November	30–40 Africans are hospitalized
Fevers	Mesopotamia	1825	August	3 months of rain, 50 are sick including whites
Diseases	Island	1825	September	No explanation given
Chicken pox	Mesopotamia	1825	March	Affects the children of the estate
Influenza	Island	1826	June	2 months rains, 115–135 Africans are hospitalized
Venereal disease	Island	1826	January	Also pleurisy; Africans have become very sickly

Source: Barham Plantation Papers.

Table 5.2 Morbidity on Other Jamaican Estates, 1802–1812

Sickness	Estate	Date	Season	Reason/Result
Fevers	Amity Hall	1802	June	Africans sick for 3 weeks; 80 are sick daily
Fevers	Amity Hall	1802	October	Africans are still sickly
Fevers	Penrhyn	1805	September	Hard rains, 4 Africans die
Whooping cough	Amity Hall	1806	February	Children are very sick although none have died
Diseases	Amity Hall	1810	May	Many die on neighbouring estates
Sore throat	Amity Hall	1811	February	5 Africans die; 25 are sick for 6 weeks
Smallpox	Amity Hall	1812	September	African children are inoculated
Measles	Amity Hall	1812	February	Many Africans hospitalized
Sore throat	Amity Hall	1812	February	4 Africans die; other estates lose up to 50 Africans
Measles	Amity Hall	1812	March	Africans sick for 4 weeks; sugar mill closed

Source: Amity Hall and Penrhyn Plantation Papers.

Table 5.3 Analysis of Morbidity Listed in Tables 5.1 and 5.2, 1801–1826

Sickness	Amount	Type
Fevers	10	Respiratory
Smallpox	5	Infectious
Dysentery	5	Intestinal
Whooping cough	3	Respiratory
Influenza	2	Respiratory
Unspecified diseases	2	Infectious
Measles	2	Infectious
Chicken pox	1	Respiratory
Lockjaw	1	Infectious
Venereal disease	1	Infectious
Dropsy	1	Respiratory and/or intestinal

Note: Respiratory illnesses are caused by viruses that first affect the respiratory tract. Some of these diseases later become infectious. Infectious diseases, on the other hand, do not necessarily start in the respiratory tract.

Source: Barham, Penrhyn and Amity Hall Plantation Papers.

Neglect and insensitivity among plantation managers were also major factors in the poor health of the enslaved population. In places where food was provided as a means of public assistance, great injustices occurred because many planters, given the high prices of food provisions, sold the provisions that were intended for the children to their neighbours. The planters did this to reduce the high cost of provisions and to maximize plantation profits. To keep the enslaved children alive, other planters including Shand adopted initiatives like soup kitchens with adequate food prepared by elderly Africans to ensure that the children had a reasonably balanced meal at least once a day. The planters' logic was that by assisting the children, they were freeing the parents to better assist themselves. On most plantations, the healthy adults were mainly responsible for feeding themselves. In cases where food assistance was not given to the enslaved population, great calamity and mortality of the enslaved Africans resulted.[40] In order for the plantation managers of early nineteenth-century Jamaica to maintain a healthier labour force, they had to prioritize their responsibility to combat the unhealthy and unsanitary conditions in which the Africans had to work and live.

Simon Taylor – one of the wealthiest planters, an attorney and assemblyman, resident in Jamaica – acknowledged in 1807 that after forty-six years of management experience, he still had more natural decreases over increases among his enslaved population. Taylor was still stuck in the old method of management, blaming the enslaved people for their failure to reproduce more effectively, rather than castigating himself as a manager for not facilitating this.[41] He enumerated a number of diseases that were responsible for the poor health of his enslaved population. First, he identified the venereal diseases caught mainly by young enslaved women, which often went undetected, leading to tetanus or lockjaw in their newborn children. Taylor blamed the enslaved women for these diseases, claiming that all the articles needed by the midwives, such as linen flannels, had been given to them. Furthermore, he reasoned, they had been expeditiously ordered to burn candles rather than wood in their houses. Second, Taylor identified yaws, a chronic infection that affected every enslaved child at least once, especially children who lived in cold or wet parts of the country. Taylor next mentioned worms; every effort was made, he said, to inoculate the children every month, often with cabbage bark, mercury and other worm medicines. His main argument was that environmental and dietary contributors were also factors. In addition to diseases, Taylor believed that natural increases occurred more easily when enslaved populations lived in warmer climates rather than in wet and rainy places. The seaside was one such area, he said, since they could receive a better diet of fish and wash their yaws in salt water.[42]

Taylor further believed that diseases such as Cuationes, namely the Lypra Arbabicum, and elephantiasis, along with smallpox, measles and yaws could be combated successfully by careful attention to the social and material environments of the enslaved Africans.[43] Yet he saw it as an insult to planters for the Crown to insist that they change their pattern of management and devote their time to the care and health of enslaved Africans, when it would require so much less effort to rear new labourers under the conditions that he had just described.[44] Most planters had already determined that the easiest option of all was to purchase enslaved Africans, despite the fact that purchasing was like a lottery. A planter could easily lose a great number of his Africans during the first three years through yaws, worms, ulcers and the like. Planters knew to purchase a small number at a time and to ensure that they were well cared for during the seasoning process. Comfortable houses were also an important factor. Their homes had to be warm and kept clean and free from chiggers, a kind of tropical flea, which got into their feet and led to painful sores.

The 1807 Abolition Act, with its emphasis on rearing enslaved Africans, was very costly to planters. Before 1807, the planters had already calculated the percentage of Africans that might be lost in the seasoning process and beyond and, most important, how much profit would still be made. Under the Abolition Act, they would have less choice in the kinds of enslaved Africans that they purchased. In addition, they would now have the dreaded task of administering discipline and inculcating good work ethics. Whenever enslaved Africans died, which some certainly would, they would not be easily replaced. For this reason, prior to the passing of the abolition bill, Taylor stated that migration to North America might be the best option for planters.

In an 1801 letter, Taylor described the kind of meticulous care that was most needed to transform captured Africans into productive and responsible workers. He wrote that upon their arrival in Jamaica, most enslaved Africans developed an itching, which appears to have been ringworm. This condition, labelled as "craw craw", was eliminated with brimstone, gunpowder and lime juice. This form of ringworm, if not treated immediately, could lead to a large ulcer on the leg. Any enslaved person with even the smallest scratch on his feet had to be attended to as urgently as possible to prevent this. Yaws was the other danger. This was a dreadful disorder that usually took around twelve months to cure. It killed many enslaved Africans. Taylor believed that one could not put great stock in the survival of new enslaved Africans until after their first three years of seasoning. It was only then, he said, that planters could rent them out, if they could find employment for them. Planters could easily make around thirty to forty pounds per jobber per year, despite having to feed them, clothe them, and pay doctors' bills and taxes. With patience and good care, Taylor wrote, small groups of around ten Africans purchased at a time were the route to prosperity.[45]

Taylor's implicit message was that the enslaved Africans were merely objects for commercial gain. The managers of Jamaica acknowledged the unhealthy climate in which most of the Africans lived and worked, but based on the management structure, in which most attorneys were hired hands, the long-term health and development of enslaved Africans were not their ultimate concern, despite the abolition of the slave trade. The Africans were capital to be used to produce wealth, and in the process they would become "Creolized and civilized". Taylor himself stated that the security of Jamaica after abolition lay not with the enslaved Africans, but with the white troops needed to combat the Africans' incivility and barbarism. In his view, it was most important that every effort be made to keep the white population healthy and meet their material needs, since they were the backbone of society.[46]

George Hibbert, one of the agents for Jamaica in Great Britain, in response to the criticism that much of Jamaica still needed to be diversified in coffee and provisions to feed the island, agreed but argued that the island was still a major health hazard. He indicated that next to a dependable enslaved African population, the other major issue that had to be addressed urgently was that of health. Seeing that free people of colour were now exempt from forced labour, he wrote, it would be best to encourage emigrants from Ireland or other popular districts to settle in Jamaica and cultivate the land. They had to be placed in the healthiest environments, such as the higher-altitude areas, as they could "not subject them to the hazards of the climate or the degradation of cooking on the same footing as enslaved Africans".[47]

The neglect of the material and environmental health of the enslaved Africans was not limited to private persons seeking to maximize profits; it was evident even among officers of the Crown. Officer Hutchinson, the acting head of customs services in Jamaica, was left with the responsibility for the welfare of forty-four enslaved Africans who were being imported illegally onto the island. Hutchinson put them all to work on his own personal coffee plantation, where they seem to all have either died or been sold. He claimed, however, that some absconded, while the others disappeared (table 5.4). To cover up his actions, Hutchinson hired a practising physician to give written evidence that all forty-four enslaved Africans had received excellent health care but had eventually died. As proof, the physician listed the date on which each died along with their causes of death.[48] But William Bullock, the chief justice of Jamaica, in response to Lord Bathurst's enquiry into the fate of the Africans, held Hutchinson responsible and indicated that they were all dead except for a Negro woman, Duchess, and her female child.[49] The governor, the Duke of

Table 5.4 Africans Condemned in the Vice-Admiralty Court up to 31 August 1816

Number of Africans	Date of Arrest	Results
5	9 December 1808	2 were resold and 3 absconded.
2	28 July 1809	No account on how they were disposed of.
15	29 August 1809	10 absconded, 4 were sold and 1 died.
15	4 August 1810	All were placed on Mr Hutchinson's coffee plantation. Medical certificates were then given to show that 13 had died.
5	31 August 1813	They were bailed out and given to the owner, Captain Bayley, who took them to the island of St Bartholomew.
1	27 February 1816	Acting collector did not know where the enslaved African was. He argued that he never received him or her from the seizing officer in Falmouth.

Source: CO 137/144, 6.

Manchester, in an evaluation of the circumstances surrounding the enslaved Africans' disappearance, castigated Hutchinson for blatant neglect. In addition, he stated that Lord Bathurst was unhappy with the deaths of the Africans and was convinced that they all died out of wanton neglect. Lord Bathurst even recommended that Hutchinson no longer be given any more enslaved Africans to care for and stressed that a similar incident should not be repeated.[50]

The ambiguous management structure on many Jamaican plantations also contributed to the environmental and material neglect of the enslaved Africans. Many of the absentee owners in Great Britain did not insist that the

Consolidated Acts that had been enacted by the Jamaican assembly be adhered to or practised on their plantations. For example, based on Jamaican law, each plantation was required to have its own hospital. There were no methods of ensuring compliance by either the Jamaican government or the absentee owners, to make certain that the hospitals were adequate in terms of space and treatment of the sick.[51] Regulation was oftentimes left to hired managers who had their own agendas. Some pushed their bosses for greater improvements, while others did nothing because they were being told daily to economize. In 1803, the attorneys at Island estate suggested to Barham that the hospital was in a swampy location and should be relocated near the great house, where the air was healthier.[52] In August of 1810, the managers at Mesopotamia recommended to Barham that they build six small long houses in different parts of the estate to protect the enslaved Africans from rain. These houses were to be shingled to offer the maximum protection. They also recommended that the hothouse be upgraded by adding a room to each end upon a stone foundation. The present hothouse, they said, was inconvenient and confined. They completed the entire project within a year. The new hothouse had a large room to hold medical stock, and there was a room on each side, one for males and the other for females. It also had a piazza of sixty feet by ten feet with two small rooms at each end, one for a medicine shop and the other for the doctor's office.[53] These initiatives were from the attorneys, not Barham, and took long in coming.

Despite these positive steps on the part of Barham's attorneys, they had minimal impact in terms of ensuring proper health care for the enslaved Africans. Table 5.5 illustrates the failure by Barham's management team to reduce mortality and increase fertility. The table shows that Island plantation had far fewer deaths than Mesopotamia. However, both plantations had more decreases in their enslaved population and as a result both experienced fluctuating production figures, as seen in figures 5.1 and 5.2. Both figures further demonstrate the disastrous effects of declining fertility and increasing mortality rates on plantation production, primarily as a result of the plantations' continual loss of valuable members of their workforce. Unhealthy plantations resulted in declining production and, eventually, productivity.

A further example of the failure of plantation managers to maintain a healthy enslaved workforce comes from Simon Taylor's property after his death in 1813. At Holland plantation in 1815, the plantation doctor confirmed

Table 5.5 Enslaved Population of Mesopotamia and Island, 1799–1831

Year	Slaves M	Increase	Decrease	Result	Slaves Is	Increase	Decrease	Result
1799	371	5	7	-2	211	1	5	-4
1800	369	–	3	-3	207	0	0	0
1801	366	–	–	-12	207	7	3	4
1802	354	6	16	-11	211	–	–	–
1803	343	1	10	-9	207	5	5	0
1804	334	11	8	3	207	5	5	0
1805	337	–	2	-2	204	3	8	-5
1806	335	7	8	-1	199	9	4	5
1807	334	6	11	-5	204	–	–	-2
1808	329	4	11	-7	202	0	5	-5
1809	322	5	13	-8	197	10	7	3
1810	314	8	15	-7	200	3	3	0
1811	307	6	7	-1	200	3	5	-2
1812	306	5	8	-3	198	3	7	-4
1813	303	5	9	-4	193	5	2	3
1814	299	9	18	-9	196	–	–	–
1815	346	–	–	–	n/a	–	–	–
1816	338	4	17	-13	n/a	–	–	–
1817	325	7	13	-6	188	4	3	1
1818	319	6	14	-8	189	4	5	-1
1819	311	–	–	-5	188	3	3	0
1820	306	7	12	-5	188	2	3	-1
1821	421	6	10	-4	187	4	6	-2
1822	417	–	–	-10	185	2	3	-1

Table 5.5 continues

Table 5.5 Enslaved Population of Mesopotamia and Island, 1799–1831

Year	Slaves M	Increase	Decrease	Result	Slaves Is	Increase	Decrease	Result
1823	n/a	–	–	-6	184	2	3	-1
1824	401	–	–	-9	184	2	3	-1
1825	392	6	13	-7	180	–	–	–
1826	385	8	20	-12	n/a	–	–	–
1827	373	7	17	-10	n/a	–	–	–
1828	363	7	17	-10	178	4	5	-1
1829	353	11	13	-2	350	–	–	–
1830	351	7	22	-15	n/a	–	–	–
1831	336	–	–	–	340	–	–	-5

Notes: "M" stands for Mesopotamia and "Is" for Island. In the years 1815 and 1821, additional Africans were purchased for Mesopotamia and in 1829, the Windsor Africans were finally added to Island estate.

Source: Barham Plantation Papers and Plantation Crop Accounts.

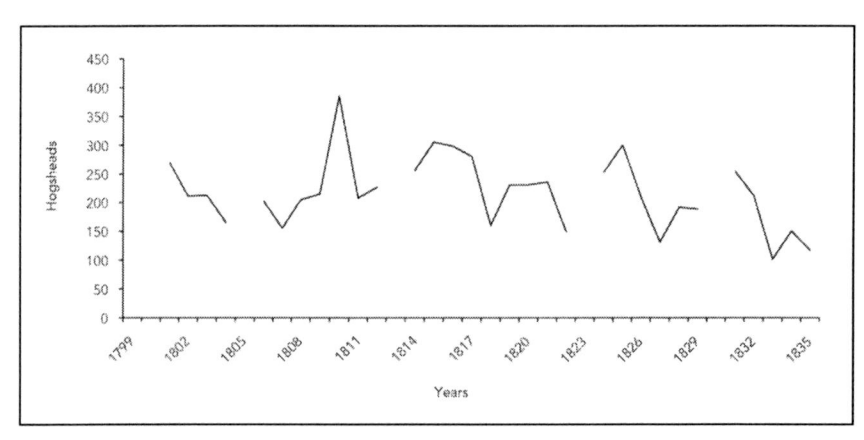

Figure 5.1 Sugar production at Mesopotamia plantation, 1799–1835
Source: Crop Accounts, Jamaica Archives.

Health and Reproduction   *139*

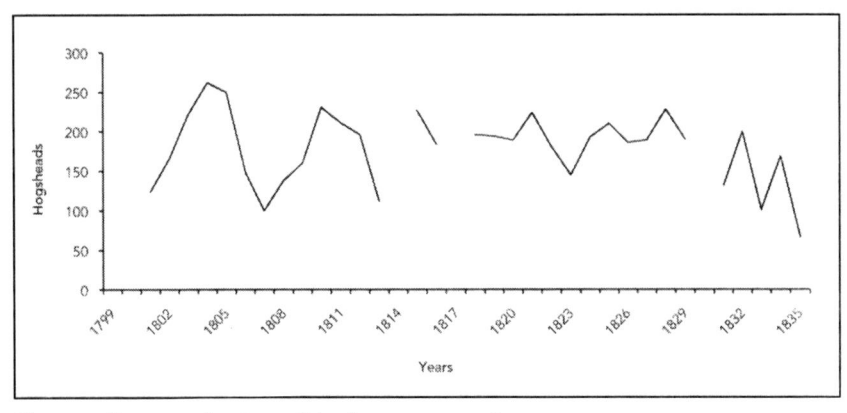

Figure 5.2 Sugar production at Island estate, 1799–1835
Source: Crop Accounts, Jamaica Archives.

that the unhealthy conditions of the Negro houses was the principal cause of the whooping cough attack that had killed several very fine children on the estate. It had also severely affected the neighbouring plantations. John Shand reassured the heirs, the Watson Taylors, that the late Simon Taylor had been aware of the unhealthy housing and had set apart a dry open space of nearly 40 acres into which the houses were to be moved. A fire that had occurred eighteen months previously and destroyed many of the Negro houses was the main reason the enslaved people had not yet been moved.[54] Although Shand erected the new homes and eventually persuaded the enslaved Africans to resettle, in 1818, the succeeding acting attorney, Richard William Harris, still expressed frustration at the unhealthy state of the island and its severe impact on the health of his enslaved labourers. He admitted that maintaining their health had been up to that point his greatest difficulty. He was very conscious of the implication of losing enslaved Africans, as they were quite difficult to obtain. At St Mary's plantation in 1817, there was a population decrease of four. At Pearl River plantation, there was no increase, even among the thirty to forty enslaved women in their most fertile years. One of the initiatives, then, that Harris wanted to discuss with the Shands was the renting of more jobbers to save the enslaved Africans of the plantation from the fatigue of labour.[55]

Health and Nutrition

The failure of the planter class in Jamaica to feed the enslaved Africans more nutritiously further contributed to the ill health of the latter. The argument proposed by some historians of a happy coalition between the interests of masters and their Africans in regards to diet is a myth; the reality is that if the Africans had not fed themselves, they would have starved to death.[56] Although the plantation papers that I have examined are in no way a full representation of Jamaica, there is no evidence to support the claims that the Jamaican planters provided balanced nutrition to their enslaved Africans. The evidence shows that the onus for obtaining nutritious meals for most of the year was on the enslaved Africans; the plantation provided minimal sustenance. With the constant fluctuations in the weather, the Africans continually faced depleted provisions. The plantations' emergency plan was to purchase supplies from any source they could find to save the starving African population. Their only other last resort was to feed the enslaved people off the cane crop, which the planters considered nutritious but which was woefully inadequate.[57]

When the weather destroyed the Africans' provisions in non-crop seasons, the planters usually panicked, especially if food provisions could not be procured. Such a scenario usually resulted in serious illness for the enslaved Africans as they scurried to eat whatever they could find, including unripe provisions that made them sick. Oftentimes, they resorted to stealing as well in order to avert starvation. It was in such situations that the planters escalated their illegal trading, defying British policy.

Some plantation managers, however, to avoid purchasing food and other necessities in desperate times when it was most expensive, especially from local merchants, resorted to initiatives such as pooling their finances and purchasing provisions in massive quantities. In 1802, one of Barham's attorneys, Sam Jefferies, given the scarcity of provisions that the island was experiencing due to severe drought, even sent a few puncheons of rum to New York in exchange for cornmeal.[58] William Rodgers, another of Barham's attorneys, asked for permission to purchase lumber from New York since a number of local attorneys were organizing the purchase. He stressed that lumber in Jamaica was too expensive.[59]

The planters' strategy in that period seems to have primarily revolved around the concept of plantation self-sufficiency. This meant that the enslaved

Africans had to feed themselves largely from their own provision grounds, receiving only minimal food from the planters. The planters used this strategy to maintain profitability of their estates. The plan, however, didn't account for the constant changes of the weather in Jamaica. These disrupted the planters' strategy of self-sufficiency and forced them to purchase extra supplies for which they never budgeted. As a result, they often came under criticism from the absentee owners for such high contingency costs. On such occasions, they would often defend their actions as completely necessary because the enslaved Africans were starving. At Mesopotamia in 1812, when the plantation faced such a weather-related calamity, Barham's managers thanked him for sending out extra Irish provisions and assured him that because of the crisis each family would now receive one and a half pounds of fresh beef daily.[60] It is clear from the plantation's own accounts that the average enslaved African was not given fresh beef daily. This only occurred in cases of emergency or on special occasions such as Christmas. For example, in both 1810 and 1815, the managers of Mesopotamia purchased two hogsheads of saltfish and fresh beef for the Africans because it was the Christmas season.[61]

Even on Simon Taylor's plantations, where the attorneys constantly stressed that the enslaved Africans had to perceive that they were cared for and loved, they still had to be self-sufficient in providing their own food supplies from their provision grounds. Mrs Watson Taylor, the niece of Simon Taylor, spoke in glowing terms of her care for her Africans and called on John Shand to adopt her approach as part of his management policy. She wanted the managers to be particularly sensitive to the children. She sent little sheets, bed gowns and capes for the pregnant enslaved women to motivate them and to show the estate's support of their condition.[62] On one occasion, she endorsed John Shand's initiative to have a portion of the estate lands sold and to rent out the jobbing services of the enslaved Africans who lived there. But she told Shand that he would have to take into account the opinions of the enslaved Africans for the initiative to be profitable.[63]

With all of Mrs Watson Taylor's humane gestures, however, the enslaved Africans still had to find their own daily provisions. The attorneys on one of her plantations noted that it was a nightmare to procure enough food for the enslaved Africans during the three crop months of May through July. The other nine months of the year, the Africans had no difficulty procuring an abundance of their own provisions. The three-month crop period was a most difficult time for the plantation as the scarcity of food resulted primarily from the overtime work of the enslaved in preparing the entire sugar crop for export on time. As such the enslaved Africans' provision grounds were neglected due to the heavy demands on their time. In such seasons, the plantation attempted to provide for the enslaved; however, the children, especially those in large families, were the worst affected as the plantation supply was usually limited.[64] This was the reason many enslaved Africans were left to eat their own provisions even before they were ripe, and this practice resulted in dysentery and other bowel complaints. Supported by the Watson Taylors, Shand supplied the Africans with enough rice and flour to carry them through those tough months. On one particular occasion in 1816, after a flood had devastated the Africans' provisions, Holland estate distributed as much as seven barrels of flour weekly. Lyssons did the same. At the other Watson Taylor plantations, the enslaved Africans received assistance, but not to the same extent.[65]

Most of the plantation records for Jamaica, unlike those from other parts of the British West Indies, have no record of the amount of provisions given to the Africans daily or weekly. It appears that attempts were made to conceal this information. In an 1832 parliamentary report from the Committee on the Extinction of Slavery chaired by Foxwell Buxton, attorney William Taylor, who had resided in Jamaica for fifteen years (1816–31) and managed three estates in the parishes of Vere, Clarendon and St Andrew, refused to provide details on the quantity of food given daily to the estates' seven hundred Africans. He argued that the information was sensitive. He confirmed, however, as a former attorney in three parishes and from his knowledge of other plantations, that the enslaved Africans had to sustain themselves largely through their provision grounds. In most cases, he reported, they were given only an allowance of pickled fish every two weeks and a bonus of saltfish at Christmas. He would not state exactly how much pickled fish was given or to whom, since plantations differed in this regard. He also confirmed that the only enslaved Africans who were fed consistently by the plantation were those who, through some disability, were not able to work their own provision grounds. Otherwise, plantations were eager to have as many of their enslaved Africans as possible produce their own provisions. Taylor believed that self-sufficiency among enslaved people was the norm except in the parish of Vere, where the enslaved Africans were supported directly from the corn granary. The land at Vere was too fertile for provision grounds to be competing with plantation staples. As a result, Vere was the only Jamaican parish to adopt a ration-allotment system like that of Barbados and to grow provisions like corn and sugar simultaneously. The enslaved Africans at Vere were also very successful at rearing poultry in their gardens.[66]

The material life of the enslaved Africans in the parish of Vere was most interesting. Higman notes that Vere was the only parish to move from a natural population decrease to an increase between 1817 and 1832.[67] Only four of the other sixteen parishes – Manchester, St Ann, Port Royal and St Elizabeth – showed natural increases in the same period.[68] Vere was the only sugar plantation parish among these, however; the other parishes had predominantly pens and coffee plantations. The registration returns of 1829 illustrate the levels of natural increases in the parish of Vere in comparison with other parishes (table 5.6).

Table 5.6 Increases and Decreases of Enslaved Africans in Five Parishes, 1817–1829

Years	Parishes	Male Slaves	Female Slaves	Slave Increase	Slave Decrease	Impact
1817–20	St George	n/a	n/a	1044	1,089	-45
1825	Westmoreland	10,325	10,806	405	626	-221
1826		10,318	10,765	426	626	-200
1827		9,816	10,454	440	564	-124
1828		9,921	10,368	394	428	-34
1825–28	Port Royal	3,344	3,313	523	403	+120
1829		n/a	n/a	n/a	n/a	n/a
1825	Vere	4,025	3,844	n/a	n/a	n/a
1826		4,050	3,983	n/a	n/a	+164
1827		4,048	3,983	n/a	n/a	-2
1828		4,010	3,870	n/a	n/a	-151
1829		3,980	3,898	n/a	n/a	-2
1829	Manchester	8,260	10,118	1,300	840	+460

Note: The other parishes reported that they had inadequate data to send to the governor.

Source: CO 137/169, 249.

William Taylor's testimony also helps illuminate the role of poor management at the Amity Hall plantation. Amity Hall experienced a natural decrease in their enslaved population in the early nineteenth century, as well as a drastic decline in their production, as seen in figure 2.4. While the parish of Vere, where Amity Hall was located, overall showed natural increases in enslaved Africans, the Amity Hall plantation had natural decreases and negative sugar production. The fact that Amity Hall's enslaved population was in decline while those in the rest of Vere were increasing highlights the relationship between plantation management and the health of the labourers.

Vere stands out as an excellent parish for sugar cultivation particularly when contrasted with Clarendon, one of its neighbouring sugar-planting parishes.[69] The land at Vere was fertile and flat, like Barbados, in contrast with Clarendon's land, which was less fertile and more mountainous. As a result, replanting cane required much more digging in Clarendon, especially in the mountainous areas, than in Vere. The latter parish allowed for continuous ratooning, which made sugar production easier. As ratooning did not work very well in Clarendon, enslaved Africans there spent around four months a year digging cane holes for planting.[70] Furthermore, in Clarendon, the canes had to be cleaned, or "trashed", two or three months before they were cut. The lower leaves, which were dry, were removed to admit the sun in order to ripen the cane. But in Vere, this seems not to have been necessary because the soil was already warm; if the sun were to shine strongly on trashed cane there, it would be more likely to spoil it.[71]

There were several other contributing factors in the superiority of the enslaved Africans' material conditions in Vere over those in Clarendon and even in St Andrew and other parts of Jamaica. The manner in which the enslaved Africans dressed was one of these. Many of the women wore muslin and Leghorn bonnets, and the men wore trousers and broad cloth hats. It also appears that the enslaved of Vere were more successful in engaging in trade, specifically in exchange for their poultry. They engaged with hucksters who travelled by ship all the way from Kingston to a market in Vere specifically to purchase poultry. In comparison, the sugar districts of Clarendon were much more remote, being sixteen miles from the coast and thirty miles from Spanish Town. They were not near to markets specializing in any particular product.[72] The food provisions for the enslaved Africans in Vere seem to have also been much more stable than in the rest of the island. They were given weekly rations not only of cornmeal, but also of corn, which was the parish's main provision item. Corn could withstand the vicissitudes of the weather, unlike plantains or yams, because it was not planted on mountain plots. Furthermore, because it was processed into cornmeal in the granary, it was longer lasting than plantains, yams and other ground provisions that could not be processed. Based on the above factors, it seems fair to conclude that the environmental and material conditions of Vere reduced the labour demands on the enslaved Africans there and increased their nutrition in comparison to other geographical areas of Jamaica.

Given that Vere was such a flourishing parish, it seems clear that the management at Amity Hall held the chief responsibility for the plantation's declining production and health. Frederick Goulburn's report to his brother Henry in 1818, when he visited the estate and compared the respective management of Samson and Richards, is a case in point. Frederick Goulburn stated clearly that upon examination of the enslaved Africans, their lack of a proper diet was obvious. This was one of the reasons that Amity Hall had not recorded any natural increases for the previous twenty years under Samson's management.[73] In two years under Richards's management, the plantation had recorded a natural increase of as many as twenty. This supports the claim of Samson's mismanagement.[74] Furthermore, three other plantations in the parish of Vere that were often used as comparisons also recorded natural increases, as shown in tables 5.7 and 5.8.

Richards was an exemplary manager. He seems not to have had negative beliefs regarding the morality of the enslaved Africans. Unlike his contemporaries, he advanced the weekly allowance of corn from four to seven quarts for an increased period of two months. Furthermore, recognizing its fundamental importance to the health of the enslaved Africans, he increased the quantity of land given to the African population for provision grounds. In addition to the 18 acres allowed by Samson, Richards gave them an extra 15 acres.[75]

By contrast, the plantation suffered under Samson's management. For example, he adopted the practice of planting fresh canes annually, even though the soils were suited to ratooning. This was very burdensome to the enslaved Africans, who had to dig the cane holes. Samson may have adopted the plough, but this is doubtful, as he was always making claims for hired labour. He chose to avoid ratooning for economic reasons. He believed, as did some other planters, that freshly planted canes produced larger crops on the whole.[76]

Table 5.7 Increases and Decreases of Enslaved Africans at Bog Estate, Vere, 1803–1817

Year	Births	Deaths	Increase	Decrease
1803	12	6	6	0
1804	12	4	8	0
1805	15	10	5	0
1806	15	6	9	0
1807	18	16	2	0
1808	19	18	1	0
1809	21	10	11	0
1810	24	17	7	0
1811	17	18	0	1
1812	23	21	2	0
1813	17	14	3	0
1814	10	15	0	5
1815	13	9	4	0
1816	16	9	7	0
1817	11	11	0	0

Source: Amity Hall Papers, 304/Box 52.

Table 5.8 Increases and Decreases of Africans at Three Estates in Vere, 1825–1831

Year	Increases Hillside	Increases Brazeletto	Increases Bog	Decreases Hillside	Decreases Brazeletto	Decreases Bog
1825	11	3	–	8	2	–
1826	5	1	–	1	1	–
1827	19	4	–	6	3	–
1828	13	5	21	10	2	10
1829	11	4	12	9	7	19
1830	13	5	14	8	3	7
1831	6	4	7	1	2	11

Source: Amity Hall Plantation Papers.

He felt his commission would suffer if he depended on ratoons.

Samson's management style seems dubious in light of the implications of the 1807 Abolition Act. Goulburn was warned – when he was considering hiring Samson as attorney – that Samson was not managerial material.[77] Frederick Goulburn's report confirms such a view since he laid the fault for the woes of the estate on Samson's management strategy. After stating that Henry Goulburn had the best land in the parish, his brother wrote:

> Your plantation has been badly managed as your fences are in bad order, your cane has been plundered to a considerable degree, the weeds have been badly cleared from the field and your canes are very thin – suffering from stunted growth. Your Negro houses are miserable huts . . . your Negroes themselves bear every appearance of being badly fed and show every outward sign of being much discontented with their present attorney.[78]

Table 5.7 further shows Richards's skilled management. The Bog estate was the plantation that Richards managed before he went to Amity Hall and which he continued to manage even while at Amity Hall. The natural increases in population that the estate experienced under his management are impressive.

Health and Gender

The other critical area in which many of the planters failed was in maintaining the health of their enslaved women. By around the early nineteenth century, women predominated in the workforce on most Jamaican plantations, as shown in table 5.6. By 1817, there were only seventy-four more African males than females in Jamaica. This was a drastic decrease from 1807, with the end of the slave trade. Before that, the planters had maintained the male advantage artificially by purchasing African males from the slave ships.[79] By 1829, for every one hundred enslaved females in Jamaica, there were 96.4 males. By 1832, for every one hundred enslaved females, there were 94.5 males.[80] Hilary Beckles and Barbara Bush argue that by the 1820s, enslaved women predominated in the category of fieldworkers since they had less chance than the males of moving into the skilled areas.[81]

The planters of Jamaica did not develop a systematic programme to ensure that their enslaved women remained healthy and reproduced naturally. They seem to have left the reproduction of the enslaved women to chance. When the women did not reproduce naturally, the planters severely castigated them with the usual labels – "promiscuous" and "licentious". Even as experienced a planter as Simon Taylor attributed the women's resistance to reproduce to their immorality. He believed that they had caught venereal diseases as young women and were deliberately concealing them with the aid of an African doctor who had given them "medicinal plants" to use. In cases where venereal disease was not disguised, African women were treated with mercury. Taylor believed that even though an enslaved woman might be labelled as "healthy", she eventually passed on her sickness to her children, who at birth appeared healthy but by age nine or ten immediately became sick and died.[82] While Taylor saw the problem as deeply rooted in childhood, other planters continued to believe that the women's polygamous lifestyles, their frivolous dancing around the country at night and their alcohol consumption were the main reasons for the natural decreases in population.[83]

It is not surprising that they solely blamed the enslaved women for their problems, given the fact that the planters' initiatives to spur population increase failed miserably. These were not a part of a coordinated attempt at effective gender management. Some planters did give incentives to pregnant women and midwives whenever a child lived beyond a certain age.[84] At Mesopotamia in 1802, the planters granted the enslaved women their wish of having their babies on the plantation. The attorneys built a maternity room for birthing children and provided changes of baby clothes as encouragement.[85] They also gave a gratuity of one pound to each enslaved woman, and one pound to the midwife and her assistant. But in spite of the incentives, the increases did not materialize.[86] Such measures were insufficient, as other important needs of the enslaved women were not addressed.

By 1809, the attorneys admitted to Barham that they had tried everything, including providing overseers who were more humane and who had good records of population increases on their former plantations. They had even warned the midwives against neglect. The planters did not understand, however, that the real issue was convincing the enslaved women of the advantages they could accrue of "breeding" babies given the horrors and misery of slavery. Unable to grasp this, the planter class returned to its belief that the low birth rate was one of the casualties of sugar cultivation and the licentiousness of enslaved women.[87]

At Lord Penrhyn's plantations, the story was similar. Penrhyn indicated in 1804 how disappointed he was at the low birth rate. On one of his plantations where there were thirty-eight women of childbearing capacity, none had produced children. Furthermore, out of an enslaved population of 229 women, only eleven had children. At King's Valley, another of Penryhn's plantations, an incentive was offered to both the mother and the midwife when they delivered the baby to the attorney after the first month. This still did not produce natural increases.[88] By 1819, the incentive had been increased to three pounds to be shared between the mother and the midwife for the safe delivery of a child. The three pounds, which later became standard on Penrhyn's plantations, were an improvement on the six shillings and eight pence given to the midwife and the three shillings and four pence given to the mother in 1804. The mother and the child were also given a young chicken as additional incentive.[89] However, as the attorneys indicated later, the fertility rates still did not increase.[90]

As helpful as these incentives may have been to the enslaved Africans, the women knew that they were measures to trick them into childbearing and not genuine initiatives by the planters. Further, the incentives were inconsistent. The planters had still failed to reduce the Africans' long work hours or improve their living and working environments. On some plantations, the managers claimed to have reduced their heavy workload for what they termed "lighter work", but such claims were misleading. For one thing, attorneys differed on what constituted "lighter work". In 1804, Fearon described this as hoeing, building fences, planting and picking oil nuts and boiling oil for the use of the estate.[91] Another of Penrhyn's attorneys, David Ewart, interpreted it as carrying out the trash from the mill or boiling house, since this was customary all over the island. He assured Penrhyn that the enslaved women only had to stoop in the act of taking up the trash basket, and in many cases they assisted each other. To justify his position, he stated that the load was not heavy, especially the day trash from the coppers, and that it was not hard labour, as the carriers were many and the distances were short. Ewart even initiated a plan to have light carts run on an iron railway to preserve his field labour force, which was dominated by women, and avoid any chance of damaging their health.[92] Ewart also stated that he chose women of stronger constitution and that the women did not have to stoop much, since the canes were placed on a bench raised a foot or two above the height of the mill bed. In addition, he said, he employed two female feeders to a mill and a third woman to replace the canes if they did not successfully go through the mill during processing. On larger estates where they made up to thirty hogsheads of sugar per week, he said, planters employed three female feeders: two fed the mill while the third rested, in alternating roles. He did not consider it too much labour for two women to be feeding a mill that generated around fifteen to twenty hogsheads of sugar per week.[93]

Ewart's initiatives did not work, however, as they did not lead to an increased enslaved population. A proper evaluation of what "lighter work" meant was not possible with the ambiguous management structure and the conflicting interests between absentee owners and managers. In reality, no aspect of fieldwork was light, as the enslaved Africans hardly had time to rest. At Mesopotamia, for example, they did not even get the entire day of Sunday to themselves as stipulated by the 1817 Consolidated Slave Laws. They were required by the plantation managers to do "light work" on Sunday evenings during crop time.[94] Furthermore, pregnant women in the first gang who became pregnant were placed in the second gang to perform what the managers considered "light work".[95] The second gang's work was not light, however, since it had the second strongest workers next to the first gang. Attorney Blyth had to justify the decision to place pregnant women in the second gang, as the doctors had recommended removing them from all labour. But many of the local plantation managers really believed that if the women were given light work, they would become idle and mischievous.

As further evidence that the enslaved women's health was secondary to economic concerns in the eyes of the planters, pregnant women at Mesopotamia were only removed from field labour six weeks before giving birth and had to return to work a month after the child's birth.[96] Attorney Morris from Island estate, who also gave pregnant women "light work" or relocated them to the pen, ironically argued that "greater relaxation would not contribute to their happiness or increases naturally".[97] His objection was founded on his sexist notion that enslaved women did not deserve free time and would not know how to make use of it.[98]

Managers who expressed some feeling of humanity towards enslaved Africans in general had little humanity for enslaved women when it came to encouraging them to have children. Morris pointed out that he would only feed women with two or more children for a few days out of each week. Even women with many children were not given total freedom from labour because the managers felt they were likely to become idle.[99] Some attorneys believed that whatever concessions they made to enslaved women had to be earned, rather than guaranteed through planter initiatives. For example, Morris stated that he would "agree with them holding property but only as a security for their continued good behaviour".[100] He wanted to change the practice of giving five to six pounds to every new child presented to him after twelve months, he said, because the enslaved Africans merely used the money to buy finery. Instead, he would give women who reared two or three children a heifer.[101] When the racial views of attorneys such as Morris are further examined, it is clear that they believed that they were doing the enslaved Africans a favour by rewarding them for "good behaviour", despite the fact that the Africans were an enslaved people whose labour and resources were forced from them. They did not realize that their reluctance to lighten the load of women bearing children was leading to greater resistance from the women.

This lack of awareness helps to explain the fact that, up to 1825, most attorneys had their field gangs predominantly made up of women digging cane holes.[102] Only pregnancy prevented women from being assigned this task. Morris wrote in 1825, "Since the Negroes began to dig cane holes many of them flinch from that kind of work. Half of the gang would wish to be excused."[103] William Taylor, in his testimony to the Committee on Slavery, argued that the digging of cane holes was very injurious to the enslaved Africans. Also, he had repeatedly heard overseers confirm that their chief objection to the ending of slavery was that they would never again get their cane holes dug cheaply. Under a new system of paid African labour, they contended, workers would require immense inducement to perform this function.[104]

In addition to the arduous job of digging cane holes, Taylor believed that the flogging of enslaved females and the constant night work that all enslaved Africans had to do were significant contributors to their ill health.[105] He stated in his testimony that the average workday of an enslaved African amounted to approximately eighteen hours. Their labour routine was so hard that most of the time they could not get to their provision grounds other than during their lunch break, which lasted an hour and a half. They had devised a way to cope with this time limitation: the men worked the provision grounds while the women prepared lunch.[106] Most Jamaican planters could have lessened the long work hours on sugar plantations by abandoning night work, as had been done in Barbados, Antigua and the Windward Islands. The Jamaican managers maintained it because they wanted to make profits both for themselves and their owners. Only a few Jamaican sugar planters abandoned night work and resorted to the use of technology such as the plough to reduce the amount of cane hole digging required.

Absentee planters in Great Britain must also shoulder some of the responsibility for the overworking and inadequate diet of their enslaved Africans. Joseph Foster Barham, one such planter, provides a case in point. In 1806, William Wilberforce strongly encouraged Barham to support his plan to import Chinese labourers into Jamaica. Such a paradigm shift, he argued, would eventually replace the system of enslavement of Africans and result in greater plantation efficiency. Wilberforce also suggested to Barham, as a second option, that he experiment with "task work", wherein the enslaved Africans would be paid when they completed certain assigned tasks. Such an initiative would render the whip useless and improve productivity. He also recommended that in tandem with removing enslaved women from field labour as soon as they were pregnant.[107] Barham refused all of these initiatives, instead finding other scapegoats for his plantation's woes. Among these scapegoats was nature itself, for designing Jamaica's bad climate and diseases as its way of preventing overpopulation. He was also extremely harsh towards the enslaved women, claiming that their inadequate moral character led to their weak emotions and intellect.[108]

Barham, along with many other absentee plantation owners, did not consider the important initiatives, such as that of reducing manual labour and the use of the whip and implementing alternative forms of labour, such as task work. These initiatives could have significantly improved the health of their enslaved workforces. Nor did they consider the extent to which a vastly improved diet could improve their plantations' production and encourage natural population increases. They made these oversights to the great detriment of their plantations.

CHAPTER 6

Management Initiatives

THE CONTINUOUS DEBATE OVER THE profitability of slavery in the Caribbean remains intriguing. B.W. Higman has argued consistently that slavery in Jamaica was not an inefficient form of labour because the planters had maximized labour output and increased the productivity of the enslaved workers.[1] Higman attributes the declining production and the natural population decreases of the enslaved Africans in early nineteenth-century Jamaica more to the effects of the 1807 Abolition Act.[2] He also states, however, that by 1834, there was an increase in the productivity of individual enslaved workers, a view that J.R. Ward supports. However, Higman concedes that the Jamaican planters paid an immense penalty for the increased productivity. After 1807, they had placed more creole slaves along with enslaved women in field labour towards this end, but as a result, the creole slaves became incensed and led the 1831 Christmas Rebellion.[3]

It is evident that the Jamaican plantation managers of early nineteenth-century Jamaica tried various strategies to maintain or restore their plantations to productive levels. One of the important initiatives they undertook was the introduction of steam engines to speed up the process of sugar production. The steam engines replaced the outdated and inefficient wind and cattle mills. Rebecca Scott and Veront Satchell have argued convincingly that the use of an enslaved labour force was not necessarily incompatible with the proliferation of technology.[4] The Jamaican planters had become convinced that the new steam engines would maximize production and productivity and thus save the precious institution of slavery. However, in spite of their optimism and their willingness to apply new technology to the archaic system of slavery, their efforts were largely futile.

The Introduction of Steam Engines

Several of the plantations examined in this study acquired steam engines in the early 1800s. However, instead of increasing the plantations' production and productivity levels, the engines created additional problems for plantation managers. Edward Long, in his treatise on planter management in Jamaica, called for a textbook to help planters acquire the art of good management based on the peculiar conditions of Jamaica. Plantation management was primarily learned through trial and error, he wrote. Many inexperienced planters and managers learned the art of management from copying their neighbours or being coached by experienced planters. In the end, Long concluded, the inexperienced managers came to realize that copying was not always the best strategy.[5]

Trial and error was certainly at play in the introduction of the steam engine in Jamaica. Between 1800 and 1830, Jamaican managers purchased fifty-one steam engines from Boulton and Watt of Birmingham, the leading British exporter of steam engines. The other major exporter to Jamaica was Fawcett and Littledale of Liverpool.[6] British Guiana was the only other British West Indian territory that rivalled Jamaica in purchasing Boulton and Watt steam engines. Planters there bought fifty-one steam engines, with Trinidad and Grenada purchasing four each.[7] The engines seem to initially have been used to water the crops against the severe dry weather that the island encountered regularly. The planters were also aware that the steam engine could be used to power the mills in the processing of cane and the boiling of sugar. It was also an excellent tool for the grinding of corn into cornmeal.

The applications of the steam engines and the problems associated with this new technology were best exemplified by an assessment of their operations on Lord Penrhyn's plantations. In 1804, Fearon decided that he wanted to follow through on the purchase of a steam engine at Denbigh, a purchase that the former attorney, Mr Falconer, had been planning to make. Intending to use it primarily for irrigation, Falconer had dug a well. He had reached a depth of seven feet when he encountered quicksand, which he misread as the bed of the river. He had also laid guttering tubes throughout some cane pieces to water the plants. After Fearon succeeded Falconer, he tried twice to water the cane from the well but was unsuccessful. He concluded that the well could not collect enough water to meet the requirements for irrigation. The well emptied quickly, in as little as ten minutes, during the dry season. During the rainy season, when the experiment was conducted again, the water lasted only thirty minutes. Fearon sought the advice of both Mr Richards of Bog estate in Vere, who later went to Amity Hall as manager, and Mr Mitchell, the proprietor of Moorland estate in Vere. Mitchell had installed a much larger steam engine and had used it only for grinding canes, not for irrigating his fields.[8] He confided to Fearon that he was very dissatisfied with the steam engine and that he was prepared to sell it. His estates were not near a good water supply for the effective watering of the cane fields, and further, he had decided that he would develop his rotative mill (a windmill) for future use. He felt the mill did a better job and was equally productive and less costly than the engine.

Fearon nevertheless decided to adopt the steam engine. Seamington, the engineer, had assured him that it would be better installed at Denbigh than it had been at Moorland, and thus it would take off the canes much more quickly.[9] In February 1805, the steam engine was installed at Denbigh. Fearon was happy to learn that it worked wonderfully, but he decided that he would not yet use it to grind corn; he wanted to see how successful Richards's operation was at Bog before importing the corn stones. This was not a problem for Fearon, as in the meantime he was using an Indian corn mill for grinding corn for the children on his estate.[10]

A month later, the steam engine still worked well. Fearon decided to support the engine with his windmill, since it was operating better than many on the neighbouring estates. He thus restored the windmill, which he had not used for years.[11] Fearon then had two mills complementing each other. At crop time, he used the windmill during the day, and when the winds died down, by 5:00 p.m., he resorted to the steam engine. By around 8:00 p.m., sugar production was finished for the day, which helped ease the burden on the enslaved Africans by protecting them from fatigue. By using the mills for only part of the day, Fearon could prevent significant wear and tear and the heavy consumption of fuel. Furthermore, he had the added assurance that if one of the mills were damaged he would still be able to resort to the other.[12]

The steam engine, however, only lasted just over a year after its installation. It ran out of the coal that fuelled it and no more was readily available on the island. Prior to the engine's installation, Fearon had thought he had an adequate amount of coal. He hadn't known that the engine consumed so much fuel in its operation. He had taken all necessary steps to ensure that the mill was well installed and not malfunctioning. To do so, he had acquired the services of Mr Jeffery from Penrhyn's King's Valley estate in Westmoreland. Jeffery had sent his mechanic to examine the steam engine, and the mechanic had approved of its construction and its power for grinding cane.[13] The reality was that the engine was malfunctioning because it should not have burned so much coal so quickly when it was used in such a limited way, only at night. What Fearon learned, as would other Jamaican managers, was that these early steam engines were not economically viable; they consumed a lot of fuel and did not produce more efficiently than the mills they were meant to replace.

In 1815, attorney John Shand decided that he wanted to establish another steam engine on the Denbigh plantation. He had weighed all the advantages and disadvantages and saw it as necessary; an unknown disease had been spreading among the animals on the estate, and thus the cattle mill was not able to take off the crop efficiently. Shand went to great lengths to indicate to the plantation owner that the installation of a steam engine was more advantageous than it had been in the past, as there were now many steam engines all over the country. Formerly, it had been necessary to import engineers at heavy expense, and if the engineer died, the work had to be suspended until another engineer could be brought in. However, the widespread acquisition of steam engines inspired many mechanics to settle in Jamaica, and they were competent and ready to set up engines and keep them operating for a moderate salary.[14]

The introduction of the steam engine at Denbigh was no panacea for the plantation's ills, as it was unable to halt the decline in the plantation's sugar production. Denbigh's crude production, as seen in figure 6.1, shows continuous decline, even after 1815 when Shand implemented the additional steam engine. This drastic decline stemmed mainly from the plantation's failure to maintain a stable enslaved population. In 1808, Denbigh had 356 enslaved Africans; by 1828, they had only 225 (table 6.1). Within 20 years, they had lost 131 enslaved Africans. With such a decrease in the enslaved population, even their steam engine couldn't prevent a drop in overall production. Levels of slave productivity at Denbigh between 1808 and 1828 were under one hogshead of sugar, except for the years 1818–20 (table 6.1). While it could be argued that the steam engine helped to increase productivity in those years, it is also clear that reliance on the steam engine without attention to the procurement of adequate labour was useless.

Not only were the earlier steam engines at a disadvantage because of irregular maintenance, but they were also examples of the trial-and-error methods to which Edward Long referred in his treatise on planter management. The mechanic sent out by the company for the 1804 steam engine at Denbigh died in 1806 from excessive rum drinking. This seems to have been a regular practice among the mechanics.[15] Further, the earlier engines, like the one at Denbigh, ran on coal, which was not as cost effective as the mixture of wood and bagasse (the dry pulpy residue left after the extraction of juice from the cane) that fuelled the later ones.[16] Coal imports increased significantly when the first steam engines were adopted and the plantations' operating costs rose markedly at a time when they could least afford it.[17] The earlier steam engines also required very expensive ironwork, as well as the services of additional enslaved Africans.[18] Some managers found that the engines fell out of favour with their staff because they demanded too much attention from them.[19] The failure of the earlier steam engines inspired the Jamaicans to innovate with an improved version of the cattle mill. Fearon described this improved cattle mill as equivalent to new technology that allowed four steers and four mules to do the work of twelve animals by a process called "double motion". The new mill could produce twenty-five hogsheads of sugar per week, the same as the steam engine, because both instruments made the same number of revolutions in one minute.[20] In 1806, Fearon boasted that this new cattle mill was unheard of among mechanics. He wrote that it was to be set up at one of the plantations the following week, and that depending on the success of its operations, he wanted to implement one at Denbigh. Fearon was excited because he was convinced that this new cattle mill would save labour for both the enslaved Africans and the plantation stock. He even planned to send to Lord Penrhyn a model of the new mill. He was convinced that it was at the cutting edge of technology and ought to be submitted to the Board of Arts and Sciences to become a major instrument among scientists and used to various ends, such as in the coalmines.[21] He further argued that several leading gentlemen of character who had been eyewitnesses of the improved cattle mill's power and execution were also convinced and had recommended the mill as a most valuable machine with great superiority over the common cattle mill.[22]

While this new invention may have suited sugar production, its overall uses were limited on estates. The new power was not animal but steam. The introduction of the steam engine brought renewed hope to some planters, who

Table 6.1 Levels of Productivity at Denbigh, 1808–1828

Year	Hhds	Slaves	Productivity
1808	216	356	0.60 hhds
1811	321	n/a	n/a
1812	350	n/a	n/a
1814	163	290	0.57 hhds
1815	197	287	0.70 hhds
1816	138	273	0.50 hhds
1817	243	264	0.92 hhds
1818	270	259	1.04 hhds
1819	282	253	1.11 hhds
1820	262	252	1.03 hhds
1821	209	257	0.81 hhds
1822	131	n/a	n/a
1823	85	n/a	n/a
1824	154	n/a	n/a
1825	26	n/a	n/a
1826	203	n/a	n/a
1827	162	232	0.70 hhds
1828	197	225	0.87 hhds

Source: Penrhyn Papers.

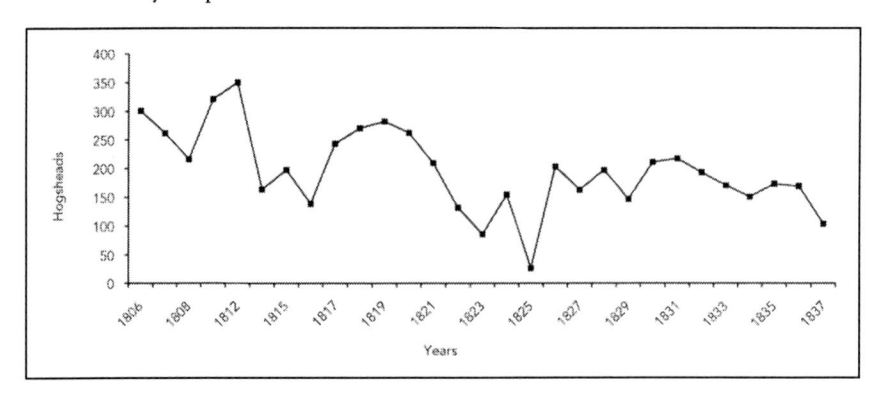

Figure 6.1 Sugar production at Denbigh, 1806–1837
Source: Crop Accounts, Jamaica Archives.

believed that its multi-purpose functions could raise their production quotas and also guarantee better material provisions for their enslaved people. As a result, they almost abandoned their older wind and cattle mills. Eventually, however, they were forced to acknowledge that their new technology was too costly and could not guarantee superior production over improved versions of their old mills, which were less expensive.[23]

At the estates of the late Simon Taylor, the failure of the steam engines to work properly after installation was embarrassing to the new owners, the Watson Taylors. By 1815, a steam engine built by Boulton and Watt was already at Lyssons estate.[24] Holland estate purchased their steam engine around 1817 or 1818, and Shand recommended to the Watson Taylors the purchase of another engine for the St Mary's property. They agreed to this in the hope of making three hundred hogsheads of sugar, as had been common under Simon Taylor.[25] Not long after the engine at Holland was installed, however, the attorneys indicated their disappointment with certain defects. They told the Watson Taylors that they had contacted the manufacturers to have the defects repaired, and they hoped that these would be rectified in proper time for the estate to count on the full benefit of the engine in its production.[26] The manufacturers, Graham and Bupton, adjusted the original wheels for the grinding of cane, a task for which it was not constructed originally. Differences between the Jamaican mechanics and their British counterparts emerged over the specific pressure necessary for a sugar mill. William Shand summed up the attorneys' side of the dispute by concluding that the cogs were not designed properly and that the wheels did not have the strength to power the engine based on the plans of the British mechanics.[27]

Not long afterward, Shand expressed additional disappointment over the steam engine at Lyssons. The binding of the iron plates led to them being broken, resulting in the failure of the machine. He wrote to the Watson Taylors that he would try to have it repaired to take off the crop, but in case he could not, he was already informed of other alternatives.[28]

Amity Hall in Vere also had its fair share of problems with the steam engine. In 1813, Thomas Samson requested a steam engine estimated to cost around £1,400 plus labour costs. In his petition to Henry Goulburn, he stated that around six of his neighbours already had steam engines. In addition, he wrote, "Amity Hall had plenty of water to run the engine sufficiently".[29] This was surprising, as Mr Mitchell of Moorland estate in Vere had reported his disappointment over the lack of water to run the engine. Samson was surely following his six neighbours who had steam engines rather than doing a detailed analysis of its feasibility. Samson further stated that the steam engine would augment the breeze mill and allow him to harvest the crop in three months, February to April, rather than the customary six months. He would also save on stock; the estate could place around thirty steers on the market, which would help in defraying expenses. In addition, he could trade some of the plantation's sugar to help cover the engine's freight. Finally, Samson argued that with both the steam engine and the windmill, the plantation would be sufficiently prepared to reap crops without the use of cattle. This would reserve the cattle for carrying cane from field to market.[30]

The steam engine brought a host of added costs, however. In 1817, the installers commenced the infrastructure for a ten-horsepower steam engine imported from Fawcett and Littledale for over one thousand pounds sterling. In 1818, the steam engine became operational. Samson's plan was similar to Fearon's: he would resort to the steam engine when the wind was too calm to propel the windmill. He would use the windmill on all other occasions.[31] Within two years of the steam engine's installation, the plantation attorney, Mr Richards, concluded that it had been improperly installed, as it was burning too much fuel. Consequently, he had to stop production and revert to the windmill. He then employed a mechanic to adjust the steam engine properly to avoid excessive use of coal. Richards's conclusion was that although the steam engine "was very lovely" and was one of the best in the country for its size, the engineer had benefited from Samson's ignorance and had him writing unnecessarily to England for increased hogsheads of coal.[32] In 1825, when Mr Bayley, the new attorney for Amity Hall, reported on the plantation, he indicated that the boiler for the steam engine was badly worn and would not last much longer, unlike the windmill, which was in excellent condition.[33] Bayley received a new boiler for the steam engine in 1826. However, in 1830, two additional problems developed. First, the two-sided Zeller grudge gears broke and replacements had to be ordered from Liverpool. Second, the Zeller grudepin fell out and the attorney had to send it to Kingston for repairs.[34]

In early nineteenth-century Jamaica, a time when many plantations were riddled with debt, the implementation of the steam engine turned out to be a costly experiment. It did not lead to the dramatic increase in production or productivity that had been expected. In the end, some planters reverted to

Table 6.2 Amity Hall Production Figures, 1802–1837

Years	Hogsheads
1802–7	370
1808–13	370
1814–19	279
1820–25	196
1826–31	170
1832–37	189

Source: Crop Accounts and Plantation Papers.

their faithful wind and cattle mills. As useful as the steam engine was in speeding up the processing of the crops, it was not the answer to the planters' economic dilemmas. As Richards rightly argued, most attorneys on sugar plantations were technically ignorant, and as a result the plantations paid dearly. This was part of their continued lesson in plantation management that Long had alluded to earlier. This probably explains why the attorneys became silent on the contribution of the steam engine in their correspondence. It was not the miracle that they had been waiting for to boost sugar output.

The disappointing results of the introduction of the steam engine can be seen in Amity Hall's pre- and post-1817 production levels (table 6.2). It is clear from these figures that the steam engine did not boost the plantation's production. The only period that saw an increase in production was the last five years shown in the table, 1832–37. In fact, in the period following 1817, when the steam engine was introduced, production began declining.

Diversification

In addition to adopting new technologies such as the steam engine, most planters also attempted to diversify their agricultural operations. Diversification had been an essential element of plantation life in Jamaica since the seventeenth century. The crops they cultivated in addition to sugar cane included coffee, ginger, cotton, cattle, tobacco, lumber, pimento and ground provisions.

Although these items did not replace sugar and its by-product rum in the export market in the seventeenth and eighteenth centuries, they nevertheless played a supporting role and led to a vibrant domestic trade.[35] By the early nineteenth century, the nature of diversification changed as declining profits from sugar production became evident. Sugar planters desperately searched for other viable export staples, which would function in tandem with sugar and even replace it if possible.[36] The most promising alternative to emerge was coffee. Coffee exports grew from 1.6 million pounds in 1791 to 28.5 million pounds in 1808, partly because of favourable market opportunities coming from the fall of St Domingue. The restrictions placed on coffee in the European markets, however, ultimately resulted in its decline. Thus, in 1815, coffee prices in the world markets fell drastically, as did those of sugar.[37] Logwood and tobacco were two other staples that planters cultivated in the hope of penetrating the export market, but neither was able to attain the same level of growth that coffee had. They nevertheless became significant as supporting staples.

The planters' inadequate response to the changing economic context of the late eighteenth and early nineteenth centuries lay at the centre of their failure to find viable export alternatives. The two most important resources available to planters were land and enslaved labour. Neither of these resources was efficiently developed and maximized for long-term growth. Henry Goulburn, for example, failed to capitalize on the production of coffee and logwood when Samson recommended these in the very early 1800s, when they were selling at very good prices. Many of the other Jamaican planters also squandered such opportunities. Barham, for example, only started experimenting with growing coffee on his plantations in the 1820s, when the international prices of that commodity were in a downward spiral and Great Britain had reduced the protective tariff for coffee planters.[38]

In 1821, Barham, in his belated haste to plant coffee, turned to his Island plantation in St Elizabeth, since that parish had better soil for it.[39] He planted 12 acres of coffee. The plantation's attorney, Mr Morris, reminded Barham that coffee cultivation called for additional enslaved Africans. Morris also told Barham that he feared that the soil and weather at Island were much too cold and wet for coffee to be successfully produced there. Yet the experiment went ahead. The trees bloomed well and the coffee bore rather heavily, but Morris was not pleased with the beans' appearance, considering them a bit too yellow, and he wondered whether Barham would even recover his labour costs. The coffee eventually improved in appearance with the mild seasons, and Morris concluded that it was worth a fair trial although its cultivation required much labour and attention to keep the berries clean and prevent them from falling and rotting.[40]

Barham had, however, planted the coffee pieces at Island without proper attention to adequate infrastructure, and poor weather in December 1823 destroyed the existing roads to the coffee fields. Morris was unable to tend to the berries or even to inspect the fields, which was a serious setback in light of the constant attention the coffee crop needed.[41] Although the quality of the picked coffee was disappointing, the three casks sold on the London market in 1824 yielded fifty-nine shillings and six pence per bag. The coffee yielded a small profit of £45.12.9, since Barham's labour costs were minimal. In 1825, four casks of coffee yielded a similar profit of £45.8.9, despite a small decline in the cost of coffee that year.[42] Morris blamed the soil at Island for the poor quality of the coffee, describing the sub-soil as "marly-clay" that killed the coffee when the roots reached it.[43] It is clear that Morris was experimenting with the coffee crop and learning through trial and error.

Kathleen Monteith has opined that the demise of many coffee planters in Jamaica was a result of both external and internal factors. Externally, Napoleon's Continental Blockade of British goods in the European market, the keen international competition from other coffee-producing countries and the reduction in British protectionism in the 1820s were all factors. Internally, she argues, many coffee planters facilitated their own demise through bad agricultural practices and the use of inadequate technology. For example, their dependence on the hoe, rather than using other lighter instruments, led to soil erosion; whenever rain fell, especially in eastern Jamaica, it washed away their topsoil and thus destroyed the coffee trees. As another example, in many instances fertilizers were inconsistently used. Monteith concludes that the planters' lack of technological innovation coupled with the harsh international realities of the time hastened the demise of some of the coffee plantations. This was especially true after 1815, when inefficient plantations gave way to more efficient ones.[44]

The most critical point is that the rapid acceleration of coffee exports in early nineteenth-century Jamaica was more circumstantial than a deliberate planter strategy. As international coffee prices rose due to the destruction of St Domingue, the coffee industry in Jamaica grew significantly, benefiting from the high prices. The industry also benefited from the reduced duties – from eighteen pence to six pence per pound – implemented in 1783.[45] Thus, coffee exports from Jamaica, which had been rising steadily in the eighteenth century, rose dramatically in the late eighteenth and early nineteenth centuries, from 1.6 million pounds in 1791 to 28.5 million pounds by 1808.[46] However, as soon as Jamaica faced intense competition from not only the newly acquired British territories in the Caribbean but also Mauritius, coffee exports declined as the coffee industry in Jamaica was not structured to survive without strong economic protection.[47]

Many of the coffee farmers, to their credit, implemented the task system of labour over the gang system used by the sugar planters. In the task system, enslaved labourers were rewarded for completing particular assignments. This was an initiative to increase efficiency and reduce the cost of supervision. Some coffee planters even paired enslaved Africans with each other based on their levels of performance and gave them rewards commensurate with the volume of work done.[48] The coffee planters, to a great extent, did more in the reorganization of labour than many of the sugar planters. But the harsh reality was that without British protective tariffs, their exports would continue to decline from the intense competition in the international coffee market.

Joseph Foster Barham and his attorney Mr Morris were an example of how outclassed and trapped the Jamaican plantation managers had become. Barham chose to experiment with coffee in hope of finding an alternative to sugar in the 1820s, when its price was very low and the British protective tariffs had been removed. The small profit that he made even at that late stage confirmed that he had missed out on what could have been an economic breakthrough if he had diversified into coffee earlier, when the conditions were more favourable. He, like many of his contemporaries, spent his energies petitioning for continued economic protection for sugar at the expense of diversifying and producing other staples so efficiently that the withdrawal of economic protection would not bring them to ruin.

Barham's attempt at planting coffee in the 1820s was symptomatic of a common trend of that period, when many Jamaican planters were realizing that they desperately needed an alternative to sugar and scurrying to develop other staples. By then, however, it was too late; they had not prioritized their plantations' infrastructure nor reorganized their labour to make themselves more competitive in the new economic order of free trade.

Morris, as attorney of Island plantation, must also share some of the blame for Barham's failure. He lived in a coffee parish[49] and yet even as late as the 1820s, he was still not familiar with the mechanics of growing coffee and was still learning the art through trial and error as described by Edward Long. Interestingly, one of the most productive areas of coffee cultivation in Jamaica lay between the May Day Mountains of Manchester and the St Elizabeth plains. Island plantation was somewhere in the middle of this geographical region. Morris maintained that its soil was not ideal for coffee production, but coffee planters in the vicinity had developed an outstanding reputation. The port of Black River, for example, had become well-known by 1808; the town was described by one planter as the fastest-developing and most prosperous town anywhere in the British West Indies. This was due to the growing affluence of coffee planters and pen keepers.[50] Alligator Pond in Manchester was another growing port made popular by coffee planters and cattle ranchers.[51] Despite Morris's assertion that his soil was not ideal for growing coffee, it was clear that as an attorney he had not yet developed the agricultural knowledge nor had he prepared the proper infrastructure to make Island plantation competitive in an early nineteenth-century free trade market where protection was slowly being removed.

Another staple that most Jamaican planters failed to develop as a viable export item was lumber – in particular, logwood. Most of the plantations' crop accounts depict small amounts of logwood being exported. Penrhyn's plantations are a good example of this (table 6.3). At Mesopotamia, one of Barham's estates, logwood was one of the items that the plantation constantly depended on for export, and outside of sugar and rum, only cattle sales surpassed it. Table 6.3 shows, by contrast, that among Penrhyn's four plantations, Denbigh was the only one that procured logwood more than once. Even then, it did so inconsistently, unlike Mesopotamia.

The difficulty of access to the wooded areas of plantations seems to have been one of the critical factors that impeded the growth of the logwood industry. To better understand this, the topography of the plantations has to be understood. The greater part of plantation lands in Jamaica, as explained in chapter three, was wooded and mountainous. It was challenging to access lumber or logwood from such land; for one thing, there were very few roads for transporting the wood from these areas. At Amity Hall, for example, Samson had plentiful timber at Carpenter's Mountain that could have been valuable

Table 6.3 Logwood Production on Penrhyn and Barham's Plantations, 1803–1835

Year	Penrhyn's Estates	Logwood (tons)	Barham's Estates	Logwood (tons)
1803	Coates Pen	67.0	Mesopotamia	36.75
1804	n/a		Mesopotamia	41
1806	Thomas River	34.5	Mesopotamia	34.5
1806	Denbigh	59.0	n/a	
1808	n/a		Mesopotamia	33
1809	n/a		Mesopotamia	10
1810	n/a		Mesopotamia	36.5
1811	n/a		Mesopotamia	56
1812	n/a		Mesopotamia	56
1814	Denbigh	32.0	Mesopotamia	15
1815	Denbigh	62.5	n/a	
1816	n/a		Mesopotamia	37.5
1817	Denbigh	65.0	n/a	
1818	n/a		Mesopotamia	10
1819	Denbigh	40.0	n/a	
1821	Denbigh	3.0	n/a	
1822	n/a		Mesopotamia	52.5
1824	Denbigh	18.0	Mesopotamia	30
1825	n/a		Mesopotamia	42
1826	n/a		Mesopotamia	7
1827	n/a		Mesopotamia	16
1832	Denbigh	12.0	n/a	
1834	n/a		Mesopotamia	10
1835	n/a		Mesopotamia	15

Source: Crop Accounts and Plantation Papers.

to him, but he could not procure it in mass quantities because of the logistical difficulty of doing so. He concluded that it was easier, although less economical, to purchase lumber from the Americans than to retrieve it from his own property.[52] He relied on plantation lumber only for special projects, such as building the foundation for the steam engine, and for other plantation necessities when money had to be saved.[53] He was able to export a limited quantity of logwood, but this was on a temporary rather than a consistent basis.

The other major reason for the lack of development of a logwood industry was the difficulty of procuring enslaved labourers. Rodgers blamed inadequate labour at Mesopotamia for the estate's inability to collect a greater volume of logwood in the 1820s. Because of this shortage, he had employed jobbers to prepare the logwood for export. Rodgers assured Barham that with the little jobbing labour they could employ, they would still continue to export logwood in small quantities, averaging ten tons.[54] But even before the 1820s, Mesopotamia only exported the quantities of lumber that it did because of hired labour. Estates that were financially strapped could not engage in any depth in a logwood industry because they could not pay jobbers or spare any of the enslaved Africans who were working on sugar production. On the whole, there was little assurance that the use of jobbers would bring profitability to the production of logwood.[55]

Planters had other reservations about the profitability of logwood as well. Some were concerned that they would lose out if their wood was not sufficiently cured and it appeared "too green", as the wood was sold by appearance.[56] Many were also apprehensive about the price. A ton of logwood was sold on the market from seven to eleven pounds.[57] The unavailability of price quotations for jobbing labour made it difficult to calculate the profitability of the logwood venture. Planters felt that if they could not find a way to procure sufficient quantities of logwood by using their own enslaved labour force, then the venture was most likely unprofitable. If the production of logwood was dependent on hiring additional labour, then one can conclude that the procurement of adequate labour was a major problem of the planters. Why should they continue to depend on enslaved labour which left them with limited options? Planters needed to diversify and become efficient if they were to compete in the new commodity markets.

The example of Mr Webb from Island estate further highlights the dilemma of the planter class in their continued dependence on an enslaved labour force. In 1809, with the price of staves becoming so high that he was paying as much as eighty pounds per foot, Webb decided that he would explore local alternatives. The Santa Maria tree, which was plentiful on his property, was one possibility, but he was not sure how durable its wood was.[58] Certain additional problems hindered his procurement of local wood. For example, he had to find large sums of money to pay jobbers to prepare the lumber, since his enslaved people were already engaged planting sugar. Webb's example shows that the very expenses that managers tried to save on the one hand led to greater costs on the other, since the plantations remained committed to forced labour in the production of sugar.

In an attempt to pull their plantations out of the rut of dependency, the planters tried to return to tobacco production for export by adopting measures to capitalize on the export market. Tobacco was one of the initial crops grown in the British Caribbean in the seventeenth century, but it was eventually marginalized because it was less profitable than sugar and could not compete with North American tobacco. With the failure of coffee at Island plantation, Morris became convinced that tobacco export was feasible. Tobacco grew in small quantities and only a few persons engaged in its trade, such as the Maroons of St Elizabeth. The Maroons travelled to Alligator Pond in South Manchester and Pedro Plains in St Elizabeth, where they purchased it and sold it to the manufacturers. The tobacco was then used to manufacture cigars in Kingston for export. However, Jamaican cigars were of inferior quality in comparison to Havana cigars and were only used by those who could not obtain other makes.[59] Thus, although the Jamaican cigars were exported to Britain, they had little impact on the export market.

Barham also explored the planting of tobacco on his plantations. But the manager at Mesopotamia told him frankly that he would not consider producing tobacco, even for the domestic market. He argued that Westmoreland was far too wet and that it was best grown in a parish such as Vere, or other places such as Santa Cruz in St Elizabeth and the May Day Mountains of Manchester. Other estate managers, however, including Rodgers, believed that if estates were to seriously engage in tobacco cultivation, it could very well become their economic saviour.[60] Nevertheless, he did not foresee most planters making serious attempts to diversify into tobacco production; sugar was so entrenched in their minds that he was convinced they would have a great fear of trying another staple. Thus, for miles around Mesopotamia, as far as one could travel, the greater part of the land remained in sugar cane. The planters continued to spend between five hundred and one thousand pounds on jobbing labour annually. For the most part, sugar remained primary to the area and the greatest amount of resources was put into it.[61]

The British policy of promoting free trade and gradually withdrawing economic protection affected the Jamaican planter class psychologically. They could not see themselves finding either a suitable replacement to sugar or a strong supporting crop without continued economic protection. In 1828, George Hibbert, the agent for Jamaica in England, was petitioned by the Jamaican authorities to investigate the claim that foreign cigars entering Britain were given economic preference. The Jamaican cigar makers had to conform to a British law that stated that cigars sent to Britain had to be placed in packages of not less than 450 pounds net with no further subdivisions. Turkish and Colombian cigar makers were exempt from the British laws; the contents of their packages could weigh as little as 320 pounds. Packages from Guatemala were also exempt; their packages could be as little as 90 pounds. Hibbert found the arguments of the Jamaican cigar makers to be true. He was to pressure the Board of Trade to grant them exemptions that would allow them to reduce their package weights. Since the islands were not allowed to purchase foreign goods, the planters felt it was unjust for Great Britain to favour alien countries over its own colonies.[62]

To support their petition, the planters drew on the experiences of one of their colleagues, W. Espeut from the parish of St George. Espeut had originally been a coffee planter, but like many others, he had switched to planting tobacco because coffee prices were low. He, like other planters, wanted tobacco to become an important staple item and believed that he could compete with his international competitors. He had been a successful tobacco planter for the last two years; however, the recent trade laws were crippling him. He had two hundred thousand cigars to be shipped, but based on British law, he could not send them in containers weighing less than 450 pounds net. One thousand cigars weighed around 6 pounds. Thus, 450 pounds consisted of seventy-five thousand cigars. First, Espeut didn't know where to find containers that would accommodate such a volume without creating additional problems in shipping. Second, he feared that the sheer size of his containers would cause the cigars to be broken or begin fermenting. The planters brought this example to the Board of Trade to show that there was a great likelihood that colonial cigars "would be declared unfit to compete with those many quantities that found their way into England from Havana".[63] For the West Indian tobacco planters to compete, they needed smaller packages of between 24 and 112 pounds net.

The Board of Trade failed to grant Espeut a direct answer, saying that regulatory issues belonged to another department.[64] Their refusal to dispel Espeut's claims seemed to be validating them. Furthermore, the Board's choice not to comment on trade policy seemed to support the Jamaicans' view that Britain gave foreign commodities the advantage. But even if this was the case, it should not have been surprising to the Jamaican planters, as they had had the same experience with both sugar and coffee. This should have awakened them to the reality that their operations in Jamaica had to become much more efficient since Great Britain was moving towards free trade. Consequently, they had to become much more sensitive to the needs of their enslaved populations and introduce initiatives such as "task work".

Pens

Pen keeping, along with its auxiliary services, was another significant area of diversification. It tremendously bolstered the plantation's domestic economy. In terms of its operations in Jamaica, it trailed only behind sugar and coffee. Verene Shepherd has argued that in the pre-sugar era, pen keeping in Jamaica had its own independent dynamism, but it was later marginalized by the growth of sugar. From the eighteenth to the early nineteenth century, it was a mere adjunct to the dominant sugar economy.[65] By the latter date, two kinds of pens had emerged. First, there were pens that were independently owned and operated as alternatives to sugar plantations. These pens were generally restricted to the parishes of St Ann, St Elizabeth, Westmoreland, St Catherine and Clarendon. Although they were independently managed, they were still interwoven into the sugar industry and the domestic market for their economic viability. The second kind of pens that emerged were those that were adjuncts to sugar plantations. These were usually located near the sugar plantations and they served the various needs of the sugar industry. They might be used to season enslaved Africans; recuperate sick enslaved Africans; grow plantation provisions; breed and fatten plantation stock; or serve as a midway or rest station to the wharfs or ports. These plantation pens largely developed in the sugar parishes, namely St Thomas in the East, St Mary, Hanover and Trelawny. They sought to complement the sugar plantations by making them more self-reliant and efficient.[66]

One of the best examples of this synergy between the sugar plantations and their pens was the economic relationship between Golden Grove plantation and Bachelor's Hall Pen. In 1833, Golden Grove plantation accrued income from the following sources: the sale of sugar and rum; the sale of ten old cattle to Holland estate for £70; £75 for rent of their land to Pleasant Hill estate; and £34.10 for rent to Stokeshall. The plantation purchased from Bachelor's Hall Pen a number of supplies, including ground provisions, coffee, arrowroot, plantains and fresh beef. Bachelor's Hall seems to have made a profit of around £900 from the sale of its items, mainly to Golden Grove.[67] In 1835, Golden Grove sold to Bachelor's Hall Pen twelve old cattle for £72, while Bachelor's Hall sold to Golden Grove £73,829 in beef, ground provisions, plantains, coffee and arrowroot.[68]

Not all plantation pens were complementary to their sugar operations. Some were more like millstones around the planters' necks because they had been ruined by bad management and needed much capital for their restoration. In 1804, Rowland Fearon apologized to Lord Penrhyn for the very poor condition of his stock at both the Kupius and Pennant estates. He blamed the overseer for neglecting the health of the stock. Although the amount of stock was still high on both plantations, Fearon lamented that many of the animals looked meagre and that he had had to send twenty of them to be fattened, at extra cost to the plantation. At another plantation, he found the stock completely inadequate and ordered several of them to be drenched and sent to pasture at a considerable cost. At Penrhyn's other two plantations, Denbigh and Coates Pen, the stock and pasture were in good condition.[69] Two years later, in 1806, Fearon wrote that he had succeeded in improving the pens, as he had promised. He stressed that he had been impeded by the loss of two top-quality bulls that had perished in the shipwreck of the *Britannia* as they were being imported. Nevertheless, he wrote, he would endeavour to acquire two good bulls locally to improve on the plantation's stock. Fearon later bought two bulls for seventy and sixty pounds, respectively, and argued that they would be a great acquisition for the stock. He wrote that he now had to ensure that all the pens had proper pasture. He would have to remove the stock and distribute them to other pens with abundant pasture. After that, he would use the opportunity to replant grass in the pens.[70]

At Mesopotamia in 1805, Joseph Foster Barham made recommendations to improve the pen in order to increase the plantation's production from 350 to 400 hogsheads of sugar annually.[71] But as late as 1823, the pen was still inefficient. The attorneys, too, were disappointed, especially because they had acquired new stock from the Green River plantation. This stock had brought little gain to Mesopotamia because it was old and also needed to be fattened. In the end, half of the Green River stock died.[72] In 1825, the new attorney, Rodgers, stated that he was doing his best with the enslaved labourers he had and that he needed to improve the pen. The demands on the estate were so great and the estate's own enslaved labour force so inadequate that he felt he could not commit to the pen without neglecting the work on the plantation. He assured Barham, however, that he had maintained a good balance between the two. He had refurbished the pens with the adequate amount of grass needed. Later, he would divide the section of the estate called P&Q into four pastures. He had already repaired the outside fences and he intended to run a stone wall through the centre from the Cornwall line. This would only require two fences to be completed. He had already planted section Q in grass; he had built the stone wall and a crop of logwood had been planted. He had put in 45 acres of grass.[73]

The planters' difficulty in procuring an adequate enslaved labour force even to perform the ordinary plantation tasks meant that proper attention was not given to the development of the pens; sugar continued to be given priority. As a result, many plantation pens suffered neglect from lack of adequate material resources and labour. Many pens were not able to fully supplement the incomes of the sugar plantations, although they still played a critical role in providing other essential plantation services. The Pepper and Bona Vista pens in St Elizabeth, which operated as a single, independently managed plantation, show that the incomes of sugar plantations could have been bolstered if they had been efficiently managed (tables 6.4 and 6.5).

The Pepper and Bona Vista pens had an enslaved population of 295 in 1832 and were efficiently managed pens. Their horses steadily increased between 1826 and 1835. They did lose 198 horned stock in 1833, a significant reduction (an explanation was not given for this unusual demise), but the births and casualties (deaths) for both horses and horned stock remained rather stable

Table 6.4 Pepper and Bona Vista Crop Accounts, 1826–1838

Year	Horses	Births	Decrease	Sold	Casualty	Horned Stock	Births	Decrease	Sold	Casualty
1826	222	45	40	27	13	640	129	140	117	23
1827	227	53	49	30	19	629	154	143	118	25
1828	232	73	55	40	15	640	112	135	107	28
1829	252	63	58	37	21	617	116	108	97	11
1830	257	59	57	30	27	625	178	86	72	14
1831	259	67	66	42	24	717	102	66	45	21
1832	260	59	66	37	29	753	124	158	133	25
1833	256	66	60	26	34	745	58	241	43	198
1834	264	38	61	32	29	594	74	143	119	24
1835	245	47	61	39	22	549	74	139	118	21
1836	231	53	57	45	12	504	57	108	77	31
1837	237	46	43	18	25	453	71	124	68	56
1838	242	52	36	19	17	400	73	43	17	26

Source: Pepper and Bona Vista Estate Book.

Table 6.5 Value of Sales at Pepper and Bona Vista, 1826–1835

Year	Value to Nearest Pound
1826	5,285
1827	5,471
1828	6,662
1829	4,631
1830	4,835
1831	5,683
1832	3,832
1833	5,698
1834	5,494
1835	4,017

Source: Pepper and Bona Vista Estate Book.

otherwise. The reasons given in the crop accounts for the casualties were listed as follows: debility, stealing, drowning, severe purging, poisoning, killing, spraying and extreme dry weather. In 1831, sixteen horned cattle died from "poverty", or illnesses resulting from starvation. Shortness of supplies led the management to slaughter seven cows to feed the enslaved Africans that year, far beyond the two cows that were usually given to them annually. Overall, however, it would appear that the operation of the pens between 1826 and 1835 remained stable and they continued to make a reasonable income, as seen in table 6.5.

The failure of Jamaican plantations to find an efficient niche crop in their attempts at diversification in the early nineteenth century was aggravated by the decline in the price of rum. Traditionally, rum sales were a vital commodity that contributed to the profitability of many plantations. They provided the income required to meet the contingencies of the estates, which included buying ground provisions and the purchasing of enslaved Africans. An assessment of the extant statistics shows clearly how drastically rum prices fell by the 1820s. From 1804 to 1807, estates received on average between three and five shillings per gallon for their rum.[74] In 1816, rum prices seem to have decreased slightly at an average of two to four shillings per gallon.[75] However, by 1823 a planter complained that rum prices were so low that he received only one shilling and six pence a gallon for his rum. The only outlet he had was to smuggle it in small barrels to South America.[76] The declining prices indicated that there was reduced demand for the product. Because the United States, which traditionally bought excess West Indian rum, was restricted from trade with the British West Indies, the price of that commodity plummeted. It reached an extremely low price after 1815, when the North Americans stopped taking most of the rum produced in Jamaica. By that time, the North Americans had developed their own alternative alcohol industry, including corn spirits. John Shand estimated that the North Americans, who previously took around 128,571 hogsheads of Jamaican rum before the Revolutionary War, were no longer buying rum in 1815. Furthermore, the state of Louisiana was well on its way to developing sugar and rum industries. Great Britain as well, Shand wrote, could no longer be relied upon to supply its troops in Canada with rum. In recent times they had made very limited purchases.[77]

An assessment of the problems of rum sales at Amity Hall further illustrates the crisis of managing estates that were financially strapped. In 1803, Amity Hall had a small production of sixty-four puncheons of rum. This was inadequate to pay for the plantation's contingencies. As a result, Samson planted 50 acres of corn to be sold locally to help with the contingencies.[78] In 1808 and 1812, conditions were not improved, and even the costs of transporting the rum to Kingston had reached such high levels that most planters preferred to export their rum than to sell it locally on the Kingston market.[79] In 1808, Samson paid £211.18 to transport a quantity of rum to Kingston. By 1813, the figure had jumped to £279.1 for the same amount.[80] In 1815, he proposed to Goulburn that the dwindling income from rum sales was too small to pay the contingencies and purchase labour.

It was the procurement of adequate amounts of labour, however, that posed the greatest difficulty to the Jamaicans in their attempts at diversification. In 1825, George Hibbert, the island's agent in London, sent information before Lord Auckland concerning the suitability of Jamaica for growing the mulberry tree. He wrote that two specialists, Dr Redstan and Mr Green, had agreed that the tree would flourish in the higher regions of Jamaica since there was still plenty of land there that could be used to cultivate it. In addition, he said, the infrastructure for such a project was available. For example, building expenses in Jamaica were moderate, as materials such as timber could be obtained easily on the spot and other materials could be purchased from the island's merchants at a modest price. Hibbert acknowledged, however, that the major problem was that of adequate cheap labour, as the cost for the labour of tradesmen to prepare the infrastructure would be double that of slaves. However, if enslaved Africans could be found, the venture could be successful, as they would be paid a minimum wage of two shillings and six pence per day. Unfortunately, an adequate enslaved labour force was not available in Jamaica for such a venture. Hibbert admitted that slavery had successfully destroyed the desire for agricultural work even among the free blacks and the free coloureds.[81]

The Board of Trade and Plantations finally responded that although they had a serious interest in developing the mulberry plant, Jamaica stood a slim chance of attracting their investment. The major limitation was the high cost of labour. To relieve this cost, they would have to introduce white settlers, such as groups of Maltese families who wished to immigrate to Jamaica to cultivate the trees. Ceylonese workers were also considered, since their climate and soil were similar to those in Jamaica.[82]

The Jamaican planters made many other attempts to find a niche crop that would strongly support their sugar operations, but these attempts mainly failed. The other items that they attempted to produce included maize, arrowroot, and ginger.[83] Some planters even entered into areas of manufacturing, such as limestone production and sugar refining in Kingston.[84] On Penrhyn's plantations, the workers produced a particular kind of oil. The product never became a major plantation item. It occupied around a quarter acre of his land and was described as excellent, but it was expensive to purchase.[85]

The planters' initiatives to find an alternative staple to sugar and coffee in the international market generally failed. Some plantations, however, were able to diversify into other staples or offer additional services to the local markets to keep themselves financially solvent. Coates Pen, one of Penrhyn's plantations, was a prime example of this. As its cattle sales started to decline, the plantation started producing lime, making puncheons and, most important, providing transportation or wainage services to neighbouring plantations.[86] As a result of these initiatives, Coates Pen was able to recover a significant amount of the revenue that was being lost in cattle sales. Other plantations producing sugar and coffee, however, were not so fortunate. They experienced declining production because the fundamental problem they faced, but which they hardly accepted, was not one of technology but one of recruitment and maintenance of slave labour. Without adequate slave labour and with declining sugar, coffee and rum prices and the gradual withdrawal of protective tariffs, it became extremely difficult to remain competitive.

Epilogue

THROUGHOUT THIS STUDY, ATTENTION has been focused on white plantation managers in Jamaica and absentee owners in Britain in the first thirty-eight years of the early nineteenth century, in the pivotal context of the 1807 Abolition Act. This study has shown that many plantation managers failed in several ways. They did not make the necessary changes to their ambiguous management structure, improve the health of their enslaved labourers or take amelioration seriously in the changing environment brought about by the abolition of the slave trade. As a result, many plantations experienced declining production and productivity. Instead of finding new incentives to encourage their enslaved labourers to become more productive, reproduce children willingly and maximize the plantation's productive capacities, the planters engaged in political battles with the British Parliament and, in the end, they lost.

In their resistance to amelioration, the Jamaican assembly implemented further draconian measures to ensure that the institution of slavery would not be dismantled. The planters did whatever they could to remind their governors and civil servants that they would not bow to pressure from the British Parliament to change fundamentally their constituted way of life. They supported the Consolidated Slave Laws, which on the surface seemed beneficial to the material lives of the enslaved Africans, but were pre-emptive and served the political purpose of appeasing the British Parliament. Furthermore, the planters ensured that the laws would not be enforced and weakened them through frequent amendments. Even the magistrates and officials who enforced the laws were constantly guilty of violating them when it was politically expedient. The planters' continual violation of their own laws backfired because it led to greater resolve by the British authorities to closely scrutinize amelioration practices in Jamaica. One example that illustrates this is the case of Lecesne and Escoffery, two free men of colour who were deported from Jamaica as illegal aliens in 1825.[1] The British authorities were disappointed at the Jamaican authorities' inability to legally substantiate their claim. The incident was an embarrassment for Jamaica and just added fuel to the growing anti-slavery movement in Britain. In addition to supporting pre-emptive laws that the Jamaican authorities were not willing to enforce, the planters also ensured that legal institutions, such as the courts and the prisons, were not reformed. These state institutions remained on the side of the planters in reinforcing the continued subjugation of enslaved Africans, in a period calling for less harshness and more conciliation.

On a management level, planters introduced various initiatives to save their industries and economies from decline. They introduced the steam engine along with various planting strategies, such as the ratooning of canes. They attempted stringent economies in their plantation expenses and the reduction of planting acreages in the hopes of improving the quality of their staples exported to Britain. They also changed attorneys and overseers, diversified into coffee and tobacco, and worked on strengthening their pens. But as necessary as those changes were, they were secondary. The primary management issue after the 1807 Abolition Act was that of labour reform and the development of a less ambiguous management structure.

Many of the plantations failed miserably in their attempts to recruit and maintain adequate levels of enslaved Africans after 1807. The planters' inability to maintain the health of their enslaved populations resulted in a continuing decline in plantation staples. These declines could be slow and gradual; drastic and rapid; or unsteady, with periodic highs and lows in production. Planter-class scepticism and resistance to amelioration in the early nineteenth century further contributed to the plantations' failure to stem the economic troubles arising from the various external factors set in motion in the late eighteenth century.[2]

A less ambiguous management structure was also necessary because of the prevalence of absentee management. This ambiguity was especially pronounced among younger owners who had inherited plantations that they had never visited and that were riddled with debt. Their interests competed with those of their family members in Great Britain who relied on annuities from the plantations to maintain their wealthy lifestyles. Plantation merchants and agents, who frequently "owned" the plantations because of their indebtedness, also dictated plantation policies, as did local managers living in Jamaica who had their own agendas. Thus, on many plantations, the owner had no idea whose interests or managerial strategies were dominating the daily execution of plantation policy: the plantation clerk, the overseer, the attorney, the merchants, the owner or family members of the owner.

Despite the failure of the Jamaican authorities to institute the necessary internal reforms, the British government cannot be fully absolved of responsibility for the decline of the plantations. The Jamaican planters were caught in the transition between the old order of mercantile capitalism and the new order of global capitalism. They represented the men Adam Smith referred to who would learn the hard lesson that slavery had its advantages but sooner or later it had to give way to wage labour as a more cost-effective way to cement capitalism.[3] The Jamaican planters, in defending the institution of slavery, were acting out of self-interest. However, the British policymakers were also motivated by self-interest. In light of the new economic realities confronting them, they shifted their trade preferences from the West Indies to the East Indies. Further, they failed to provide effective leadership to colonies such as Jamaica during the first twenty-nine years of the early nineteenth century, which could have motivated the Jamaican planters to restructure their operations.[4]

Carrington and other historians of early decline are correct in arguing that the effect of the American Revolution on the British West Indies was enormous. The older West Indian economies were left with increasing costs for provisions that had once been supplied cheaply by the Americans, and they also had to live with the often expensive and inconsistent provisions from other sources. The independence of the United States also had an important effect upon Great Britain. First, Great Britain had to find a method to force the West Indian economies to become more cost effective and at the same time develop the East Indian markets to make up for the loss of the American colonies. Second, it had to administratively restructure its own political systems to take advantage of the new economic realities.[5] As such, the country was in the process of slowly fine-tuning its policies for the first twenty years of the nineteenth century in order to prepare the British West Indian colonies for change. The British authorities, under pressure for free trade by the coalition of the British sugar-refining industry and the humanitarians, created a new division of government called the Colonial Office. The Colonial Office initially lacked the leadership to properly prepare colonies like Jamaica for reform. Throughout the early nineteenth century, it was slowly developing strategies to reinforce amelioration in the slave colonies. Between 1800 and the 1830s, British West Indian policy went through several changes as the Colonial Office was forced to become more and more proactive and authoritarian in enforcing amelioration.[6] The Colonial Office was even accused by several of the Jamaican planters of violating its own constitutional principle of non-interference in the internal affairs of legislative assemblies, such as that of Jamaica.[7]

This helps to explain why, prior to the 1830s, Jamaican governors such as the Duke of Manchester and the Earl of Belmore were allowed to remain in office even though they were incapable of helping the planters in restructuring their plantations. Both Belmore and Manchester were non-confrontational leaders who did not try to engage the planters in reform. By the 1830s, however, the governor's role in Jamaica had changed; this office now had a more proactive agenda to reform every branch of the Jamaican government. This included the courts, the prisons, the workhouses and the civil service. The governor was no longer required to have any form of management over enslaved Africans. The uninformed decisions that governors Manchester and Belmore were permitted to make without suffering any negative consequences could not be made by later governors, who had to record meticulously the most minute details to be sent to the Colonial Office for verification.

The Jamaican planters had a legitimate claim in arguing that the bureaucrats in London had no idea of the inflammatory nature of amelioration or how it would destroy their colonies and their way of life. As capitalists, they had a right to block ameliorative attempts by the Crown and to resist the Colonial Office's attempts to force them into passing certain laws against their own interests. The Jamaican planters were caught in many mitigating external circumstances. But they failed to understand the nature of the mature capitalism in which Great Britain was engaged. If that country was to reconquer the economic markets from the French, it could no longer grant trade privileges to older West Indian economies saddled with debt, decline and inefficient management, despite their historical ties. In a declining economy triggered by a number of external factors, good plantation management meant looking internally at plantations and rethinking the issue of labour. After 1807, it was imperative that each enslaved African be kept alive and healthy for as

Table 7.1 Merchants' Accounts on Tharp's Plantations, 1815–1833

Year	P.J. Mills	G. Hibbert
1815	7,085.3.5	-13,239.80
1816	4,980.5.1	-13,528.18
1817	4,707.10.1	-4,965.00
1818	2,096.12.7	-16,265
1819	194.7.11	-32,336.00
1820	-1,314.13	-33,538.00
1821	2,229.18	-54,561
1822	3,760.0.7	-71,054.00
1823	-25,689.19	-47,702.00
1824	-29,547.14	-48,313.00
1825	-29,509.11	-56,930.11
1826	-35,970.00	-50,705.00
1827	-36,146.00	-46,960.00
1828	-40,828.18	-40,471.00
1829	-41,408.14	-43,057.10
1830	-42,171.10	-52,112.16
1831	-41,626.00	-65,409.00
1832	-40,553.00	-63,238.13
1833	–	-52,932.15

Note: The negative sign indicates that the plantation owed the merchant.

Source: Tharp Papers, R.55.7.130, 2–45.

long as possible. The decision to rethink labour strategies should have become even more urgent given the pattern of economic decline on most Jamaican plantations. Not only were their production figures declining, but their incomes had also fallen off drastically. Furthermore, their levels of indebtedness to their merchant financiers were also rising markedly. Even in the face of such realities, plantation managers in the early nineteenth century would not consider labour reforms, such as task work.

The crisis of debt that plantations were experiencing is clearly illustrated by Tharp's plantation accounts (table 7.1). The production figures for Tharp's eight sugar plantations were declining drastically in the early 1800s, as shown in figure 2.5. Consequently, it is surprising that the plantations' indebtedness to their two merchants, P.J. Mills and G.H. Hibbert, increased so significantly in less than two decades, as seen in table 7.1.

The Tharp plantations consisted of eight sugar plantations and two separate pens. In 1815, both Mills and Hibbert were owed around £20,000 sterling. By 1820, the debt had jumped to around £34,000. Then, in 1825, it rose to around £85,000, reaching around £94,000 in 1830 and over £103,000 two years later. These were the same plantations on which Hibbert had ordered his attorneys to practise tight fiscal management. They had had a level of success, reducing the yearly plantation expenditures from around £10,000 a year between 1818 and 1821 to around £7,000 a year between 1823 and 1828.[8] The merchants still invested in the plantations despite the rising debt. However, the attorneys had not entertained the idea of investing more of their finances in the material and socioeconomic needs of their enslaved Africans. They had not, for example, offered the enslaved Africans bonuses to produce sugar, nor initiated any plans for the enslaved women who were their chief labour force. Even after the Sam Sharpe Rebellion in 1831, Hibbert still believed that only force could keep the enslaved Africans working. He entertained the idea of appealing to the authorities in Great Britain to send out a larger military force to Jamaica for this purpose.[9] Like most of the planter class in the years after 1807, he had still not learned that the pendulum had swung. Planters now had to earn the trust of their enslaved population, as they had the power to ruin a plantation.

Figure 7.1 shows the net profits of Henry Goulburn through his accounts with both his Liverpool and London merchants. It indicates a decline in his net profits in the early nineteenth century and their overall fluctuations between the years 1805 and 1825. In 1805, Goulburn's profits were around 50 per cent, but by 1825 they had dropped to about 40 per cent. Figure 2.4 has already demonstrated the unsteady decline at Amity Hall exacerbated by a fluctuating plantation output. The decline in Goulburn's net proceeds stemmed not only from Samson's poor management but also from external factors, including the reduction in the prices of sugar and rum; the continued reduction in the drawback; the rising costs of overhead expenses in producing sugar; increased insurance and marketing charges; rising duties; and higher

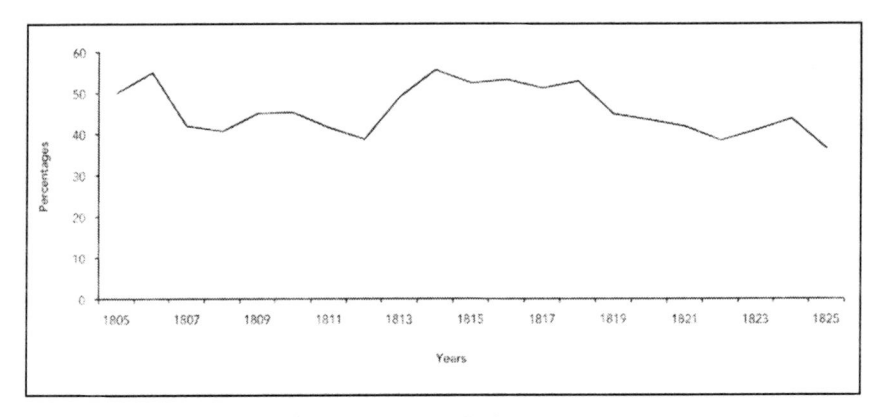

Figure 7.1 Net profits at Goulburn's Amity Hall plantation, 1805–1825
Source: Selwyn H.H. Carrington, "Statistics for the Study of Caribbean History during the Eighteenth and Nineteenth Century" (manuscript).

provisions costs from England. In the face of such pressures, managers actually had to be increasing their yearly production or their levels of productivity of each enslaved African to overcome the external factors accelerating their decline.

As we have seen, the plantation managers' best response to such external pressures would have been to re-examine internally the issue of labour management. Scholars such as Douglas Hall argue that even with the best management practices, the existence of slavery would make profitability incalculable.[10] This could very well be true; however, without the planters' willingness to rethink labour issues and their flexibility in implementing necessary reforms such as task work with pay, they had very little chance of saving their industry.

The rising external pressures on Jamaican planters affected even the most experienced and seasoned planters, including Simon Taylor, who has been classified as one of the island's leading sugar tycoons. Taylor was a member of the Jamaican assembly and had also served as an active member of the Association of West Indian Merchants and Planters. As we saw in the first three chapters, he had become disillusioned with British economic policy in the late eighteenth century. He blamed the British government for the increasing number of external factors that were reducing planters' profits; for example, between the years 1792 and 1798, the total cost of imported provisions from

England and Ireland had risen significantly, from £4,343 in 1792 to £8,444 in 1798. In addition, Taylor faced increased charges in duties, freight and insurance.[11] This meant that he had to increase his levels of production and productivity to offset these rising costs in order to make a profit. Making his situation even more troubling, Taylor also faced an internal problem at the end of the eighteenth century: he was unable to increase his production of sugar, and it declined from 1,034 hogsheads in 1792 to 707 hogsheads in 1798. It is not surprising, then, to see his net profits decline from 66.2 per cent in 1792 to 51.1 per cent in 1798.[12]

Jamaican planters like Taylor, approaching the 1800s, realized that the external factors pushing up overhead costs in the production of sugar were slowly eating away their profits. This was the reason they used the meetings of the Committee of West India Merchants and Planters to petition the British authorities. They sought help in reducing their expenses by re-instating the protective duties on their staples and increasing both the bounty and the drawback. As demonstrated throughout this study, the planters' mistake was in their failure to look internally at better labour management and reorganization. It was imperative for plantation managers in post-1807 Jamaica to maintain the health of the enslaved Africans; to entice them to become more productive; to reduce their levels of violent resistance; and to reduce abortions among their population.

Figure 7.2 illustrates the declining net profits of another Jamaican planter in the early nineteenth century. Clement Tudway's net profits fell by around 20 per cent in that period. It is, however, even more remarkable that in 1770, Tudway's Jamaican plantations gave him an overall net profit of 70 per cent.[13] By 1800, it had dwindled to 50 per cent and by 1834, it was around 30 per cent. Thus, between 1770 and 1834, his net profits declined by 40 per cent.

Amelioration programmes would most likely enhance the Jamaican planters' levels of management since they included humane measures to help the enslaved Africans. For example, in 1823, the British Parliament made eight recommendations regarding the treatment of slaves. These included establishing the office of Protector of Slaves, establishing a savings bank, compulsory manumission, abandonment of the whip and the admissibility of evidence from enslaved persons in Court.[14] The planters of Jamaica should have welcomed the implementation of these recommendations in their Consolidated Slave Laws, but they resisted, and in doing so impeded their plantations' con-

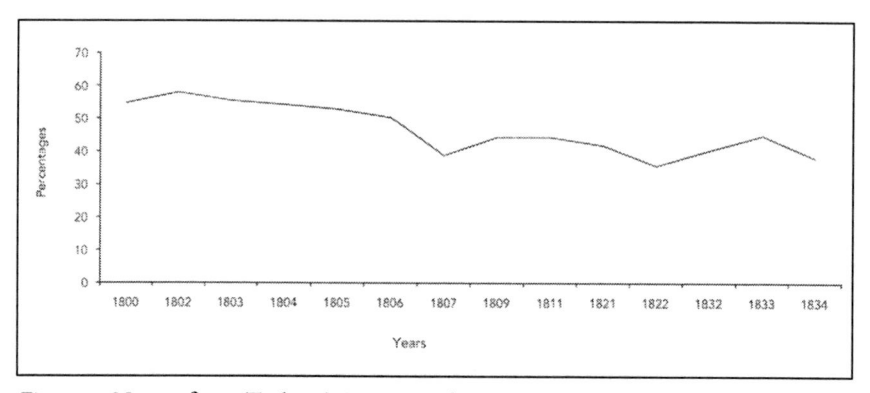

Figure 7.2 Net profits at Tudway's Jamaican plantations, 1800–1834
Source: Selwyn H.H. Carrington, "Statistics for the Study of Caribbean History during the Eighteenth and Nineteenth Centuries" (manuscript).

tinued growth. It is not surprising that many magistrates during the Apprenticeship period (1834–38) blamed the planters for the continued decline of the plantations. The planters attempted to sabotage Apprenticeship by casting the enslaved Africans as lazy, irresponsible and immoral. They spread such propaganda to ensure that they would have access to new immigrant labourers from Asia and could continue to manipulate them.

Unlike the Jamaican planters, the British authorities were committed to the growth of an efficient system of labour during Apprenticeship. As late as 1837, magistrate Peter Hulme, who was stationed in Green Island, Hanover, was sent a scale of labour charges that had been developed for his parish according to its peculiarities, such as differences in soil. These labour charges were, first of all, guidelines for the special magistrates to help them to negotiate better between management and labour. Second, and most important, they formed the basis upon which task work was to be regulated. For example, they specified that male apprentices in an able gang with a nine-hour workday should dig 90 cane holes, 4 feet square by 6 inches deep, in heavy clay soil. Meanwhile, female apprentices should dig only 30 holes, given the same conditions. In mould, marl or light soil, male apprentices were to dig 100 cane holes, while female apprentices should dig 90. When there was very light sandy soil, male apprentices were to dig 110 cane holes while female apprentices were to dig 100.[15] The guidelines also had clear specifications for every other area of plantation life, including a stipulation of nine hours of work to be done daily by the apprentices and the importance of ensuring that they received time to themselves.[16]

In addition, Hulme was told by the governor, Sir Lionel Smith, to inform the apprentices that no more than three at a time were to travel to King's House, in the eastern part of the island, to complain of the injustices of the planter class. Large groups of apprentices had been complaining personally to the governor and bypassing the magistrates. This demonstrates that the apprentices were willing to work, providing the conditions were just.[17] Another magistrate, Frederick White, working in the parishes of St Georges and St Mary, visited a number of plantations in one week and confirmed the apprentices' willingness to work, except for a few who had to be warned or punished. On several occasions, to his surprise, he agreed with their complaints regarding the inhumanity of the planters. The planters still attempted to overwork the apprentices and flog them. In one case at Golden Grove, the apprentices went on strike and resumed working only after White intervened. White also admonished the manager of Beadington estate in St Georges to treat his apprentices fairly. He threatened that otherwise, he would inflict on him the heaviest punishment that the law allowed. White wrote: "this unfeeling man has not given to these poor beings the necessities of life for some years past".[18]

The failure of the Jamaican planter class in general to reform their management practices had one other important implication. The planters left an indebted and outdated plantation culture, which after over three hundred years of operations was still dependent on Great Britain for continued economic protection. In their desire to preserve the institution of slavery, they continued to underdevelop Jamaica's infrastructure along with its human resources, and helped create the conditions for future racial conflict with new immigrant groups. The planter class could never approve of its ex-slaves finally being free. The planters had already attempted to dehumanize the enslaved Africans and in doing so, they forced Great Britain to find other labourers from the East and elsewhere. This would further advance the marginalization of the formerly enslaved Africans and their descendants.

APPENDIX 1

Injustices in the Jamaican Legal System, 1817–1822

On 24 August 1821, an attorney in Clarendon castigated the magistrates for numerous irregularities in the severe punishment of his head watchman. The attorney general agreed that a proper jury had not been convened and warned the magistrates that they would be removed if other unconstitutional occurrences took place. (CO 137/152)

On 20 March 1817, one planter, Edward Bolt, was convicted of murder. It was, however, recommended by the jury and the chief justice that he be tried for manslaughter and not murder, on the grounds that he had been "provoked". The governor sought the advice of the Colonial Office. (CO 137/144)

On 8 March 1822, one planter, Charles Newman of Manchester, killed his slave by punishing him with a large stick while he was in stocks. He disappeared from the island and charges of neglect were brought against the coroner and two magistrates in the Grand Court. They were released, as there was not sufficient evidence to have them convicted. (CO 137/144)

On 5 August 1822, one planter, Thomas Simpson, was convicted in the Cornwall Court of Assize for raping an infant under ten years old. The case was sent to the Crown to be decided, as it was argued that Simpson was at times mentally deranged and that furthermore, he had been tried by an English law, which was not applicable in the Jamaican context. (CO 137/144)

APPENDIX 2

Injustices in the Jamaican Legal System, 1826–1832

On 9 August 1826, one white person, Adam S. Mckay, was convicted of murder for killing a fellow white man under the 1826 Consolidated Laws of Jamaica, but when the 1826 law was repealed by the Crown, the judges asked that his sentence be disallowed as slave evidence in the 1826 law had been used to have him convicted. (CO 137/167)

On 22 April 1828, one fellow white planter, Henry Benjamin, accused the incoming custos or chief justice of Trelawny, William Miller, for being a tyrant who bullied his jurors for the verdicts that he wanted. The attorney general in his investigation agreed and stated that in Miller's trials no proper notes were taken or if they were, they were written in pencil, then later transcribed. (CO 137/169)

On 2 December 1830, the custos of St Andrew was accused by a fellow white person, W. Taylor, of not offering a Council of Protection to his slave, resulting in her being severely beaten by the jailor. Lord Goderich ordered that she be released and reprimanded the magistrates for being too insensitive. (CO 137/179)

On 15 May 1832, Lord Goderich again censured the magistrates and custos of St Mary for their mishandling of a murder investigation. (CO 137/181)

APPENDIX 3

Company for Importing Chinese Workers in Jamaica in 1808

The original capital was £6,000 but with power to extend shares of £500 to entitle the holder to one vote in the choice of directors:

- £1,500 to 2 votes
- £3,000 to 3 votes
- £5,000 to 4 votes
- £10,000 to 5 votes
- £20,000 to 6 votes

Directors were to be annually chosen and they were to direct the affairs of the company, appoint agents and declare dividends, etc. Bylaws were to be made as usual and shares were to be subscribed. Five per cent on the subscription was to be paid at subscribing. The remainder of such times as was to be fixed by the directors after July 1, 1808. The company contracted Mr Barham to bring to his Island estate in St Elizabeth, Jamaica, 500 Chinese with all stock, crops, utensils and the like, thereon excepting the Negroes, starting 8 July 1808. Should the Chinese not arrive by the date, this delivery would be postponed. Mr Barham was allowed interest from that date and a fair price for the labour of his Negroes, who would remain on the estate until their arrival in order to keep working. For every Chinese imported fewer than 500, Mr Barham would be allowed £20 and for every one which exceeded 500, he would be allowed an equal sum. Mr Barham engaged himself to subscribe 30,000 persons.

Notes

Introduction

1. Jamaican Assembly to Colonial Office, 14 November 1806, CO 137/121, 188.
2. All slaves who were either born in Jamaica or brought to Jamaica from the continent of Africa and forced into labour will be described as "enslaved Africans". The term will be used interchangeably with the term "Africans". For a summary of the recent debate on the reasons why Africans were chosen over other ethnicities for primarily forced labour, see David Eltis, *The Rise of African Slavery in the Americas* (Cambridge: Cambridge University Press, 2000), 1–28.
3. Colonial Office to Jamaican Assembly, January 1808, CO 137/121, 81–86.
4. Lowell J. Ragatz, *The Fall of the Planter Class in the British Caribbean, 1763–1833* (New York: The Century Company, 1928); Eric Williams, *Capitalism and Slavery* (Chapel Hill: University of North Carolina Press, 1944); Selwyn H.H. Carrington, *The British West Indies during the American Revolution* (Dordrecht: Foris Publications, 1988) (hereafter *American Revolution*); Selwyn H.H. Carrington, *The Sugar Industry and the Abolition of the Slave Trade, 1775–1810* (Gainesville: University Press of Florida, 2002). Other historians disagree with the theory of early decline and argue for a later decline from the effects of the 1807 Abolition Act; see Roger Anstey, *The Atlantic Slave Trade and British Abolition, 1760–1810* (London: Macmillan, 1975). Other prominent historians strongly support Anstey, including Seymour Drescher in *Econocide: British Slavery in the Era of Abolition* (Pittsburgh: University of Pittsburgh Press, 1977).
5. The term "planters" throughout this study refers to upper and middle managers. It includes those in England as absentees, and the steward managers in Jamaica such as overseers and bookkeepers who were responsible for the daily running of the plantations.
6. It is debatable which interest group first initiated amelioration: the West Indian planters or the British free traders. Carrington in *Sugar Industry* and J.R. Ward in *British West Indian Slavery, 1750–1834: The Process of Amelioration* (Oxford: Claren-

don Press, 1988), argue that it was the absentee planters from the 1760s. Heather Cateau in "Management and the Sugar Industry in the British West Indies, 1750–1810" (PhD diss., University of the West Indies, 1994) and Alvin O. Thompson in *Unprofitable Servants: Crown Slaves in Berbice, Guyana, 1803–1831* (Kingston: University of the West Indies Press, 2002), are very critical of the planters' motives and see their rhetoric of amelioration as pre-emptive. This study takes the position that despite its origins, amelioration was the cornerstone of British policy of reform for the British West Indian colonies by the 1790s.

7. The Colonial Office Papers are filled with examples of the British authorities complaining of the Jamaican planters' interpretation of gradual abolition. Both parties seemed to acknowledge that the gradual abolition of slavery was a goal, but what it meant and how it should be executed were not mutually agreed upon.

8. Douglas Hall, "Incalculability as a Feature of Sugar Production in the Eighteenth Century", *Social and Economic Studies* 10, no. 3 (1961): 340–52.

9. Williams, *Capitalism and Slavery*.

10. Barbara Solow, "Capitalism and Slavery in the Exceedingly Long Run", in *British Capitalism and Caribbean Slavery: The Legacy of Eric Williams*, ed. Barbara Solow and Stanley Engerman (Cambridge: Cambridge University Press, 1987).

11. See William Darity Jr, "The Williams Abolition Thesis before Williams", *Slavery and Abolition* 9, no. 1 (May 1988): 29–41; Carrington, *American Revolution*; Ward, *British West Indian Slavery*.

12. Drescher, *Econocide*; David Eltis, *Economic Growth and the Ending of the Transatlantic Slave Trade* (Oxford: Oxford University Press, 1987). Eltis agrees with Drescher and shows that Britain would have increased its colonial production by at least 24 per cent if it had not abandoned the slave trade. As a result of abolition, Britain stifled further economic expansion in its sugar colonies; Anstey, in *Atlantic Slave Trade*, agrees and argues that the ending of the slave trade was a result of a new evangelical doctrine of Christianity that emerged from the Enlightenment and which had tremendous concern for the individual rights of man.

13. Eugene Genovese, *The Political Economy of Slavery* (New York: Vintage Books, 1965), 221.

14. Rebecca Scott, "Explaining Abolition", in *Caribbean Slavery in the Atlantic World*, ed. Verene Shepherd and Hilary Beckles (Kingston: Ian Randle, 2000), 1, 101.

15. T. Roughley, *The Jamaica Planter's Guide* (London, 1823); Benjamin M'Mahon, *Jamaica Plantership* (London: Effingham Wilson, 1839).

16. "Seasoning" refers to the months of preparation for all new enslaved Africans in which they ought be prepared to take on the demands of slave labour. Dr Collins, *Practical Rules for the Management and Medical Treatment of Negro Slaves in the Sugar Colonies* (New York: Books for Libraries Press, 1971).

17. Edward Long, *The History of Jamaica* (London: Frank Cass, 1970), 1:435–56.

18. Bryan Edwards, *The History, Civil and Commercial, of the British Colonies in the West Indies*, vol. 2 (London: Stockdale, 1801), 180–81; William Dickson, *The Mitigation of Slavery* (London: Longman, 1814).
19. Lowell J. Ragatz, *The Old Plantation System in the British West Indies* (London: Bryan Edwards Press, 1925).
20. Ragatz, *Fall of the Planter Class*, 7–8. The other factors include the rivalry of newly exported tropical territories; adherence to a policy of restricted trade when it was no longer feasible; vicious fiscal legislation in the mother country; and around forty years of intermittent warfare.
21. Lowell J. Ragatz, "Absentee Landlordism in the British Caribbean, 1750–1833", *Agricultural History* 5 (1931): 7–24.
22. Carrington, *American Revolution*; Barbara Solow, *British Capitalism and Caribbean Slavery*. Two of the leading scholars who argue against early decline are Drescher, in *Econocide*, and Anstey, in *Atlantic Slave Trade*.
23. B.W. Higman, *Slave Population and Economy in Jamaica, 1807–1834* (Cambridge: Cambridge University Press, 1976).
24. Richard Dunn, "A Tale of Two Plantations: Slave Life at Mesopotamia in Jamaica and Mount Airy in Virginia, 1799–1828", in *An Expanding World: The European Impact on World History, 1450–1800*, vol. 18: *Plantation Societies in the Era of European Expansion*, ed. Judy Bieber (Aldershot: Variorum, 1997), 215–48; Michael Craton, "Death, Disease and Medicine on the Jamaican Slave Plantations: the Example of Worthy Park", in *Caribbean Slavery in the Atlantic World*; Kenneth F. Kiple and Virginia H. Kiple, "Deficiency Diseases in the Caribbean", *Journal of Interdisciplinary History* 11 (1980): 197–215.
25. Ward, *British West Indian Slavery*, 269–70.
26. Ibid., 261–62.
27. Cateau, "Management and the Sugar Industry".
28. Carrington, *Sugar Industry*.
29. Selwyn H.H. Carrington, "Management of Sugar Estates in the British West Indies at the End of the Eighteenth Century", *Journal of Caribbean History* 33, nos. 1–2 (1999): 30.
30. Ibid., 32–47.
31. B.W. Higman. *Plantation Jamaica, 1750–1850: Capital and Control in a Colonial Economy* (Kingston: University of the West Indies Press, 2005), 9–11.
32. Ibid.
33. John Campbell, "Managing Human Resources on a British West Indian Sugar Plantation, 1770–1834" (PhD diss., University of Cambridge, 1999).
34. David Ryden, "Producing a Peculiar Commodity: Jamaican Sugar Production, Slave Life, and Planter Profits on the Eve of Abolition, 1750–1807" (PhD diss., University of Minnesota, 1999), 34–35.

35. Ibid., 122–23.
36. Ibid., 124–25.
37. Ward, *British West Indian Slavery*, 263.
38. Thompson, *Unprofitable Servants*, 37. He argues that Ward only paid peripheral attention to the newer slave colonies. Furthermore, for Jamaica, from which he drew much of his statistical information, the period after 1807 witnessed more draconian measures being applied to enslaved Africans.

Chapter 1

1. Williams, *Capitalism and Slavery*; Carrington, *American Revolution*.
2. Adam Smith, *An Inquiry into the Nature and Causes of the Wealth of Nations* (1776; Reprint, New York: Modern Library, 1937).
3. Committee of West India Merchants and Planters (hereafter West India Committee Papers), April 1769–79, M915/Reel One, 7–8, 37. British West Indian merchants residing in London passed continuous resolutions in their general meetings to regain economic protection.
4. Ibid. The term "drawback" refers to the refunded duties granted to planters upon re-exportation of their original imported items.
5. Ibid., 14–15. The Ceded Islands were islands granted to Britain by France in 1763 as a result of the Peace of Paris. The islands were Dominica, St Vincent, Tobago, Grenada and the Grenadines.
6. Ibid., 25–26.
7. Ibid., 96.
8. Index of the West India Committee Papers, 96/2/12, Institute of Commonwealth Studies, London. The minutes of the August 1783 general meeting of planters and merchants were not microfilmed, as minutes of such meetings were only microfilmed after 1785.
9. Ibid., 176–82.
10. Ibid.
11. Ibid., 182–84. The term "bounty" refers to an incentive given to planters on exported items.
12. Ibid., 186.
13. Ibid., 184. Pitt's argument is that the measures were necessary to force the West Indians to restructure their plantations and thus become more efficient.
14. Ibid., 185.
15. Simon Taylor (hereafter Taylor) to Richard B. Taylor, 28 October 1801, Taylor Papers, 120/I/E/8.
16. Ibid., 7 October 1799, 120/I/C/26.
17. West India Committee Papers, 17 May 1791, 148.

18. Ibid.
19. Ibid., 30 June 1814, 318–21 and 23 February 1815, 333–42.
20. See CO 137/168, 1 August 1828, 77–78. This is the most glaring example as the island's agent, George Hibbert, was being petitioned to inform British officials how their contradictory free trade policy had encouraged the growth of foreign tobacco while completely destroying their attempts to increase their annual production of cigars for the British market.
21. Taylor to Roland Taylor, 9 October 1799, Taylor Papers, 120/I/C/26.
22. Taylor to Henry Shirley, February 1802, Taylor Papers, 120/I/E/26.
23. Ibid.
24. Shirley to John Sullivan, 3 April 1803, CO 137/110, 375–77.
25. Ward, *British West Indian Slavery*, 275.
26. Cateau, "Management and the Sugar Industry", 220–60.
27. Society for the Abolition of Slavery, 20 July 1790, Add. MS 21256, vols. 3, 5.
28. Ibid.; Carrington, *Sugar Industry*, 142.
29. Society for the Abolition of Slavery, 20 July 1790, Add. MS 21256, vols. 3, 5.
30. Earl of Camden to Lieutenant Governor Nugent, 1 August 1804, CO 137/112, 82–84.
31. Ibid., 85; Carrington, *Sugar Industry*, 204–5, shows that the cost of rearing a child to age fourteen cost around eighty pounds in the late eighteenth century. By 1785, rearing enslaved Africans became more expensive because the average price of a captive African surpassed eighty pounds.
32. Nugent to the Colonial Office, 30 August 1804, CO 137/112, 104.
33. Lord Castlereagh to the Duke of Manchester, 19 January 1808, CO 137/121, 81–84.
34. Ibid., 81; Williams, *Capitalism and Slavery*, 123. Williams also argues that Parliament had realized that the British West Indies had to become more efficient in their operations to outrival France. Thus, the abolition of slavery was to become their medicine, and they now had to look to the East Indies.
35. Private letter to Lord Wellington, 7 September 1814, Liverpool Papers, Add. MS 38416, 332–39.
36. James Stephens to Wellington, 7 September 1814, Liverpool Papers, Add. MS 38416, 340–41.
37. Ward, *British West Indian Slavery*; Michael Craton and James Walvin, *A Jamaican Plantation: The History of Worthy Park, 1670–1970* (London: W.H. Allen, 1970).
38. Cateau, "Management and the Sugar Industry", 222.
39. Ibid.
40. CO 139/50, 20 February 1801, 92.
41. CO 137/155, 28 June 1823, 18.
42. Ibid.
43. Ibid.

44. CO 137/169, 28 January 1829, 14.
45. Ibid., 10 February 1829, 83–90, 154. This allegation was made by a fellow white planter whose enslaved African was punished.
46. CO 137/162, 15 November 1825, 84–98.
47. CO 137/147, 8 October and 10 July 1814, 1–16.
48. Ibid.
49. CO 137/178, 8 April 1831, 160–63.
50. Ibid., 8 October 1829, 203–4.
51. Ibid., 2 November 1829, 253–56. This bill stated that all appointments of judges and their assistants in Jamaica should cease until a certain date, after which all new nominations by the governor and his assistant had to be candidates who were previously called to the Bar in England and practised in the Court of the King's Bench for a certain number of years. It also specified that there should be only one chief justice and the others should be assistants. They were all required to be present at all grand courts and to hear and determine all arguments for new trials, whether they arose in the same courts or the Courts of Assize. Furthermore, the chief justice or assistant judges could sit and form the several Courts of Assize. It stated that at each sitting of the Court of Assize there should be at least two such judges. CO/137/169, 17 November 1829, 253–56.
52. CO 137/173, 15 October 1830, 80.
53. Mary Turner, " 'The 11 o'clock Flog': Women, Work and Labour Law in the British Caribbean", in *Working Slavery, Pricing Freedom*, ed. Verene A. Shepherd (New York: Palgrave, 2001), 249–72.
54. The Jamaican governors of the late eighteenth and early nineteenth centuries constantly complained in their correspondence of the selfishness and stubbornness of the Jamaican planters. See, for example, CO 137/105, 217–20, which describes the difficult time that Lord Balcarres had in getting the Jamaican Assembly to accept Negro soldiers in 1801.
55. Nugent to the Colonial Office, 20 December 1803, CO 137/110, 294–95.
56. Manchester to the Colonial Office, 24 December 1823, CO 137/157, 494–95.
57. Mulgrave to Goderich, 4 August 1831, CO 137/179, 3.
58. Mulgrave to Goderich, 5 August 1832, CO 137/183, 19–20.
59. Ibid., 124.
60. Goderich to Mulgrave, December 1832, CO 137/183, 145.
61. Mulgrave to Goderich, 13 November 1832, CO/137/183, 359.
62. Ibid., 360.
63. Belmore to Goderich, 4 August 1831, CO 137/179, 2.
64. Ibid.
65. Belmore to Lord Hobart, CO/137/179, 21 November 1831, 349.
66. Ibid., CO/137/179, 3 December 1831, 386.

67. Mulgrave to Goderich, 7 October 1832, CO 137/183, 129–36.
68. See Michael Craton, *Testing the Chains* (Ithaca: Cornell University Press, 1984), 335. He gives a chronology of rebellions throughout the British West Indies from the seventeenth to the nineteenth centuries. Hilary Beckles, "The 200 Years War: Slave Resistance in the British West Indies: An Overview of the Historiography", *Jamaica Historical Review* (1982): 1–10. He argues that resistance is a common theme in Caribbean history from the time of the first Europeans.
69. Mary Turner, *Slaves and Missionaries: The Disintegration of Jamaican Slave Society, 1787–1834* (Urbana: University of Illinois Press, 1982), 48.
70. Goulburn Papers, 304/J/1. Fire initiated by the enslaved people is a common form of resistance in these papers.
71. CO 137/147, 1–81. This describes results of slave courts in twelve parishes between 1814 and 1818.
72. Turner, *Slaves and Missionaries*, 48.
73. Mulgrave to Goderich, 6 August 1832, CO 137/183, 20.
74. Committee of Correspondence to George Hibbert, 7 December 1824, CO 137/157, 47; Rodgers to Barham, 10 June 1824, Barham Papers, MS Clarendon Dep. c.358; Belmore to Goderich, 6 January 1832, CO 137/181, 29–33.
75. Belmore to Goderich, 6 January 1832, CO 137/181, 29–33.
76. Ibid., and 49.
77. Marquess of Sligo to the Colonial Office, 9 February 1835, CO 137/197, 370.
78. CO 137/189, 24 November 1833, 172–74.
79. Ibid.
80. Hugh Paget, in "The Free Village System in Jamaica", *Caribbean Quarterly* 3, no. 2 (1954): 40–51, argues that with more sensitive management from the planters, more of the Jamaican apprentices would have stayed on the plantations to work for the planters since their provision grounds were located on the estates.

Chapter 2

1. Higman, *Plantation Jamaica*; Higman, *Montpelier, Jamaica: A Plantation Community in Slavery and Freedom, 1739–1912* (Kingston: University of the West Indies Press, 1988). Higman further argues, in *Montpelier, Jamaica*, that by emancipation, absentee owners owned 540 of the 670 sugar plantations in Jamaica.
2. Ibid., 282. One person whom Higman refutes is Ragatz, "Absentee Landlordism in the British Caribbean". Ragatz identified this issue as pivotal to the continuing success of West Indian plantations.
3. See Andrew Arcedeckne vs. Beeston Long and Turner, 1821, Vanneck-Arcedeckne Papers, Vanneck-Arc/3F/5, 4–16; Goulburn Papers, 304/J/1/19–20. The attorney

Samson's alleged mismanagement of the Amity Hall plantation was stated by Frederick Goulburn and other plantation managers.

4. See Goulburn Papers, 304/J/1/19–20; Colonel John Phillips to Reverend G.W. Phillips, 5 November 1823, Tharp Papers, R.55.7.133 (1–26), 51; John Shand and Fearon to Lord Penrhyn, 15 May 1809 and 11 October 1809, Penrhyn Papers, MS 1505, 2–3.
5. See Herbert James to Crabb, 7 November 1834, Boucher-Crabb Papers; Arcedeckne vs. Beeston Long and Turner, 1821, Vanneck-Arc/3F/5, 4–16; Tharp Papers.
6. See A.E. Furness, Tharp Estate History, Cambridge County Office, Cambridge, and George Hibbert to William Tharp, 15 September 1830, Tharp Papers, R.55.7.128 (J).
7. See Thomas Samson, 1 June 1818, Goulburn Papers, 304/J/1/19, 1, 77; Taylor to Andrew Arcedeckne, 24 May 1811, Vanneck-Arc/3A/1811/1; Fearon to Penrhyn, 16 May 1806, Penrhyn Papers, MS 1423.
8. Colonel John Phillips to Reverend G.W. Phillips, 5 November 1823, Tharp Papers, R.55.7.133 (1–26), 51; William Rodgers to Joseph F. Barham, 15 December 1801, Barham Papers, b.33–38, 6; Plummer to Barham, 17 December 1801, Barham Papers, b.33–38.
9. Petition of the Jamaican assembly to Governor Mulgrave, 2 November 1832, CO 137/183, 368.
10. Ibid., 374.
11. Ibid., 384.
12. Carrington, *Sugar Industry*, 165–87.
13. Castlereagh to Manchester, 19 January 1808, CO 137/121, 81–84.
14. Henry Goulburn to Thomas Samson, 18 March 1801, , Goulburn Papers, 304/J/1/11, 7.
15. Long, *History of Jamaica*, 1:435.
16. Rodgers to Barham, 15 December 1801, Barham Papers, b.33–38, 6. Some plantations had two attorneys, such as those belonging to Barham and those managed by the Shand brothers (William and John). But even on such plantations, both managers were still absentees who occasionally visited, as they had other plantations to manage.
17. Plummer to Barham, 17 December 1801, Barham Papers, b.33–38.
18. Shand to George Watson Taylor, 11 May 1816/11, Taylor Papers, 120/V/III/B.
19. Vanneck-Arc, 26 May 1815, 3A/1813/2.
20. Simon Taylor, Taylor Papers, 120/V/III/B.
21. Shand to Thomas Graham, 11 September 1814, Penrhyn Papers, MS 1524.
22. Colonel John Phillips to Reverend G.W. Phillips, 5 November 1823, Tharp Papers, R.55.7.133 (1–26), 51.
23. Ibid.

24. R. Grant to Arcedeckne, 19 December 1818, Vanneck-Arc/3A/1818/1.
25. Higman, *Plantation Jamaica*, 67.
26. Taylor to Arcedeckne, 24 May 1811, Vanneck-Arc/3A/1811/1.
27. Ibid., 12 January 1812, 3A/1812/1.
28. Fearon to Penrhyn, 16 May 1806, Penrhyn Papers, MS 1423.
29. Taylor to David Reid, 10 March 1801, Taylor Papers, 120/I/D/53.
30. Carrington, *Sugar Industry*, 165–87.
31. Heather Cateau, "Beyond Planters and Plantations: The Negro Business" (paper presented at the Association of Caribbean Historians, Trinidad and Tobago, 2–6 April 2001), 10–11.
32. Ibid., 10.
33. James Daley to John Wemyss, 14 June 1823, Letterbook of John Wemyss, MS 250, 15.
34. Ibid., 16.
35. William Adlam to Wemyss, 26 February 1820, Letterbook of John Wemyss. He is listed as an overseer in 1820.
36. Mrs Boucher to Herbert James, 26 June 1834, Boucher-Crabb Papers, MS 377.
37. James to Crabb, 7 November 1834, Boucher-Crabb Papers, MS 377.
38. James to Crabb, 1 November 1834, Boucher-Crabb Papers, MS 377.
39. Ibid.
40. Mrs Boucher to R. Boucher, 3 August 1835, Boucher-Crabb Papers, MS 377.
41. Ibid.
42. Mrs Boucher to Crabb, 18 November 1835, Boucher-Crabb Papers, MS 377.
43. Higman, *Montpelier, Jamaica*.
44. Arcedeckne vs. Beeston Long and Turner, 1821, Vanneck-Arc/3F/5, 4.
45. Ibid., 5.
46. Ibid., 9; McCormack quoted from book 5, chapter 3 of Edwards.
47. Ibid., 13.
48. Ibid.
49. Ibid., 16.
50. Shand and Fearon to Penrhyn, 15 May 1809, 11 October 1809, Penrhyn Papers, MS 1505, 2.
51. Ibid.
52. Ibid., 3.
53. Ibid.
54. Patrick White to Barham, 21 July 1804, Barham Papers, b.33–38, 16.
55. Charles Campbell to Adam Fairclough, 20 August 1820, Tharp Papers, R.55.7.128, 1.
56. Steel and Hardyman to William Fairclough, 22 August 1816, Tharp Papers, R.55.7.128, 10.

57. Affidavit of John Tharp, 15 August 1821, Tharp Papers, R.55.7.133 (1–26), 34.
58. Plantation Accounts, 1835, Vanneck-Arc/3C/1835/1.
59. Long, *History of Jamaica*, 1:575.
60. Rodgers to Barham, 30 August 1825, Barham Papers, c.359.
61. Arcedeckne to Catherine Lambert, 19 June 1819, Vanneck-Arc/3F/4/2–3.
62. Lambert to Arcedeckne, 25 June 1819, Vanneck-Arc/3F/4/4–5.
63. Ibid., 4 August 1819, 3F/4/7.
64. Furness, Tharp Estate History.
65. Ann Tharp to William Green, 7 August 1802, Tharp Papers, R.55.7.128, 17.
66. Ibid., 1 March 1803, 19.
67. Ibid., 2 June 1803, 21.
68. Ibid., 10 August 1804, 26.
69. Ibid., 4 January 1804, 25.
70. Goulburn to Samson, 18 March 1801, Goulburn Papers, 304/J/1/11, 7.
71. Samson to Goulburn, 30 July 1806, Goulburn Papers, 304/J/1/13, 8.
72. Goulburn to Samson, n.d, Goulburn Papers, 304/J/1/9, 5.
73. All plantations had pens as adjunct entities to aid the sugar plantation in many ways and also to produce other forms of commodities, such as beef. To have a functional pen required more capital and more labour. However, if one adopted a policy of contraction, as Goulburn had done, one could do without a functional pen but would have to pay, nevertheless, other pens for services such as rearing additional cattle or having them rested and restored or even to buy beef when it was necessary at market value. Goulburn to Samson, 3 August 1813, Goulburn Papers, 304/J/1/19(1), 25.
74. Mair to Madam, 1 May 1802, Goulburn Papers, 304/J/1/8, 7a; 23 December 1802, 304/J/1/8; 20; Richards to Goulburn, 5 September 1818, Goulburn Papers, 304/J/1/20, 3.
75. Samson to Goulburn, 1 April 1814, Goulburn Papers, 304/J/1/19(1), 38.
76. Ward, *British West Indian Slavery*, 93. Ward argues that the failure of the Jamaicans to contract rather than expand their agricultural production in the late eighteenth century was one of the reasons for their decline in the early nineteenth century (91). He shows that Barbados was forced to contract in the late eighteenth century and as a result benefited in the early nineteenth century (62–64).
77. Carrington, *Sugar Industry*, 121. He discusses the many dependent variables which constitute the complexity of the British West Indian sugar industry.
78. Higman, *Slave Population and Economy*, 102.
79. Susannah Goulburn to Henry Goulburn, n.d., Goulburn Papers, 304/J/1/18, 1.
80. Samson to Goulburn, 19 November 1802, 304/J/1/8, 18; 27 January 1803, 304/J/1/9, 2; 1 July 1803, 304/J/1/9, 8.
81. Samson to Goulburn, 10 September 1803, Goulburn Papers, 304/J/1/9, 9.

82. Ibid., 6 November 1804, 304/J/1/11, 13. The remainder of the debt owed was mainly to Kingston merchants: Messrs. Dick Mgall & Co., £721.3.8 and £600.13.8, respectively.
83. Ibid., 10 April 1802, 304/J/1/8. One Mr Mair, a neighbouring planter who was recommended by Susannah Goulburn to run the plantation, informed her that Samson had an average of thirty jobbers being used on the plantation, who were paid a high salary of three shillings and four pence per day. He denied later to Henry Goulburn that he had so many jobbers: 304/J/1/14, 12 September 1807, 10. The other expenses were £1178 for cattle, £580.25.7 for lumber, £280.28.9 for wharfage, £54.8.5 for Irish supplies, £181.21.9 for the balance carried forward from 1806 and the remainder for salaries.
84. Ibid., 11 October 1805, 304/J/1/12, 12.
85. Ibid., 28 April 1813, 20 July 1813, 304/J/1/19(1), 17, 33.
86. Ibid., 25 October 1814, 42.
87. Ibid., 12 January 1815, 46.
88. Ibid., 27 May 1814, 40. He complained that he could not find enslaved Africans to buy; thus, he had to resort to his usual hired labourers.
89. Ibid., 22 February 1816, 60.
90. Ibid., 9 January 1818, 14 March 1819, 304/J/1/19(1).
91. Ibid., 1 June 1818.
92. Ibid., 9 January 1821, 304/J/1/20, 18.
93. Ibid., 5 September 1818, 304/J/1/20, 5.
94. Ibid., 20 September 1811, 304/J/1/18, 7.
95. Ibid., 304/J/1/24, 60.
96. Cateau, "Beyond Planters and Plantations", 9.
97. Goulburn to Samson, 1 June 1818, Goulburn Papers, 304/J/1/19(1), 77.
98. Furness, Tharp Estate History.
99. Hibbert to Tharp, 15 September 1830, Tharp Papers, R.55.7.128 (J).
100. Ibid., 3 May 1831.
101. Ibid. Deficiency Laws were laws that required plantations to have a certain number of whites residing on a plantation in relation to enslaved Africans. This was a security initiative to discourage the prevalence of enslaved resistance. Plantations that breached the law were charged a fine as a means of discouraging the practice.
102. Ibid., 5 January 1831.
103. Ibid., 6 June 1832.
104. Ibid., 1 May 1833.
105. Furness, Tharp Estate History. He estimates that the yearly average of sugar produced from 1795 to 1800 was around 1,500 hogsheads.
106. McPherson to Goulburn, Goulburn Papers, 304/J/1/24, 56–58.
107. Vanneck-Arc/3C/1803/11.

108. Arcedeckne vs. Beeston Long and Turner, 1821, Vanneck-Arc/3F/1821/5.
109. Vanneck-Arc/3C/1835–1838/1.
110. A. Norcott to governor, 1 December 1834, CO 137/194, 5.
111. John Nelson Bond to governor, 1 December 1834, CO 137/194, 6–7.
112. Higman, *Slave Population and Economy*. Higman argues that declining production was multifaceted and examines the role of a declining enslaved population as one of the contributing factors to economic decline. However, this study argues that the prevention of a declining enslaved population was a component of plantation management. Thus, the planters cannot be fully absolved.
113. Carrington, *Sugar Industry*, 137.

Chapter 3

1. U.B. Phillips, "A Jamaica Slave Plantation", *American Historical Review* 19, no. 3 (April 1914): 550.
2. Ibid., 556–57.
3. Ibid., 557.
4. Ibid., 550–51.
5. Craton and Walvin, *Jamaican Plantation*, 173.
6. Gangs were work groups of field slaves organized by planters primarily based on age and relative strength. Thus the strongest and healthiest group of slaves constituted the first gang, and the less strong and healthy field slaves composed the second and third gangs. The strength and health of each gang largely determined their daily tasks on the plantation; the hardest work was reserved for the strongest and most healthy.
7. Craton, "Death, Disease and Medicine", 805.
8. Ibid.
9. Craton and Walvin, *Jamaican Plantation*, 168–69; B.W. Higman, *Jamaica Surveyed: Plantation Maps and Plans of the Eighteenth and Nineteenth Centuries* (Kingston: Institute of Jamaica Publications, 1988), 102.
10. Craton and Walvin, *Jamaican Plantation*, 169.
11. Ibid., 186. See also 185–88. Rose Price was related to all of his executors as a result of his marriage to Diane Elizabeth Lambert. Charles, the Earl of Talbot was his brother-in-law, while John Talbot and Henry Lord Viscount were the sons of Charles and thus his nephews. Lord Baron Sherburne was the uncle of Rose Price as a result of his marriage.
12. Deeds Transfer and Assignment of Securities, 14 October 1812, Island Record Office (IRO) 618/191, 191; Rose Price to his children, 27 January 1817, IRO 665/31, 31.
13. Deeds Transfer and Assignment of Securities, 14 October 1812, IRO 618/191, 191.

14. Price to his children, 27 January 1817, 665/31, 31–34; Craton and Walvin, *Jamaican Plantation*, 187.
15. List of Apprentices, 1836, Worthy Park Plantation Books, Jamaica Archives, 4/23/7.
16. Will of Sir Rose Price, 28 November 1834, IRO 116/11; Craton and Walvin, *Jamaican Plantation*, 185, 188.
17. Richard Carter to Price, 17 May 1817, IRO 658/215.
18. Worthy Park Plantation Books, 4/23/4, 280–81.
19. Ibid., 278–79.
20. Worthy Park Plantation Book, 1792–96, AC 4035, Library of Congress.
21. Craton and Walvin, *Jamaican Plantation*, 201.
22. Ibid., 187, 205.
23. "Pen" (sometimes spelled "penn") was the Jamaican term used for a cattle ranch.
24. Craton and Walvin, *Jamaican Plantation*, 174–77.
25. Worthy Park Plantation Book, 1811–17, 4/23/4.
26. Worthy Park Plantation Book, 20 October 1792, AC 4035, 38.
27. Ibid., 46–47.
28. Worthy Park Plantation Books, 7 November 1836, 4/23/7.
29. Craton and Walvin, *Jamaican Plantation*, 175, 201.
30. Long, *History of Jamaica*, 2:435.
31. Of the three time periods after 1800 for which data was available for table 3.5 and figure 3.3, the second period, 1821–24, was the only period in which the ages of death were not always shown in the plantation journals. For example, in 1821, the ages of 2 of the 12 deceased were not recorded and in 1822, the ages of 9 of the 20 deceased were not recorded. Of the 63 deceased for the 1821–24 period, only 11 ages were not recorded. This means that the findings of the 1821–24 time period would not have been significantly different, as its conclusions were similar to that of the other two periods, for which full information was given.
32. Craton, "Death, Disease and Medicine", 799. Craton, in his later work on Worthy Park, shows that the main causes of death between the years 1795 and 1838 were old age and debility.
33. Carrington, *Sugar Industry*, 202–5.
34. Taylor to George Hibbert, 8 January 1807, Taylor Papers, 120/I/1, no. 6; Samson to Goulburn, 18 January 1806, Goulburn Papers, 304/J/1/13, 1; Grant to Barham, 10 April 1809, Barham Papers, c.358. Stephen Fuller to the Colonial Office, "Two Reports from the Jamaican House of Assembly", 1788, highlights the opinion of various medical practitioners.
35. Fuller, "Two Reports from the Jamaican House of Assembly", 31.
36. Ibid., 32. Examples of abortion can be seen in other plantation papers, such as those of Goulburn, Barham and Penrhyn.
37. Ibid.

38. Craton, "Death, Disease and Medicine", 796.
39. Most plantations had children's gangs in addition to the traditional three gangs, for the purpose of assimilating children into plantation life and culture. They would often perform lighter plantation tasks, such as weeding grass for cattle and picking up trash. On most occasions they would be under the supervision of older, superannuated slaves.
40. Slave List of the Worthy Park Plantation, 1824, Worthy Park Plantation Book, 4/23/5.
41. Slave List of the Worthy Park Plantation, 1836, Worthy Park Plantation Book, 4/23/7.
42. Ibid.
43. Ibid.
44. Worthy Park Plantation Book, 1792–96, AC 4035, 44.
45. Carrington, *Sugar Industry*, 146.
46. Worthy Park Plantation Book, 1821–24, 4/23/5, 5.
47. Worthy Park Plantation Book, 1792–96, AC 4035, 1.
48. Ibid., 44.
49. Worthy Park Plantation Book, August–December 1792, AC 4035, 38–40.
50. Ibid., 42–43.
51. Worthy Park Plantation Book, 1791–1811, 4/23/3.
52. Craton and Walvin, *Jamaican Plantation*, 172–73.
53. Worthy Park Plantation Books, Vestry Accounts, AC 4035 and 4/23/4.
54. CO 441/4/4, nos. 3–4, 5–7.
55. Craton and Walvin, *Jamaican Plantation*, 171–72.
56. Ibid., 171.
57. Ryden, "Producing a Peculiar Commodity", 114.
58. Ibid., 128.
59. Ibid., 114; B.W. Higman, "The Spatial Economy of Jamaican Sugar Plantations: Cartographic Evidence from the Eighteenth and Nineteenth Centuries", *Journal of Historical Geography* 13 (1987): 26.
60. Craton and Walvin, *Jamaican Plantation*, 191.
61. Worthy Park Manumission Records, Jamaica Archives, 1B/11/6/19. Over the seventy volumes containing the information, three volumes could not be seen, as they were badly damaged.
62. Worthy Park Plantation Book, 1830–37, 4/23/6.
63. Ibid.
64. Manumission Records, Jamaica Archives, 1B/11/6/23, 152; IRO 632/249.
65. Ibid., 1B/11/6/23, 152; IRO 632/249.
66. Worthy Park Plantation Book, 1821–24, 4/23/5; IRO 728/188.
67. Worthy Park Plantation Book, 1830–37, 4/23/6.

68. Bygrave to Price, 18 December 1824, IRO 728/190.
69. Worthy Park Plantation Book, 1837, 4/23/7, 19.
70. Governor of Jamaica to the Colonial Office, CO 137/184, 4.
71. Worthy Park Plantation Book, 1838, 4/23/7, 24, 27.
72. CO 441/4/4, nos. 3, 5.
73. Craton and Walvin, *Jamaican Plantation*, 188–91.

Chapter 4

1. Wedderburn and Grant to Barham, 25 February 1806, Barham Papers, b.33–38, 20.
2. Ibid.
3. Samson to Susannah Goulburn, 5 March 1802, Goulburn Papers, 304/J/1/8, 4.
4. Ibid., 3 September 1802, 21.
5. Ibid., 15 December 1803, 304/J/1/10, 14.
6. Ibid., 12 January 1804, 304/J/1/11, 2.
7. Ibid., 23 January 1805, 304/J/1/12, 10a.
8. Ibid., 30 July 1804, 304/J/1/11, 7.
9. Carrington, *Sugar Industry*, 176.
10. Rodgers to Barham, 25 September 1801, Barham Papers, b.33–38, 4–5.
11. Sam Jefferies and Rodgers to Barham, 12 November 1805, Barham Papers, b.33–38, 19.
12. John Webb to Barham, 30 September 1801, Barham Papers, b.33–38, 5.
13. Ibid.
14. Webb to Barham, 14 August 1816, Barham Papers, c.358, 38.
15. Grant and Blyth to Barham, 14 October 1816, Barham Papers, c.358, 39.
16. Fearon to Penrhyn, 8 October 1804, Penrhyn Papers, MS 1343.
17. Fearon to George Pennant, 7 January 1805, Penrhyn Papers, MS 1361.
18. Carrington, *Sugar Industry*, 186.
19. Rodgers to Barham, 17 February 1826, Barham Papers, c.359.
20. Ibid.
21. Slave List for King's Valley Estate, 1806, Penrhyn Papers, MS 1455.
22. Slave List for King's Valley Estate, 1808, Penrhyn Papers, MS 1477.
23. David Ewart to Pennant, n.d., Penrhyn Papers, MS 1477.
24. Radnor Plantation Journal, MS 180, 2.
25. Ibid.
26. Ibid., 107.
27. Rodgers to Barham, 11 March 1825, Barham Papers, c.359.
28. Blyth to Barham, 11 April 1819, Barham Papers, c.358.
29. Ibid., 17 October 1819. 56 of the 104 enslaved Africans were accustomed to working on coffee plantations and thus were not accustomed to working in the lowlands on

a sugar plantation. In addition, Mesopotamia's attempt to purchase many young African women to encourage a natural population increase meant that they also had to take a number of older women as well (Blyth to Barham, 9 June 1823, Barham Papers, c.358).
30. Ibid.
31. Rodgers to Barham, 3 June 1825, Barham Papers, c.359.
32. Ibid., 18 February 1825.
33. Shand to Arcedeckne, 16 July 1814, Vanneck-Arc/3A/1814/1.
34. Fearon to Pennant, 7 January 1805, Penrhyn Papers, MS 1361.
35. Samson to Goulburn, 1 April 1814, Goulburn Papers, 304/J/1//19(1), 38.
36. Adlam to Wemyss, 7 December 1819, Hermitage Estate Book, MS 250, 1–2.
37. Ibid., 2.
38. Ibid., 3.
39. Ibid., n.d., 11–12.
40. Ibid., 1 February 1824, 19.
41. Webb to Barham, 30 September 1801, Barham Papers, c.357.
42. Grant to Barham, 3 September 1814, Barham Papers, c.358.
43. Ibid., 14 October 1816, c.358.
44. Ibid., 15 June 1818, c.358.
45. Ibid., c.361, 1816/17.
46. Plantation Accounts, Penrhyn Papers, MS 1529–77.
47. Ibid.
48. Mair to Susannah Goulburn, 10 April 1802, Goulburn Papers, 304/J/1/8, 7a. Mulattoes, however, could cost as much as £200 per person; Attorney Falconer in 1805 was willing to pay as much to obtain his two female mulattoes (Fearon to Pennant, 13 August 1805, Penrhyn Papers).
49. Samson to Goulburn, 27 May 1814, Goulburn Papers, 304/J/1/19(1), 40.
50. In 1814, Moreland estate in Vere, one of the plantations to which he often referred, produced 355 hogsheads of sugar, while Amity Hall produced only 309.
51. Samson to Goulburn, 24 February 1815, 47.
52. Ibid., 6 October 1815, 54.
53. Ibid., 28 March 1816, 61.
54. Ibid., 16 October 1817, 69.
55. Ibid., 12 April 1818, 76 and 9 July 1818, 81.
56. Ibid., 1 June 1818, 77.
57. Nugent to the Colonial Office, 30 August 1804, CO 137/112, 104.
58. Samson to Goulburn, 7 August 1802, 304/J/1/8, 12. Susannah Goulburn complained that runaways were at about 20 to 25 at one time, which was without precedence on the island. This cost the plantation over £750 a year, not including the cost of paying men to catch them (n.d, 304/J/1/8, 1).

59. Ibid, 4 October 1804, 304/J/1/11, 14.
60. Radnor Plantation Journal, MS 180, 6.
61. Samson to Goulburn, 18 January 1806, 28 April 1813 and 29 September 1827, Goulburn Papers. Other plantation papers, such as the Barham Papers, make a similar argument.
62. Ibid.
63. Genovese, *Political Economy of Slavery*, 23, 53, 181, 275.
64. Merchant to Barham, 1 July 1806, Barham Papers, b.33–38.
65. Colonel Mc Cawley to Barham, n.d., Barham Papers, c.366.
66. Ibid., 6.
67. Task work was the allocation of specific tasks by a planter to a group of enslaved Africans. At the end of a task, the planter would provide compensation to the enslaved Africans. Generally, the enslaved Africans worked at their own pace; however, if they were hired for a task they usually worked at a faster pace to complete it quickly so as to be compensated sooner.
68. In *Mitigation of Slavery*, Dickson indicates that such an experiment was done in Barbados by a planter and was successful; House of Commons, "Report from Select Committee on the Extinction of Slavery throughout the British Dominions", *Parliamentary Papers*, vol. 20 (721), 1832. Some Jamaican planters admitted that task work would have been a better system of labour and that a few planters who had attempted it had found it to be better.
69. Barham Papers, n.d., c.366.
70. Island estate contained 3,200 acres of land and 200 enslaved Africans. The plantation produced 270 hogsheads of sugar per year but it was believed that with sufficient labour, it could produce 350 to 400 hogsheads. There was also a tract of fine wooded land which if settled would produce 250 or 300 hogsheads more. The aforementioned number of Chinese was judged to be fully adequate to achieve this. It was also judged that Island could be adapted for the cultivation of rice, a favourite Chinese food. The estate had a water mill and was situated at the head of Black River, which was for the greater part navigable.
71. Morris to Barham, 5 November 1822, Barham Papers, c.358.
72. Ibid., 10 February 1821.
73. G. Gilbert to governor, 21 October 1823, CO 137/155, 64. Gilbert was the bookkeeper for the New Yarmouth plantation in the parish of Vere, and he wrote to the governor as a concerned citizen regarding amelioration.
74. Long, *History of Jamaica*, 2:410–11.
75. Grant and Blyth to Barham, 7 March 1825, Barham Papers, c.359.
76. Rodgers to Barham, 25 August 1804, Barham Papers, c.357.
77. Grant and Wedderburn to Barham, 10 August and 4 September 1809, Barham Papers, c.357.

78. Ibid., 11 August 1809.
79. Ibid., 16 March 1813.
80. Fearon to Pennant, 1807, Penrhyn Papers, MS 1484.
81. Ewart to Pennant, 10 January 1808, Penrhyn Papers, MS 1495.
82. Ibid., 14 April 1808 MS, 1499.
83. Ira Berlin and Philip D. Morgan, *The Slaves' Economy: Independent Production by Slaves in the Americas* (London: Frank Cass, 1991). The concept of negotiation between masters and slaves has become popular in the historiography and has led to the conclusion by some historians that the enslaved Africans had become contented with slavery.
84. Crop Accounts for Pepper and Bona Vista Pens, 26 August 1837.
85. Salmon to Crabb, 15 August 1836, Boucher-Crabb Papers, MS 377.
86. Ibid., 14 June 1836.
87. Ibid.
88. Ibid.

Chapter 5

1. Ward, *British West Indian Slavery*; Higman, *Slave Population and Economy*.
2. B.W. Higman, *Slave Populations of the British Caribbean, 1807–1834* (Baltimore: Johns Hopkins Press, 1984), 308–11; Ward, *British West Indian Slavery*; Richard Sheridan, *Doctors and Slaves: A Medical and Demographic History of Slavery in the British West Indies, 1680–1834* (Cambridge: Cambridge University Press, 1985).
3. Higman, *Slave Populations*, 311.
4. Higman, *Slave Populations*; Ward, *British West Indian Slavery*; Sheridan, *Doctors and Slaves*.
5. Richard Sheridan, "Strategies of Slave Subsistence: The Jamaican Case Reconsidered", in *From Chattel Slaves to Wage Slaves*, ed. Mary Turner (Kingston: Ian Randle Publishers, 1995), 64.
6. "Marginal" in this context means that not only were they geographically located in the mountains, but they were also rocky and primarily infertile.
7. Sheridan, "Strategies of Slave Subsistence", 64.
8. Mary Turner, "Slave Workers, Subsistence and Labour Bargaining: Amity Hall, Jamaica, 1805–1832" in *The Slaves' Economy: Independent Production by Slaves in the Americas*, ed. Ira Berlin and Philip Morgan (London: Frank Cass, 1991), 93–94.
9. Ibid.
10. Ibid.
11. Higman, *Slave Populations*, 349–55.
12. Ward, *British West Indian Slavery*, 90–91.
13. Ibid., 267.

14. See the following plantation papers: Goulburn, Barham and Tharp. Other plantation papers in which there is less frequent communication amply support these plantation papers. Such papers include Vanneck-Arcedeckne, Hermitage, Radnor and Worthy Park.
15. Fearon to Penrhyn, 14 July 1804, Penrhyn Papers, MS 1327, 1.
16. Ibid., 12 May 1808, MS 1501.
17. Shand to Pennant, 4 June 1814, Penrhyn Papers, MS 1518.
18. Plummer to Barham, 9 February 1802, Barham Papers, b.33–38.
19. Ibid., 27 April 1802.
20. Ibid., 7 January 1803.
21. Ibid., 31 July 1803.
22. Webb to Barham, 10 June 1807, Barham Papers, b.33–38.
23. Jefferies, Grant and Blyth to Barham, 6 April 1802 and 26 April 1817, b.33–38, c.358.
24. Samson to Susannah Goulburn, 5 June 1802, Goulburn Papers, 304/J/1/8, 10. The figure eighty might on the one hand be an exaggeration, as in a December correspondence it was learned that some of the enslaved Africans were feigning a fever as a form of resistance to Samson. It seems unlikely, however, as this report was sent in June and the correspondence between June and December makes no mention of so many enslaved Africans being sick.
25. Rodgers to Barham, 30 May and 3 August 1802, Barham Papers, b.33–38.
26. Grant and Blyth to Barham, 26 May 1817 and 15 June 1818, Barham Papers, c.358.
27. Plummer and Webb to Barham, 31 July and 4 August 1802, b.33–38.
28. Morris to Barham, 9 June 1826, c.359.
29. Ewart to Penrhyn, 6 August 1807, Penrhyn Papers, MS 1477.
30. Shand to Pennant, 6 November 1815, MS 1542, 1555.
31. Shand to Watson Taylor, 6 November 1815, Taylor Papers, 120/V/III/B/4.
32. Sheridan, *Doctors and Slaves*, 13.
33. Ibid.; Higman, *Slave Populations*; Craton, "Death, Disease and Medicine"; Kiple and Kiple, "Deficiency Diseases".
34. Higman, *Slave Populations*, 272; Craton, "Death, Disease and Medicine", 803.
35. Sheridan, *Doctors and Slaves*, 41, 70.
36. Ibid.
37. Higman, *Slave Populations*; Craton, "Death, Disease and Medicine"; Ward, *British West Indian Slavery*, 285; Sheridan, *Doctors and Slaves*.
38. Higman, *Slave Populations*, 347; Craton, "Death, Disease and Medicine", 805; Ward, *British West Indian Slavery*, 285.
39. Shand to Pennant, 26 October 1814, 1527, Penrhyn Papers.
40. Ibid.
41. Taylor to Hibbert, 8 January 1807, Taylor Papers, 120/I/I/6.
42. Ibid.

43. Ibid.
44. Taylor to Reid, 10 March 1801, Taylor Papers, 120/I/D/53.
45. Ibid.
46. Taylor to Hibbert, 18 June 1807, Taylor Papers, 120/I/I/29.
47. CO 137/161, 6 June 1825, 91.
48. CO 137/144, 9, 31 December 1816.
49. Ibid., 7.
50. Ibid., 3.
51. Higman, *Slave Populations*, 267.
52. Plummer to Barham, 16 March 1803, b.33–38.
53. Grant and Wedderburn to Barham, 11 August 1810 and 14 July 1811, Barham Papers, c.358.
54. Shand to Taylor, 7 October 1815/3, Taylor Papers, 120/VIII/B/3.
55. Richard Harris to Watson Taylor, 5 March 1818, Taylor Papers, 120/VIII/D/14.
56. Sheridan, "Strategies of Slave Subsistence", 61–62.
57. See Amity Hall Papers; Taylor Papers.
58. Jefferies to Barham, 2 April 1802, Barham Papers, b.33–38.
59. Rodgers to Barham, 4 July 1801, Barham Papers, b. 33–38.
60. Grant and Blyth to Barham, 19 October 1912, Barham Papers, b.33–38.
61. Ibid., 2 January 1810 and 13 November 1815.
62. Watson Taylor to Shand, 2 November 1815, Taylor Papers, 120/VIII/A/3.
63. Ibid., 6 May 1818/12.
64. Shand to Watson Taylor, 16 September 1815, Taylor Papers, 120/VIII/B/2.
65. Ibid., 31 March 1816, 9.
66. P. Ford and G. Ford, eds., *A Guide to British Parliamentary Papers*. (Shannon: Irish University Press, 1972), 7–8, 40.
67. Higman, *Slave Population and Economy*, 102.
68. Ibid.; Sheridan, "Strategies of Slave Subsistence", 32. He also discusses the overall natural increases in the parish of Vere.
69. As early as 1673, Vere was separated from the parish of Clarendon. In the Counties and Parishes Act of the *Laws of Jamaica*, 23 April 1867, Vere was returned to the parish of Clarendon.
70. Ford, *British Parliamentary Papers*, 13.
71. Ibid., 40.
72. Ibid., 19.
73. Frederick Goulburn to Henry Goulburn, 22 February 1818, Goulburn Papers, 304/J/1/20, 3.
74. Richards to Henry Goulburn, 12 July 1817, Goulburn Papers, 304/J/1/20, 2.
75. Frederick Goulburn to Henry Goulburn, 22 February 1818, Goulburn Papers, 304/J/1/20, 3.

76. Fearon to Penrhyn, 16 March 1805, Penrhyn Papers, MS 1366, n.p.
77. Frederick Goulburn to Henry Goulburn, 22 February 1818, Goulburn Papers, 304/J/1/20, 3.
78. Ibid.
79. Higman, *Slave Population and Economy*, 71.
80. Ibid., 72.
81. See Barbara Bush, *Slave Women in Caribbean Society, 1650–1838* (Kingston: Heinemann Caribbean, 1990); Hilary Beckles, *Natural Rebels: A Social History of Enslaved Black Women in Barbados* (New Brunswick, NJ: Rutgers University Press, 1989).
82. Taylor to Hibbert, 8 January 1807, Taylor Papers, 120/1/1/6.
83. Ibid.
84. Grant and Wedderburn to Barham, 11 August 1810, Barham Papers, c.358.
85. Rodgers to Barham, 16 April 1802, Barham Papers, b.33–38.
86. Ibid., 5 July and 22 September 1802.
87. Grant and Blyth to Barham, 10 April 1809, 16 June 1809 and 13 October 1817, c.358, c.358.
88. Ewart to Penrhyn, 6 August 1807, Penrhyn Papers, MS 1477.
89. Fearon to Penrhyn, 30 October 1804, Penrhyn Papers, MS 1349; Ibid., 8 December 1804, MS 1355.
90. Penrhyn Plantation Accounts, Kupius, 1576, Coates Pen, 1578.
91. Fearon to Penrhyn, 8 December 1804, Penrhyn Papers, MS 1355.
92. Ewart to Penrhyn, 6 August 1807, Penrhyn Papers, MS 1477.
93. Ibid.
94. This law stipulated that the enslaved Africans be given twenty-six free days per year, excluding all Sundays. In non-crop time they were also to be given Saturdays. During crop time, however, they were to receive two Saturdays for themselves.
95. Blyth to Barham, 14 September 1814, Barham Papers, c.358.
96. Ibid.
97. Ibid.
98. Ibid.
99. Morris to Barham, 26 December 1814, Barham Papers, c.358.
100. Ibid.
101. Ibid.
102. Rodgers to Barham, 5 August 1925, Barham Papers, c.359; Morris to Barham, 13 September 1825, Barham Papers, c.359.
103. Morris to Barham, 13 September 1825, Barham Papers, c.359.
104. Parliamentary Report, 721, 1831–32, in Ford Ford, *Guide to British Parliamentary Papers*, 25.
105. Ibid., 27–28.
106. Ibid., 38.

107. William Wilberforce to Barham, 26 August 1806, Barham Papers, c.366.
108. Barham to Wilberforce, n.d., Barham Papers, c.366.

Chapter 6

1. Higman, *Slave Population and Economy* and *Plantation Jamaica*.
2. Higman, *Slave Population and Economy*, 221.
3. Ibid., 221–22.
4. Ward, *British West Indian Slavery*, 261; Rebecca Scott, *Slave Emancipation in Cuba: The Transition to Free Labor, 1860–1899* (Princeton: Princeton University Press, 1985); Veront Satchell, "Steam for Sugar-Cane Milling: The Diffusion of the Boulton and Watt Stationary Steam Engine to the Jamaican Sugar Industry, 1809–1830", in *Jamaica in Slavery and Freedom*, ed. Kathleen Monteith and Glen Richards (Kingston: University of the West Indies Press, 2002), 242.
5. Long, *History of Jamaica*, 1:435.
6. Satchell, "Steam for Sugar-Cane Milling", 242.
7. Ibid., 243.
8. Fearon to Penrhyn, 14 July 1804, Penrhyn Papers, MS 1327, 4–5.
9. Ibid., 4 August 1804, MS 1329, 5.
10. Ibid., 9 February 1805, MS 1361.
11. Ibid., 7 January 1805, MS 1361. When he tried the rotative mill then at Denbigh for half an hour, it twisted its shaft, which united the cogwheel to its rotors.
12. Ibid., 16 March 1805, MS 1366.
13. Ibid., 25 April 1806, MS 1422.
14. Shand to Pennant, 23 April 1815, MS 1534.
15. Veront Satchell, "The Early Use of Steam Power in the Jamaican Sugar Industry, 1768–1810", in *Caribbean Slavery in the Atlantic World*, 524.
16. Satchell, "Steam for Sugar-Cane Milling", 247.
17. Fearon to Penrhyn, 4 October 1806, Penrhyn Papers, MS 1435.
18. Ibid.
19. Satchell, "The Early Use of Steam Power", 524.
20. Fearon to Penrhyn, 4 October 1806, Penrhyn Papers, MS 1435.
21. Fearon to Penrhyn, 16 May 1806, Penrhyn Papers, MS 1423.
22. Ibid.
23. Carrington, *Sugar Industry*, 160.
24. Satchell, "Steam for Sugar-Cane Milling", 248–49.
25. Shand to Watson Taylor, 2 November 1815 and 16 May 1818, Taylor Papers, 120/VIII/A/3, 12.
26. Ibid., 4 November 1818, 120/VIII/D/17.

27. William Shand to Watson Taylor, n.d., Taylor Papers, 120/VIII/E/2.
28. William Shand to Watson Taylor, n.d., Taylor Papers, 120/VIII/E/3. In this letter, the word "mill" is used. This most likely refers to a steam engine, since the plantation had one by 1815 and Shand wrote of having this "mill" repaired to take off the crop of 1818.
29. Samson to Goulburn, 10 December 1803, Goulburn Papers, 304/J/1/10, 6a–13; 15 October 1813 and 10 February 1814, 304/J/1/19(1), 3, 35–36.
30. Ibid., 9 June 1815, 51.
31. Ibid., 12 December 1817, 72–74.
32. Richards to Goulburn, 8 May 1819, Goulburn Papers, 304/J/1/20, 17.
33. Ashley to Goulburn, 18 August 1832, Goulburn Papers, 304/J/1/23, 2.
34. Bayley to Goulburn, 12 March 1825, 3 March 1826 and 7 February 1830, 304/J/1/21, 1, 17, 105.
35. Verene Shepherd, "Trade and Exchange in Jamaica in the Period of Slavery" in *Caribbean Slavery in the Atlantic World*, 355; Sheridan, "Strategies of Slave Subsistence", 13–14.
36. Carrington, *Sugar Industry*. He credits the American Revolution as the watershed moment for the beginning of British West Indian decline.
37. Petition of the Jamaican Assembly, n.d., CO 137/134, 278.
38. Kathleen Monteith, "The Coffee Industry in Jamaica" (MA thesis, University of the West Indies, 1991), 270.
39. Grant and Blyth to Barham, 10 February 1821, Barham Papers, c.358; Morris to Barham, 6 May 1823, Barham Papers, c.358.
40. Morris to Barham, 6 May 1823, Barham Papers.
41. Ibid., 10 December 1823.
42. Ibid., 7 August 1824 and 13 October 1825, Barham Papers, c.359.
43. Ibid., 15 February 1825, Barham Papers, c.359.
44. Monteith, "The Coffee Industry in Jamaica", 152–60.
45. Ibid., 18.
46. Petition of the Jamaican Assembly, n.d., CO 137/134, 178.
47. S.D. Smith, "Sugar's Poor Relation: Coffee Planting in the British West Indies, 1720–1833", *Slavery and Abolition* 19, no. 3 (December 1988): 68–89.
48. Monteith, "The Coffee Industry in Jamaica", 106–7.
49. Jamaican House of Assembly Letterbook, 1B/5/13, 455. In a list of coffee settlements in fourteen parishes (there were no returns from three parishes), St Elizabeth had the second highest number of coffee plantations, with sixty-three. They were behind St Ann with seventy-two. St Elizabeth thus has to be considered a coffee parish.
50. Ewart to Penrhyn, 10 January 1808, Penrhyn Papers, MS 1495.
51. Ibid.
52. Samson to Goulburn, 22 June 1808, 304/J/1/15, 8.

53. Ibid.
54. Rodgers to Barham, 30 August 1825 and 17 February 1826, Barham Papers, c.359.
55. Grant and Blyth to Barham, 11 August 1810 and 31 December 1816, Barham Papers, c.359.
56. Ibid., 4 September 1809.
57. Mesopotamia was offered between eight and ten pounds per ton for logwood; in 1805, a coffee estate in St Catherine was paid eleven pounds per ton for 24.5 tons total (Letterbook of William Jovett, 23 April 1805, Letter 28). In 1817, Denbigh was paid seven pounds per ton (Denbigh Plantation Account, 1817, Penrhyn Plantations, 1558).
58. Webb to Barham, 8 February 1809, Barham Papers, c.358.
59. Morris to Barham, 15 February 1825, Barham Papers, c.359.
60. Rodgers to Barham, 11 March 1825, c.359.
61. Ibid.
62. Committee of Correspondence to Hibbert, 1 August 1828, CO 137/168, 77.
63. Ibid., 77–78.
64. Ibid., 145.
65. Verene Shepherd, "Pens and Pen-keepers in a Plantation Society, 1740–1845" (PhD diss., University of Cambridge, June 1988), 1.
66. Ibid., 53–54.
67. Plantation Accounts, 1833, Vanneck-Arc/3C/1833/1.
68. Ibid., 3C/1835/1. The crop accounts for both plantations in the Jamaica Archives give yearly accounts of the economic relationship between them.
69. Fearon to Penrhyn, 14 July 1804, Penrhyn Papers, MS 1327, 2–6.
70. Ibid., 16 May 1806, MS 1423.
71. Webb to Barham, 28 August 1805, Barham Papers, b.33–38.
72. Blyth to Barham, 9 June 1823, Barham Papers, c.358.
73. Rodgers to Barham, 30 August 1825, Barham Papers, c.359.
74. Fearon to Lord Penrhyn, 14 July 1804, MS 1327; Armstrong to Lord Penrhyn, 31 October 1807, MS 1485.
75. Davidson and Graham to Lord Penrhyn, 3 June 1816, MS 1544.
76. McCormack to Arcedeckne, 12 October 1823, Vanneck-Arc/3A/1823/1. Fifty-six gallons of rum are equivalent to one hogshead, and one puncheon of rum is equivalent to 240 gallons.
77. Shand to Pennant, 14 January and 11 March 1815, Penrhyn Papers, MS 1530, 1532.
78. Samson to Goulburn, 1 July 1803, 304/J/1/10, 7.
79. Ibid., 3 May 1808, 29 July 1808 and 7 January 1812, 2, 6–9.
80. Ibid., 28 April 1813, 18.
81. Hibbert to Governor of Jamaica, 9 June 1825, CO 137/161, 93–94.
82. Lord Auckland to Lord Bathurst, 1 August 1825, CO 137/161, 302.

83. Morris to Barham, 15 February 1825, Barham Papers, c.359.
84. Grant and Blyth to Barham, 4 May 1821, Barham Papers, c.358; Ewart to Penrhyn, 10 January 1808, Penrhyn Papers.
85. Fearon to Penrhyn, 16 May 1806, MS 1423.
86. Crop Accounts of Penrhyn Plantations, 1B/11/4, Jamaica Archives.

Epilogue

1. Manchester to Earl of Bathurst, 15 September 1825, CO 137/160, 131–37.
2. These external factors included the American Revolution and its impact on trade, including rising overhead costs for the British West Indian planters; the change in economic doctrine of the British government towards free trade and the implications of this for British West Indian sugar; the preference of London industrialists and the British government for the cheaper East Indies sugar; and a reduction in the British West Indians' drawback and bounties.
3. Smith, *Wealth of Nations*.
4. D.J. Murray, *The West Indies and the Development of Colonial Government* (Oxford: Clarendon Press, 1965), 109–26.
5. Ibid.
6. Ibid., 151.
7. Ibid., 145.
8. A.E. Furness, introduction to the Tharp Estate Papers, Cambridge University Library.
9. Hibbert to Tharp, 6 June 1832, Tharp Papers, R.55.7.128 (J).
10. Douglas Hall, "Incalculability as a Feature of Sugar Production during the Eighteenth Century", *Social and Economic Studies* 10, no. 3 (1961): 340.
11. Carrington, *Sugar Industry*, 258.
12. Ibid.
13. Selwyn H.H. Carrington, "Statistics for the Study of Caribbean History during the Eighteenth and Nineteenth Centuries" (manuscript).
14. The other measures were the abolition of the Sunday markets, the promotion of marriage among the enslaved population, an end to enslaved Africans being sold as public debts and an end to the breaking up of enslaved families.
15. Governor to Peter Hulme, 24 June 1837, Diary of John Hulme, circular 1028, reel 420/1.
16. Ibid.
17. Ibid., 28 September 1836, circular 99.
18. Diary of Frederick White, 3–9 August 1834, reel 481, 13.

Selected Bibliography

Primary Sources

British Library, London

Huskisson Papers. Add. MSS 38734–70. These offer vital information on British policy.

Liverpool Papers. Add. MSS 38416. These offer important information on British policy and on trade.

Long, Edward. Manuscript copies of *History of Jamaica* with corrections and additions. Add. MSS 12402–4.

Society for the Abolition of Slavery. Minutes. Add. MS 21256. Vol. 3. 1790–1806. These contain discussion and strategies to be employed in passing the 1807 Abolition Act.

Institute of Commonwealth Studies, University of London

Committee of West India Merchants and Planters. Minutes. West India Committee Papers. M915/Books 1–12. 1769–1832. These papers discuss the strategies, concerns and opinions of the absentee planters in Great Britain in relation to British economic policies and their effects on their plantations.

Island Record Office, Jamaica

Deeds. Nos. 507–740. 1803–26.
Wills. Nos. 79–116. 1808–34.

Jamaica Archives, Spanish Town

Accounts Produce (Crop Accounts). 1B/11/4/Nos. 28–81. 1800–1838. These contain the actual items produced yearly on absentee-owned plantations. The following plantations were examined: Worthy Park, Thomas River, Kupius, Denbigh, Coates Pen, Mesopotamia, Island, Golden Grove, Bachelor's Hall, Pantre Pant, Potosi, Lansquinet,

Wales, Covey, Merrywood, Good Hope, Chippenham Park, Radnor, Hermitage, Amity Hall, Bog, Brazilleto, Pepper and Bona Vista.
Jamaica. House of Assembly. Journals. Committee of Correspondence Minute Book. 1B/5/12. 1795–1846. Correspondence between the Jamaican Assembly and their agent in Great Britain.
Jamaica. House of Assembly. Journals. Letterbook. 1B/5/13. 1794–1800.
Worthy Park Manumission Records. 1B/11/6/19–64. 1792–1828. These contain data on the volume and nature of manumissions at Worthy Park.
Worthy Park Plantation Book. AC 4035, Library of Congress. 1792–96.
Worthy Park Plantation Books. 4/22–23. Books 4–7. These contain plantation accounts and other relevant information for the following years: 1783–87, 1787–91, 1791–1811, 1798–99, 1811–17, 1821–24 and 1813–38.

National Library of Jamaica, Kingston

House of Commons. "Report from Select Committee on the Extinction of Slavery throughout the British Dominions: With the Minutes of Evidence, Appendix and Index". *Parliamentary Papers*, Vol. 20 (721). 1832.
Letterbook of John Wemyss. Hermitage Estate Book. 1819–1824. MS 250. This describes the problem of management and inadequate labour on a coffee plantation.
Letterbook of William Jowett Titford, MD. 1802–1807. Diary of a young white apprentice working on a coffee plantation. MS 1900.
Radnor Plantation Journal. 1821–1826. MS 180. This includes the daily tasks of the various gangs on a coffee plantation.

Plantation Papers, United Kingdom

Barham Papers. Clarendon Deposit, b.33–38, c.357–366, 375–378, 381, 386, 388–389, 428. Bodleian Library, Oxford. These letters between Sir Joseph Foster Barham and his estate managers contain information and problems related to nineteenth-century plantation management.
Goulburn Papers. Acc. 319, 426. Surrey Record Office, Kingston upon Thames. This contains correspondence regarding plantation activities, policy problems and concerns between the years 1800 and 1838.
Penrhyn Papers. 1233–1593. University College of North Wales Library, Bangor. This contains letters from Richard Pennant, Lord Penrhyn on all aspects of plantation management.
Taylor Papers. 120/I/B–H (1798–1807) and 120/VIII/A–E (1815–19). Institute of Commonwealth Studies, London. These letters discuss the effects of the 1807 Abolition Act, the Registry Bill, health, technology and plantation management.
Tharp Papers. R.55.7.121–133. Cambridge Record Office, Cambridge. These letters high-

light the internal conflicts among plantation owners, merchants and their estate managers in Jamaica.

Vanneck-Arcedeckne Papers. Boxes 1/4, 1/23–24, 2/33, 37, 56–59, 60. Cambridge University Library, Cambridge. These letters highlight the internal conflicts between plantation managers, owners and merchants.

Colonial Office Papers, Public Record Office, Kew Gardens

CO 137/105–214. Correspondence between the Colonial Office and Jamaica. 1800–1836.
CO 138/35, 138/38. Entry Books of Commissions, Instructions and Correspondences.
CO 139/50, 139/52A. Acts passed by the Jamaican Assembly.
CO 441/4/4. Nos. 1–4. Worthy Park Maps.

University of the West Indies Library, Kingston

Hulme, Dr John Rhodes. Special Magistracy Papers under the Abolition of Slavery Act, 1833. Hanover, Jamaica, 1832–38. MR 420.
Pepper and Bona Vista Estate Books.
White, Frederick. Diary of Frederick White, a Magistrate in Jamaica, August 1, 1834–February 8, 1835. MR 481.

Secondary Material

Anstey, Roger. *The Atlantic Slave Trade and British Abolition, 1760–1810*. London: Macmillan, 1975.
Ashton, T.S. *An Economic History of England: The Eighteenth Century*. London: Methuen, 1955.
Aufhauser, Fitzroy, "Slavery and Technological Change". *Economic History Review* 34 (1974): 36–50.
Barham, Joseph Foster. *Considerations of the Abolition of Negro Slavery and the Means of Practically Effecting It*. London: J. Ridgway, 1823.
Beckles, Hilary McD. *Natural Rebels: A Social History of Enslaved Black Women in Barbados*. New Brunswick, NJ: Rutgers University Press, 1989.
———. "The 200 Years War: Slave Resistance in the British West Indies: An Overview of the Historiography". *Jamaica Historical Review* (1982): 1–10.
Berlin, Ira, and Philip D. Morgan, eds. *The Slaves' Economy: Independent Production by Slaves in the Americas*. London: Frank Cass, 1991.
Brathwaite, Edward Kamau. "Caliban, Ariel, and Unprospero in the Conflict of Creolization: A Study of the Slave Revolt in Jamaica in 1831–32". In *Caribbean Slavery in the Atlantic World*, edited by Verene Shepherd and Hilary Beckles. Kingston: Ian Randle, 2000.

———. *The Development of Creole Society in Jamaica, 1770–1820*. Oxford: Clarendon Press, 1971.

Breeden, James O., ed. *Advice among Masters: The Ideal in Slave Management in the Old South*. Westport, CT: Greenfield Press, 1980.

Bush, Barbara. *Slave Women in Caribbean Society, 1650–1838*. Kingston: Heinemann Caribbean, 1990.

Campbell, John. "Managing Human Resources on a British West Indian Sugar Plantation, 1770–1834". PhD diss., University of Cambridge, 1999.

Campbell, Mavis. *The Dynamics of Change in a Slave Society*. London: Associated University Presses, 1976.

Carrington, Selwyn H.H. *The British West Indies during the American Revolution*. Dordrecht: Foris Publications, 1988.

———. "Management of Sugar Estates in the British West Indies at the End of the Eighteenth Century". *Journal of Caribbean History* 33, nos. 1–2 (1999): 27–53.

———. *The Sugar Industry and the Abolition of the Slave Trade, 1775–1810*. Gainesville: University Press of Florida, 2002.

Cateau, Heather. "Management and the Sugar Industry in the British West Indies, 1750–1810". PhD diss., University of the West Indies, 1994.

Cateau, Heather, and Selwyn H.H. Carrington, eds. Capitalism and Slavery *Fifty Years Later: Eric Eustace Williams – A Reassessment of the Man and His Work*. New York: Peter Lang, 2000.

Collins, Dr. *Practical Rules for the Management and Medical Treatment of Negro Slaves in the Sugar Colonies, by a Professional Planter*. New York: Books for Libraries Press, 1971.

Craton, Michael. "Death, Disease and Medicine on Jamaican Slave Plantations: The Example of Worthy Park". In *Caribbean Slavery in the Atlantic World*, edited by Verene Shepherd and Hilary Beckles. Kingston: Ian Randle, 2000.

———. *Empire, Enslavement and Freedom in the Caribbean*. Kingston: Ian Randle, 1997.

———. "Jamaican Slave Mortality: Fresh Light from Worthy Park, Longville and the Tharp Estates". *Journal of Caribbean History* 3 (1971): 1–27.

———. *Sinews of Empire: A Short History of British Slavery*. New York: Anchor Books, 1974.

Craton, Michael, Alvin James and David Wright. *Slavery, Abolition and Emancipation*. London: Longman, 1976.

Craton, Michael, and James Walvin. *A Jamaican Plantation: The History of Worthy Park, 1670–1970*. London: W.H. Allen, 1970.

Crafts, N.F.R. *British Economic Growth during the Industrial Revolution*. Oxford: Clarendon Press, 1985.

Deer, Noel. *The History of Sugar*. 2 vols. London: Chapman and Hall, 1949.

Dickson, William. *The Mitigation of Slavery*. London: Longman, 1814.

Drescher, Seymour. *Econocide: British Slavery in the Era of Abolition*. Pittsburgh: University of Pittsburgh Press, 1977.

Dunn, Richard. "Dreadful Idlers in the Cane Fields: The Slave Labor Pattern on a Jamaican Sugar Estate, 1767–1831". *Journal of Interdisciplinary History* 17 (1987): 795–822.

———. "A Tale of Two Plantations: Slave Life at Mesopotamia in Jamaica and Mount Airy in Virginia, 1799 to 1828". *William and Mary Quarterly* 34 (1977): 32–65.

Edwards, Bryan. *The History, Civil and Commercial, of the British Colonies in the West Indies, 1793–1891*. Vol. 2. London, 1801.

Eltis, David. *Economic Growth and the Ending of the Transatlantic Slave Trade*. Oxford: Oxford University Press, 1987.

Ford, P., and G. Ford, eds. *A Guide to British Parliamentary Papers*. 3rd ed. Shannon: Irish University Press, 1972.

Fortune, Stephen. *Merchants and Jews: The Struggle for British West Indian Commerce, 1650–1750*. Gainesville: University Press of Florida, 1984.

Fraginals, Manuel Moreno. *The Sugarmill: The Socioeconomic Complex of Sugar in Cuba, 1760–1860*. New York: Monthly Review Press, 1976.

Franklin, John H. *Runaway Slaves: Rebels on the Plantation*. New York: Oxford University Press, 1998.

Genovese, Eugene. *The Political Economy of Slavery*. New York: Vintage Books, 1965.

Goldin, Claudia Dale. "The Economics of Emancipation". *Journal of Economic History* 33 (1973): 66–85.

Goveia, Elsa V. *Slave Society in the British Leeward Islands at the End of the Eighteenth Century*. New Haven: Yale University Press, 1965.

Grainger, James, M.D. *An Essay on the more Common West-India Diseases; and the Remedies which that Country Itself Produces: to which are added some hints on the Management, etc., of Negroes*. Edinburgh, 1802.

Grant, Hugh F. *Planter Management and Capitalism in Antebellum Georgia: The Journal of Hugh Fraser Grant, Ricegrower*. Edited by Albert V. House. New York: Columbia University Press, 1954.

Hall, Douglas. "Absentee Proprietorship in the British West Indies to about 1850". *Jamaican Historical Review* 4 (1964): 15–35.

———. "Incalculability as a Feature of Sugar Production in the Eighteenth Century". *Social and Economic Studies* 10, no. 3 (1961): 340–52.

Heuman, Gad J. *Between Black and White: Race, Politics and the Free Coloreds in Jamaica, 1792–1865*. Westport, CT: Greenwood Press, 1981.

Higman, B.W. *Montpelier, Jamaica: A Plantation Community in Slavery and Freedom, 1739–1912*. Kingston: University of the West Indies Press, 1998.

———. *Plantation Jamaica, 1750–1850: Capital and Control in a Colonial Economy*. Kingston: University of the West Indies Press, 2005.

———. *Slave Population and Economy in Jamaica, 1807–1834*. London: Cambridge University Press, 1976.

———. *Slave Populations of the British Caribbean, 1807–1834*. Baltimore: Johns Hopkins University Press, 1984.

———. "The Spatial Economy of Jamaican Sugar Plantations: Cartographic Evidence from the Eighteenth and Nineteenth Centuries". *Journal of Historical Geography* 13 (1987): 17–39.

———. "The West India Interest in Parliament, 1807–1833". *Historical Studies* 13 (1967): 1–19.

Hunt, E.K. *History of Economic Thought: A Critical Perspective*. 2d ed. New York: HarperCollins, 1992.

Jordan, G.W. *An Examination of the Principles of the Slave Registry Bill*. London: T. Cadwell and W. Davies, 1816.

Kiple, Kenneth F., and Virginia H. Kiple. "Deficiency Diseases in the Caribbean". *Journal of Interdisciplinary History* 11 (1980): 197–215.

———. "Slave Child Mortality: Some Nutritional Answers to a Perennial Puzzle". *Journal of Social History* 10 (1977): 284–309.

Klingberg, Frank J. *The Anti-Slavery Movement in England*. New Haven: Yale University Press, 1926.

Knight, Franklin W., ed. *General History of the Caribbean*. Vol. 3. London: UNESCO, 1997.

———. *Slave Society in Cuba During the Nineteenth Century*. Madison: University of Wisconsin Press, 1970.

Lascelles, Edwin, et al. *Instructions for the Management of a Plantation in Barbados and for the Treatment of Negroes*. London, 1786.

Lewis, Matthew. *Journal of a West India Proprietor, 1775–1818*. New York: Oxford University Press, 1999.

Lindsey, Jean. "The Economic and Social Development of the Pennant Estates in Jamaica". *Caernarfonshire Historical Society Transactions* 44 (1983): 59–96.

Long, Edward. *The History of Jamaica*. Vols. 1–2. London, 1774. Reprinted, London: Frank Cass, 1970.

Look Lai, Walton. *Indentured Labor, Caribbean Sugar: Chinese and Indian Migrants to the British West Indies, 1838–1918*. Baltimore: Johns Hopkins University Press, 1993.

Mahon, Benjamin. *Jamaica Plantership*. London: Effingham Wilson, 1839.

Management and Labor Legislation in the Plantation Industry. Malaysia: Incorporated Society of Planters, 1978.

McDonald, Roderick A. *The Economy and Material Culture of Slaves*. Baton Rouge: Louisiana State University Press, 1993.

———, ed. *West Indies Accounts: Essays on the History of the British Caribbean and the Atlantic Economy*. Kingston: University of the West Indies Press, 1996.

Mellor, G.R. *British Imperial Trusteeship, 1783–1850*. London: Faber and Faber, 1926.

Metzer, Jacob. "Rational Management, Modern Business Practices and Economies of Scale in the Antebellum Southern Plantations". *Explorations in Economic History* 12 (1975): 253–70.

Mintz, Sidney W., and Douglas Hall. *The Origins of the Jamaican Internal Marketing System.* Papers in Caribbean Anthropology 1, no. 57 (New Haven: Department of Anthropology, 1960).

Monteith, Kathleen E.A. "The Coffee Industry in Jamaica, 1790–1850". MA thesis, University of the West Indies, 1991.

———. "The Labour Regimen on Jamaican Coffee Plantations during Slavery". In *Jamaica in Slavery and Freedom: History, Heritage and Culture*, edited by Kathleen E.A. Monteith and Glen Richards. Kingston: University of the West Indies Press, 2002.

Morgan, Philip D. "Work and Culture: The Task System and the World of Lowcountry Blacks, 1700–1880". *William and Mary Quarterly* 39 (1982): 563–99.

Murray, D.J. *The West Indies and the Development of Colonial Government, 1801–1834.* Oxford: Clarendon Press, 1965.

Parry, John H. "Plantation and Provision Ground: An Historical Sketch of the Introduction of Food Crops into Jamaica". *Revista de Historia de America* 39 (1955): 1–20.

Patterson, Orlando. *The Sociology of Slavery: An Analysis of the Origins, Development and Structure of Negro Slave Society in Jamaica.* London: MacGibbon and Kee, 1967.

Peloso, Vincent. *Peasants on Plantations: Subaltern Strategies of Labor and Resistance in the Pisco Valley, Peru.* Durham, NC: Duke University Press, 1999.

Phillips, Ulrich Bonnell. *American Negro Slavery.* Baton Rouge: Louisiana State University Press, 1966.

———. "A Jamaica Slave Plantation". *American Historical Review* 19, no. 3 (April 1914): 543–58.

Pinckard, George. *Notes on the West Indies.* 3 vols. London: Longman, 1806.

Pitman, Frank W. *The Development of the British West Indies, 1700–1763.* Hamden, CT: Archon Books, 1967.

Pringle, J. *The Fall of the Sugar Planters of Jamaica with Remarks on their Agricultural Management and on the Labour Question in that Island.* London: Trubner, 1869.

Ragatz, Lowell J. "Absentee Landlordism in the British Caribbean, 1750–1833". *Agricultural History* 5 (1931): 7–24.

———. *The Fall of the Planter Class in the British Caribbean, 1763–1833.* New York: The Century Company, 1928.

———. *The Old Plantation System in the British West Indies.* London: Bryan Edwards Press, 1925.

Roughley, T. *The Jamaica Planter's Guide.* London, 1823.

Ryden, David. "Producing a Peculiar Commodity: Jamaican Sugar Production, Slave Life, and Planter Profits on the Eve of Abolition, 1750–1807". PhD diss., University of Minnesota, 1999.

Satchell, Veront. "The Early Use of Steam Power in the Jamaican Sugar Industry, 1768–1810". In *Caribbean Slavery in the Atlantic World*, edited by Verene Shepherd and Hilary Beckles. Kingston: Ian Randle, 2000.

———. "Innovations in Sugar-Cane Mill Technology in Jamaica, 1760–1830". In *Working Slavery, Pricing Freedom: Perspectives from the Caribbean, Africa and the African Diaspora*, edited by Verene A. Shepherd. New York: Palgrave, 2001.

———. "Steam for Sugar-Cane Milling: The Diffusion of the Boulton and Watt Stationary Steam Engine to the Jamaican Sugar Industry, 1809–1830". In *Jamaica in Slavery and Freedom: History, Heritage and Culture*, edited by Kathleen E.A. Monteith and Glen Richards. Kingston: University of the West Indies Press, 2002.

Scarborough, William K. *The Overseer: Plantation Management in the Old South*. Baton Rouge: Louisiana State University Press, 1966.

Shepherd, Verene. "Livestock and Sugar: Aspects of Jamaica's Agricultural Development from the Late Seventeenth to the Early Nineteenth Century". In *Caribbean Slavery in the Atlantic World*, edited by Verene Shepherd and Hilary Beckles. Kingston: Ian Randle, 2000.

———. "Pens and Pen-keepers in a Plantation Society, 1740–1845". PhD diss., University of Cambridge, 1988.

———. "Trade and Exchange in Jamaica in the Period of Slavery". In *Caribbean Slavery in the Atlantic World*, edited by Verene Shepherd and Hilary Beckles. Kingston: Ian Randle, 2000.

Sheridan, Richard. *Doctors and Slaves: A Medical and Demographic History of Slavery in the British West Indies, 1680–1834*. Cambridge: Cambridge University Press, 1985.

———. *Sugar and Slavery: An Economic History of the British West Indies, 1623–1775*. Bridgetown, Barbados: Caribbean Universities Press, 1974.

———. " 'Sweet Malefactor': The Social Costs of Slavery and Sugar in Jamaica and Cuba, 1807–54". *Economic History Review* 29 (1976): 236–57.

———. "The West India Sugar Crisis and British Slave Emancipation, 1830–1833". *Journal of Economic History* 21 (1961): 539–51.

Simmonds, Lorna. " 'That Little Shadow of Property and Freedom': Urban Slave Society in Jamaica, 1780–1834". PhD diss., University of the West Indies, 1997.

Smith, Adam. *An Inquiry into the Nature and Causes of the Wealth of Nations*. 1776. Reprint, New York: Modern Library, 1937.

Solow, Barbara, ed. *Slavery and the Rise of the Atlantic System*. Cambridge: Cambridge University Press, 1991.

Solow, Barbara, and Stanley Engerman, eds. *British Capitalism and Caribbean Slavery: The Legacy of Eric Williams*. Cambridge: Cambridge University Press, 1987.

Thompson, Alvin O. *Unprofitable Servants: Crown Slaves in Berbice, Guyana, 1803–1831*. Kingston: University of the West Indies Press, 2002.

Turner, Mary, ed. *From Chattel Slaves to Wage Slaves: The Dynamics of Labour Bargaining in the Americas*. Kingston: Ian Randle, 1995.

Ward, J.R. *British West Indian Slavery, 1750–1834: The Process of Amelioration*. Oxford: Clarendon Press, 1988.

Williams, Eric. "The British West Indian Slave Trade after Its Abolition in 1807". *Journal of Negro History* 27 (1942): 175–91.

———. *Capitalism and Slavery*. Chapel Hill: University of North Carolina Press, 1944.

———. *From Columbus to Castro: The History of the Caribbean, 1492–1969*. New York: Vintage Books.

Index

Note: The letters *f*, *t* and *n* indicate that the entry refers to a figure, a table or a note, respectively.

abolition, 4
   in the British West Indies generally, 5–6
   in Cuba, 5
   emancipation and, 2, 9
   in Haiti, 18
Abolition Act, 1–2, 9, 11, 178
   Barham, Joseph Foster, and, 114
   Chinese labour and, 114
   economic costs of, 133
   economic motives for, 1, 4–10
   impact of, 11–31
   Jamaican assembly reaction to, 18, 34
   Jamaican planter class resistance to, 2, 20
   labour scarcity and, 94–95, 109, 133
   lack of economic impact from, 19, 153
   literature about, 4–10
   Lord Castlereagh's reaction to, 18
   plantation management reform and, 1–3, 18, 32–33, 147
   political context of, 25–31
   purposes of, 76
   rebellions and, 29–30
   social context of, 16–24
abolitionist movement, 4, 27. *See also* African Institution
abortions, 185
"Absentee Landlordism in the British Caribbean, 1750–1833" (Ragatz), 6
absentee owners, 2–10, 32–33, 35–44, 47, 50–51, 62, 65, 71, 92–93, 95, 105, 112, 122, 135–36, 141, 150, 152, 178–79, 193nn5–6, 199n1
Adlam, William, 40, 108–9
Admiralty Court, 56
African Institution, 17, 19
Alligator Pond, 165, 168
amelioration, 2, 6, 8, 10, 14, 16–17, 20, 24, 25, 31, 33–34, 86, 114, 178–79, 181, 185, 193n6
American Revolution, 122, 180
Amity Hall plantation, 10, 50–56, 52*f*, 53*t*, 65, 99*t*, 105, 108, 111–13, 123–24, 144–45, 147, 155, 159, 161, 161*t*, 165, 175, 184*f*
Antigua, 152
apprentices, 31, 43, 61–62, 89, 90, 101, 101*t*, 118–19, 186–87
Apprenticeship period, 28, 31, 43, 61–62, 70, 90, 116, 118, 186
Arcedeckne, Andrew, 38, 44–45, 48–49, 69, 105
arrowroot, 104, 171, 176
Arthur Seat plantation, 69, 74
Association of West India Planters and Merchants, 12, 184
attorneys, 8–10, 14, 32–33, 36–40, 43–44, 47, 53, 58, 70–71, 92, 112, 116–17, 122–24, 134, 136, 140–41, 148–49, 151, 161, 179, 200n16

230 Index

Bachelor's Hall Pen, 44, 171
Bahamas, 21
Barbados, 7, 52, 120, 121, 143, 152
Barham, Joseph Foster, 10, 36, 47, 77, 93–95, 103–5, 114, 116–17, 123, 136, 140–41, 148, 152, 162–65, 166t, 168, 172, 191
Beadington estate, 187
beans, 85, 86t
Beckles, Hilary, 147
beef, 48, 63, 83, 84f, 141, 171, 202n73
Benjamin, Henry, 190
Berbice, 120
Bermuda, 23
Black River, 165
black troops, 126
Blair, John, 69, 71
Blyth, John, 103–4
Board of Arts and Sciences, 157
Board of Trade and Plantations, 169–70, 176
Bog Estate, 146t, 147, 155
Bogue, 114
Bolt, Edward, 189
Bonthorn, Mr, 108
Boucher, Mrs, 42
Boucher, R., 42, 118
Boulton and Watt of Birmingham, 154, 159
Braitsford, James, 90
Braitsford, Thomas, 90
Brazeletto, 146t
"breeding" babies, 148
breeze mill, 160
Britannia, The, 171
British Guiana, 154
British policy, 14, 16, 140, 169, 180, 193n6
British sugar refiners, 12, 180
British West Indian Slavery, 1750–1834 (Ward), 7
Bullock, William, 69, 134
Burrowfield Pen, 125
Bush, Barbara, 147
Buxton, Foxwell, 142

Buxton, Sir Thomas, 58

Camden, Earl of, 17–18
Campbell, John, 8–9
cane fields, 3, 70, 121, 124, 155
cane fires, 123
cane holes, 62, 72f, 93–95, 110, 144–45, 151–53, 186
Capitalism and Slavery (Williams), 4
Carpenter's Mountain, 50, 55, 165
Carrington, Selwyn H.H., 7–8, 11, 34, 62, 77, 184f, 186t
Cateau, Heather, 7, 16–17, 20, 40
cattle, 51, 103–4, 161
cattle mills, 153, 156–59, 161
Cedar Grove plantation, 42–44
Ceded Islands, 12
Ceylonese workers, 176
Charles, the Earl of Talbot, 66, 68
chiggers, 133
children's gangs, 80, 82, 97, 101, 206n39
Chinese labour, 114–16, 152, 191, 209n70
Christmas, 30, 83, 100, 107t, 118, 141–42
Christmas Rebellion, 153
cigars, 168–70, 197n20
Clarendon, 37, 94, 142, 144, 170, 189
Coates Pen, 166t, 171, 176
cocoa, 124
Cocoree, 69, 87
coffee, 9, 40–42, 50–52, 98, 104, 107–9, 113, 116, 118–19, 125, 134, 135t, 143, 161–65, 169, 170–71, 176, 179, 207n29
Collins, Dr, 5
Colonial Church Union, 27, 30
Colonial Office, 1, 17, 21, 22t, 23, 25, 29t, 50, 90, 180–81, 189
Committee of West Indian Merchants and Planters, 14, 185
Committee on the Extinction of Slavery, 142, 151
Conran, Henry, 21–22
Consolidated Slave Laws, 16, 20, 113, 117, 136, 150, 178, 185–86, 190
Continental Blockade, 163

corn, 51–52, 56, 63, 85, 85*f*, 86*t*, 88*t*, 91, 93, 98, 102, 112, 117–18, 124, 145, 128*t*, 142, 245, 154–55
cornmeal, 140, 145, 154
Cornwall, 43, 103, 172, 189
cotton, 119, 161
Council of Protection, 190
Court of Chancery, 33, 42, 44–45, 54, 57
Courts of Assize, 24, 43, 189, 198n51
Crabb, Mr, 42
Craggs, Mr, 54
Craton, Michael, 63–64, 71, 80, 82, 86–87, 89, 91, 126–27
Creoles, 25, 74, 121, 153
crop accounts, 86, 174
Cuationes, 132
Cuba, 5, 21, 23, 168
culture of neglect, 18
Cummings, Susannah, 90
custodes, 26

Dale, Susana, 90
Daley, James, 40
Darnity, William, Jr, 4
Deficiency Laws, 58, 203n101
Demerara-Essequibo, 120
Denbigh, 110, 155–58, 158*t*, 165, 166*t*, 171
Derry and Russell pens, 68
disease theory, 126
division of Africans, 96*t*, 99*t*, 100*t*
Dominica, 12
Douglas, Ann, 90
Drescher, Seymour, 4
droughts, 85, 93, 117, 123–24, 140
Dry Gully, 87

Econocide: British Slavery in the Era of Abolition (Drescher), 4
Edwards, Bryan, 5–6, 116
elephantiasis, 132
Ellis, 36
enslaved Africans, 2–10, 11, 14–16, 20–21, 29, 137*t*, 138*f*
  ages of, 73*t*, 80–81, 109*f*, 205n31

birth rates of, 9, 105, 148
child care of, 1, 18, 128*t*, 131
cost of maintaining, 11, 78*t*
death rates of, 9, 64, 73*t*, 75*t*, 76*f*, 121, 126
Europeanization of, 114
fertility rates, 4, 63–64, 73–74, 73*t*, 121, 149
gender and, 147–52
health management of, 1, 18, 35, 73, 122–147
health of, 74*t*, 95–103, 122–53
illegal importation of, 9
infant mortality, 77
legal trade in, 22*t*
market value of, 111, 110*t*
natural decrease of, 45, 53, 120, 128*t*, 132, 143*t*, 144, 148
natural increase of, 7, 17, 20, 34, 45, 53, 56, 64, 103, 120, 132, 143–47, 143*t*, 146*t*, 149
nutrition of, 140–53
pardons of, 23–24
procuring, 111
productivity and, 9, 53*t*, 60*t*
punishment of, 21, 135*t*
rebellions, 18, 29*t*
seasoning of, 5, 84, 133, 194n16
starvation among, 14
women, 106*t*, 107*t*
Espeut, W., 169, 170
Ewart, David, 117, 149–50

Fairclough, William, 57
Falconer, Mr, 107, 154
Fall of the Planter Class in the British Caribbean, The (Ragatz), 6
Fawcett and Littledale of Liverpool, 154, 160
Fearon, Rowland, 39, 46, 94, 107, 123, 149, 154–55, 157, 171
field gangs, 96, 151
fieldwork, 81, 95, 97–98, 101–2, 109, 127, 147, 150

232 Index

first gang, 76, 81, 91, 97–98, 150, 204n6
flogging, 23, 151, 187
flooding, 123–25, 129t, 142
Florida, 21
France, 15, 19, 50, 181, 196n5

gang work, 6, 72f
Genovese, Eugene, 5
ginger, 104, 119, 161, 176
Golden Grove plantation, 9, 10, 38, 44–45, 46f, 61, 171, 187
Good Hope plantation, 48
Goulburn, Frederick, 145, 147
Goulburn, Henry, 36, 50–52, 54–55, 69, 71, 93, 105, 111, 113, 116, 145, 147, 159, 162, 183, 184f
Goulburn, Susannah, 54
Governor Belmore, 23–24, 30, 181
Governor Mulgrave, 34
Governor Nugent, 17–18, 25–26, 112
Graham and Bupton, 159
Grand Court, 189, 198n51
Grant, J.C., 92
Grant, Richard, 44
"great gang", 81, 97–103, 100t, 102t
great house, 37, 85, 100t, 136
Green, Mr, 175
Green, William, 49, 50
Greenfield estate, 49
Green Island, 186
Green River plantation, 172
Grenada, 12, 154
ground provisions, 63, 82, 85, 104–5, 125, 145, 161, 171, 174
Guatemala, 169
guinea grass, 72f, 88t, 93–95, 102–3
guttering tubes, 154

Haiti, 18
Hall, Douglas, 184
Hanover parish, 21–22, 28, 186
Hanson, John, 69
Harris, Richard William, 139

Hermitage plantation, 40, 41f, 42t, 108–9, 109f
Hibbert, George, 57, 58, 59, 61, 134, 169, 175, 176, 182t, 183
Higman, B.W., 6–7, 9–10, 32, 38, 44, 62, 88, 120–21, 126–27, 143, 153
Hillside, 146t
History of Jamaica (Long), 5–6
Holland estate, 125, 136, 142, 159
Honduras, 21
hothouses, 105, 108, 124, 136
House of Commons, 12, 21, 30, 34
House of Lords, 18–19
Hulme, Peter, 186, 187
hurricanes, 85, 123, 125
Hutchinson, Officer, 134–35, 135t

illegal trade, 15, 124, 140
India, 15
influenza, 124
invalids, 9, 82–83, 96–99, 100t, 101t, 102, 102t, 105
Ireland, 134
Island estate, 10, 36, 94, 114, 123–24, 136, 137t, 138f, 139f, 150, 163, 165, 167–68, 191

Jamaican House of Assembly, 1, 13, 24, 33, 78
Jamaican planter class, 4, 6, 8, 32, 62, 183
  abuses of, 20, 187
  decline of, 1, 4
  dependency on enslaved labour, 167–68
  diet of, 83–84
  indebtedness of, 33
  injustices, 189–90
  political power of, 14
  psychology of, 169
  racism of, 126
  responsibility for decline, 140, 148
  types of members, 20
  white managerial class, 82
Jamaica Planter's Guide, The (Roughley), 5
James, Charles, 90

Index   233

James, Thomas, 90
Jefferies, Sam, 140
Jeffery, Mr, 156
jobbing
    gangs, 92, 109
    jobbers, 37, 40, 92, 93, 110–11, 72*f*
    labour, 71*t*, 94, 97, 104, 167, 169

Kerr, W.M., 57
Kingston, 26, 29*f*, 144, 175
King's Valley, 95–96, 96*t*, 117–18, 124, 149, 156
Kiple, 126
Kupius, 97, 110, 171

labour
    Ceylonese workers, 176
    Chinese labour, 114–16, 152, 191, 209n70
    day, 21, 37
    hired, 70–71, 93–95, 97, 108, 110, 115, 145, 167
    motivating, 4
    task work, 6, 21, 152, 164, 170, 186
    See also enslaved Africans; jobbing
Lambert, Catherine, 48–49
Lane, James Seaton, 68
Lecesne, 179
life imprisonment, 23
Lists of Apprentices, 68
Liverpool, 183
lockjaw, 132
logwood, 165–67, 166*t*, 172
London, 183
Long, Beeston, 44
Long, Edward, 5–6, 36, 48, 73–74, 77, 117, 154, 157, 161, 165
long houses, 136
Lord Auckland, 175
Lord Bathurst, 134–35
Lord Castlereagh, 18–19, 34, 35
Lord Goderich, 26, 30, 34, 190
Lord Penhryn, 14, 37, 39, 46, 94–95, 97, 110, 117, 123–25, 127, 149, 154, 156–57, 165, 166*t*, 171, 176
Lord Wellington, 19
lumber, 14–15, 140, 161, 167
Lyons, James, 68, 74
Lypra Arbabicum, 132
Lyssons estate, 125, 159

Mair, Mr, 113
maize, 176
Maltese workers, 176
Manchester, 42, 143, 143*t*, 165, 168, 189
Manchester, Duke of, 24, 25, 134–35, 181
manumissions, 89
Maroons, 28–29
Marquess of Sligo, 31
McCawley, Colonel, 115
McCormack, Thomas, 44
Mckay, Adam S., 190
McLean, Mr, 40
measles, 132
mercantilism, 4, 11
Mesopotamia plantation, 10, 36, 48, 92, 94, 95, 103, 104, 110, 117, 124, 128*t*, 136, 137*t*, 138*f*, 141, 148, 150, 165, 166*t*, 167, 168, 172
methodology, 10
metropolitan authorities, 2
    initiatives of, 25
    resistance from Jamaican planters, 25
Mickleton Pen, 68, 70, 87–89, 88*t*
Miles, P.J., 57, 61
Miller, William, 190
Mills, P.J., 182*t*, 183
Mitchell, Mr, 159
monopoly, 12, 14
Monteith, Kathleen, 163
Montpelier, 44
Moorland estate, 159
morbidity, 127*f*
Morris, 150, 151, 162, 163, 164, 165
mulattos, 90, 108
Mulgrave, Earl of, 25–27, 31

Murray, George, 22–23

Napoleon, 163
Nassau, 23
navigation laws, 12–13, 15, 21
"Negro grounds", 87
"Negro rum", 84
Neptune, 21–22
Nethersole, Mr, 54
Newman, Charles, 189
night work, 152

Old Plantation System in the British West Indies, The (Ragatz), 6
overseers, 33, 36–37, 38, 56, 112, 148, 193n5

parish jails, 24
Parliament, 12, 178
Pearl River plantation, 139
Peirce, Ann, 90
Pennant, George, 107, 171
Pennant, Richard, 46, 47, 171
Pepper and Bona Vista pens, 101, 101*t*, 102*t*, 103, 118, 172, 173*t*, 174*t*
Phillips, F.J., Colonel, 37–38, 57
Pitt, William, 12–13
Plantain Garden plantation, 125
plantains, 84, 124, 145, 171
plantation doctors, 80, 126
Plantation Jamaica, 1750–1850: Capital and Control in a Colonial Economy (Higman), 8
plantation management
 Abolition Act and, 1–3
 absentee management, 25–44
 econometrics, 3
 emergency plans, 150
 failures, 4
 health management, 1, 18, 35, 73, 122–147
 internal conflicts and, 44–50
 land utilization, 88*t*
 management structure, 32–35
 productivity and, 15, 2–3
 restructuring, 91
 technology, 8
plantation pens, 170–77
plantations
 coffee, 107–13
 crude production versus productivity of, 2–3
 diversification of, 3, 103–7, 161–70
 leadership and, 3
 ownership of, 33
 planting methods and, 3
 soil quality and, 3
 yearly crop accounts, 10
Pleasant Hill estate, 171
Plummer, Thomas, 36
Political Economy of Slavery (Genovese), 5
Pope, Mr, 50
Portland, 29
Port Royal, 29, 125, 143, 143*t*
Portuguese, 12
Potts, Mr, 12
Practical Rules for the Management and Medical Treatment of Negro Slaves in the Sugar Colonies (Collins), 5
Price, Bessy, 90
Price, John, 65
Price, Nelly, 84
Price, Rose, 63–65, 68, 82, 86, 87, 88*t*, 89, 91, 105
Protector of Slaves, 185

Quier, John, 78, 79

race
 attorneys' racial views, 151
 labour and, 114–19
 racial stereotyping, 4, 111, 114
Radnor plantation, 98, 100*t*
Ragatz, Lowell J., 6, 11
ration-allotment system, 121–22, 143
ratooning, 179
Redstan, Dr, 175

Reed, James, 85
regional jails, 24
Registration Act, 29
Reid, David, 39
Reid, Robert, 84
Revolutionary War, 175
Richards, Mr, 112, 155, 145, 160
ringworm, 133
Rodgers, William, 36, 48, 95, 104–5, 103, 140, 167, 168, 172, 93
Roughley, 5
rum, 86, 162, 174, 175
Russell and Derry, 70
Ryden, David, 8–9, 88

Salmon, 42, 118, 119, 141
"salt-water" Africans, 74
Sampson, 51, 52
Sam Sharpe Rebellion of 1831, 2, 28, 30, 183
Samson, Thomas, 50, 54, 55, 93, 108, 111, 112, 113, 145, 147, 159, 160, 162, 165, 175, 183
Santa Cruz, 168
Santa Maria tree, 168
Satchell, Veront, 153
Scott, Rebecca, 5, 153
Seamington, 155
Seven Years' War, 6
Shand, John, 36–39, 44–45, 105, 123, 125, 127, 139, 141, 142, 156, 159, 175
Shand, William, 37–39, 44–45, 57, 159
Shand brothers, 44, 139
Shepherd, Verene, 170
Sheridan, 121, 126, 127, 127
Shirley, Mr, 50
sickness, 128*t*
Sierra Leone, 14
Simpson, Thomas, 189
"slave courts", 6
slave list, 95, 96
slave registration, 2
slaves. *See* enslaved Africans

smallpox, 127, 132
Smith, Adam, 4, 11, 180
Smith, Sir Lionel, 187
Smith, Thomas, 66, 68
Society for the Abolition of Slavery (African Institution), 17, 19
Solow, Barbara, 4
soup kitchens, 131
Spanish Town (St Jago de la Vega), 27, 37, 40, 144
Springfield plantation, 104
Spring Gardens Pen, 68, 70, 85, 85*f*, 87–89, 88*t*
St Andrew parish, 125, 142, 144, 190
St Ann parish, 143, 170
St Bartholomew parish, 135
St Catherine parish, 29*f*, 69, 170
St David parish, 125
St Domingue parish, 20, 162, 163
St Dorothy parish, 23
Steele and Hardyman, 48
St Elizabeth parish, 29*f*, 36, 40, 47, 94, 108, 114, 143, 162, 165, 168, 170, 172, 191
Stephens, James, 19
St George parish, 29*f*, 143*t*, 169, 187
still house, 123
St Jago de la Vega (Spanish Town), 27, 37, 40, 144
St Jago Pen, 51
St James parish, 31
St John parish, 78
St Mary parish, 159, 187, 190
St Mary's plantation, 139
St Vincent parish, 12, 18, 35
Stokeshall, 171
sugar, 7–8, 119
    British sugar refiners, 12, 180
    cane fields, 3, 70, 121, 124, 155
    cane fires, 123
    cane holes, 62, 72*f*, 93–95, 110, 144–45, 151–53, 186
    consumption, 12
    drawback on, 11–12

sugar (*continued*)
  East Indian producers, 13
  economic protectionism and, 5, 15–16, 162–64, 177
  international trade of, 5
  old versus new colonies, 2, 120
  price of, 6
  prices, 5, 13, 91, 116
  production, 35*f*, 46*f*, 65, 52*f*, 77*t*, 138*f*, 139*f*
  re-exported, 13
Supreme Court, 24
Surrey, 125

task work, 6, 21, 152, 164, 170, 186
Taylor, Simon, 12–13, 15, 38, 125, 132–34, 136, 139, 141, 148, 159, 184, 185
Taylor, Watson, 139, 141–42, 159, 190
Taylor, William, 142, 144, 151
Tharp, Ann, 49, 50
Tharp, John, Jr, 38, 49, 57, 59
Tharp, William, 57, 58
Tharp estates, 48, 57–62, 59*f*, 60*t*, 182*t*, 183
Thomas River, 97, 110, 166*t*
tobacco, 119, 161, 168
Tobago, 12, 18, 35
transportation (punishment), 22, 21
Trelawny, 48, 57, 190
Trinidad, 19, 154
Tudway, Clement, 185, 186*t*
Turner, George, 44
Turner, Mary, 24, 28, 29
Tydixton Park, 85

United States, 15, 15*t*, 21, 124, 167

Vassal, Custos, 21–22
Vere, 10, 50, 53, 56, 141–42, 143*t*, 144–45, 146*t*, 159, 168
Vice-Admiralty Court, 135*t*

Walvin, James, 63–64, 71, 82, 86–87, 89, 91, 126, 127
Ward, J.R., 7, 10, 16, 122, 127, 153
watchmen, 81, 83, 96, 189
Wealth of Nations (Smith), 11
Webb, Mr, 94, 167–68
Wedderburn, James, 92
Westmoreland, 36, 92, 125, 143*t*, 156, 168, 170
White, Frederick, 187
White, Patrick, 47
Wilberforce, William, 17, 19, 152
Williams, Eric, 4, 11
Wilson, Captain, 109
windmills, 151, 155, 160
Windward Islands, 152
workday, 186
work gang, 64
work rates, 121
worms, 132
Worthy Park, 3, 63–91, 66*f*, 72*f*, 84*f*, 86*t*, 88*t*, 105
  fertility rates, 73*t*
  health indicators at, 74*t*
  mortality rates, 73*t*, 75*t*, 76*f*
  productivity at, 67*t*
  sugar production at, 77*t*

yams, 84
yaws, 132, 145